CASINA BY PLAUTUS

Casina by Plautus
An Annotated Latin Text with a Prose Translation

by

Catherine Tracy

(based on the Latin text of W. M. Lindsay)

https://www.openbookpublishers.com

©2025 Catherine Tracy (exclusive of the Latin text)

This work is licensed under a Creative Commons Attribution 4.0 International No-Commercial No-Derivatives (CC BY-NC-ND 4.0). This license allows you to share, copy, distribute and transmit the text; to adapt the text for non-commercial purposes of the text providing attribution is made to the authors (but not in any way that suggests that they endorse you or your use of the work). If you remix, transform, or build upon the material, you may not distribute the modified material. Attribution should include the following information:

Catherine Tracy, *Casina by Plautus: An Annotated Latin Text, with a Prose Translation*. Cambridge, UK: Open Book Publishers, 2025, https://doi.org/10.11647/OBP.0482

Further details about CC BY-NC-ND 4.0 licenses are available at https://subjectguides.york.ac.uk/creative-commons/by-nc-nd

All external links were active at the time of publication unless otherwise stated and have been archived via the Internet Archive Wayback Machine at https://archive.org/web

Digital material and resources associated with this volume are available at https://doi.org/10.11647/OBP.0482#resources

Information about any revised edition of this work will be provided at https://doi.org/10.11647/OBP.0482

Paperback ISBN: 978-1-80511-673-8

Hardback ISBN: 978-1-80511-674-5

PDF ISBN: 978-1-80511-675-2

DOI: 10.11647/OBP.0482

Cover image: A female servant takes something from a box on the ground. Wall painting, Ares and Aphrodite, Pompeii (VII 2 23). Napoli, Museo Archeologico Nazionale, inv. 9249. Photo by ArchaiOptix (2018).

Cover design: Jeevanjot Kaur Nagpal

Contents

Acknowledgments	viii
Introduction	1
Helpful Information for Reading the Latin Text	23
Plautine Latin	23
The Rhythm of Plautus	28
Casina (Annotated Latin Text)	35
PERSONAE	36
PROLOGVS (1-88)	37
ACTVS I	47
I.i Olympio, Chalinus (89-143)	47
ACTVS II	54
II.i Cleustrata, Pardalisca (144-164)	54
II.ii Myrrhina, Cleustrata (165-216)	56
II.iii Lysidamus, Cleustrata (217-278)	61
II.iv Lysidamus, Chalinus (279-308)	71
II.v Olympio, Lysidamus (309-352)	75
II.vi Cleustrata, Chalinus, Lysidamus, Olympio (353-423)	80
II.vii Chalinus (424-436)	90
II.viii Olympio, Lysidamus, Chalinus (437-514)	92
ACTVS III	101
III.i Lysidamus, Alcesimus (515-530)	101
III.ii Cleustrata, Alcesimus (531-562)	104
III.iii Lysidamus, Cleustrata (563-590)	109
III.iv Alcesimus, Lysidamus (591-620)	112
III.v Pardalisca, Lysidamus (621-719)	115
III.vi Olympio, Chytrio, Lysidamus (720-758)	125
ACTVS IV	130
IV.i Pardalisca (759-779)	130
IV.ii Lysidamus, Pardalisca (780-797)	133
IV.iii Olympio, Lysidamus (798-814)	135

IV.iv Chalinus, Pardalisca, Olympio, Lysidamus, Cleustrata (814-854) 138

ACTVS V 142
V.i Myrrhina, Pardalisca, Cleustrata (855-874) 142
V.ii Olympio, Myrrhina, Cleustrata, Pardalisca (875-936) ... 144
V.iii Lysidamus, Chalinus (937-962) 152
V.iv Chalinus, Lysidamus, Cleustrata, Myrrhina, Olympio (963-1018) 154

Casina (in Translation) 163

About the Translation 164

Cast of Characters 167

Prologue (1-88) 168

Act I 172
I.i Scene with Olympio and Chalinus (89-143) 172

Act II 175
II.i Scene with Cleustrata and Pardalisca (144-164) 175
II.ii Scene with Myrrhina and Cleustrata (165-216) 175
II.iii Scene with Lysidamus and Cleustrata (217-278) 177
II.iv Scene with Lysidamus and Chalinus (279-308) 181
II.v Scene with Olympio and Lysidamus (309-352) 182
II.vi Scene with Cleustrata, Chalinus, Lysidamus, and Olympio (353-423) 184
II.vii Scene with Chalinus (424-436) 190
II.viii Scene with Olympio, Lysidamus, and Chalinus (437-514) 190

Act III 195
III.i Scene with Lysidamus and Alcesimus (515-530) 195
III.ii Scene with Cleustrata and Alcesimus (531-562) 196
III.iii Scene with Lysidamus and Cleustrata (563-590) 197
III.iv Scene with Alcesimus and Lysidamus (591-620) 198
III.v Scene with Pardalisca and Lysidamus (621-719) 199
III.vi Scene with Olympio, Chytrio (the hired cook), and Lysidamus (720-758) 203

Act IV 207
IV.i Scene with Pardalisca (759-779) 207
IV.ii Scene with Lysidamus and Pardalisca (780-797) 207
IV.iii Scene with Olympio and Lysidamus (798-814) 208

IV.iv Scene with Pardlisca, Olympio, Lysidamus, and Cleustrata (815-854) 209

Act V **212**
V.i Scene with Pardalisca, Myrrhina, and Cleustrata (855-874)   212
V.ii Scene with Olympio, Myrrhina, Cleustrata, and Pardalisca (875-936) 212
V.iii Scene with Lysidamus and Chalinus (937-962) 215
V.iv Scene with Chalinus, Lysidamus, Cleustrata, Myrrhina, and Olympio (963-1018) 216

ARGVMENTVM (Plot Summary)   220
Acrostic Translation of the *Argumentum* 221
(Mostly) Literal Translation of the *Argumentum* 221

Works Cited   222

Index   227

Acknowledgments

My students at Bishop's University in Sherbrooke, Quebec (Canada) are the inspiration for this book, whose good-natured tolerance for my love of Plautus allows me to keep sneaking plays like the *Casina* into the various classes I teach. With cogent questions and comments such as "is this supposed to be funny?", and "this entire plot is a lawsuit waiting to happen", my students made class discussions lively and entertaining even when we were also talking about the serious and upsetting realities of what life could be like for the less powerful in ancient Rome. My thanks in particular to my third-year Latin students, who read the play in Latin with me and helped me find mistakes in my annotations. I very much appreciated their hard work, curiosity, precision, and excellent table readings.

My former professor, Dr Amy Richlin, is always forefront in my mind when I think about the world in which Plautus wrote his comedies. When I was a doctoral student at the University of Southern California, I didn't yet know I would want to spend so much time on Plautus, but I'm glad I had the opportunity to learn from Amy how to read the Classics with an eye for the mostly silent actors in Roman history. Her book *Slave Theater in the Roman Republic: Plautus and Popular Comedy* (2017) blew me away when I first read it, and still does.

Bishop's University, located on the traditional and unceded territory of the Abenaki people and the Wabenaki confederacy, provided the time and resources I needed to write this book. My colleagues provided friendly and useful conversations, the librarians and inter-library loan staff ensured that I had every book I needed, and the Research Office gave me a publication grant to help defray the costs borne by the Open Book Publishers.

I very much appreciated the useful comments and corrections of the anonymous reviewers at OBP, and the painstaking proof-reading and generously offered help of OBP editor Dr Adèle Kreager.

And of course I am grateful to my husband Oisín Feeley, and daughter Sorcha Feeley, who sympathize when I'm stuck, and rejoice with me when I succeed. I'm so happy to have their unfailing support.

Introduction

What's so funny about the *Casina*? The plot involves:

- a married couple who apparently hate each other, each scheming to get the better of the other
- this same married couple using enslaved men of their household as proxies in their scheming against each other
- a planned marriage where the consent of the (enslaved) bride is neither needed nor considered (though her potential unwillingness does form part of the plot)
- sexual assault upon two men (Olympio and Lysidamus) by a third (Chalinus)

It is difficult to imagine that such a comedy could be written today as lighthearted entertainment: it would either be deliberately and aggressively reactionary, or the overtly comic plot would be undercut by a dark and ironic awareness of the social injustice it depicted. But the *Casina* was, as far as we can tell, intended to be a lighthearted comedy when it was performed in ancient Rome. Does this prove that its Roman audiences were all sadistic brutes who delighted in seeing vulnerable people come to harm? Mid-republican Rome, when Plautus wrote his plays, was a society where injustice and inequality were well entrenched, and it would be a mistake to imagine that Roman play-goers questioned much or any of this injustice. But, while the *Casina* reflects many of the evils of life in early second century BCE Rome, its comic elements were fundamentally based on the hilarity of reversed power relationships. The *Casina*, that is, involved "punching up" (within the norms of Roman power relations), not "punching down".[1] The characters in the play who most obviously suffer assault and humiliation are those whom the Roman audience would have identified as the ones with potentially frightening amounts of power in the real world. Their suffering is played for laughs because they hold power over people whom they have intended to abuse, until their would-be victims manage to reverse the dynamic.

This does not mean that the *Casina* was especially subversive, since the humiliation of the authority figures in the play does not hint at any revolutionary ideas about the illegitimacy of their authority. Rather, the humiliation is supposed to be deserved because the authority figures have failed

---

[1] The phrase "punching up" (often credited to the comedian Chris Rock, according to Quirk 2018: 19) became popular in 2004, and refers to comedy that satirizes the powerful, as opposed to bullying the less powerful (Farthing 2020).

to use their authority appropriately. To use another phrase from comedic theory, Plautus did not, as far as we can tell, use "charged humour", which self-consciously intends "to create a more equitable world by challenging its divisions and cultural exclusion" (Bhargava and Chilana 2023: 6). There may have been revolutionaries in Plautus's audiences that hoped for a more equitable world, but if there were they left no record. The power inversions in the plays of Plautus were always only temporary, and were, moreover, cloaked in a Greek disguise,[2] which further distanced the plot from any real-world Roman social upheaval. Nevertheless, the plot of the *Casina* is unusual in the powerful roles it gives to women, and in particular to the *matrona* Cleustrata.[3]

We, in the modern world, do not, of course, need to share wholeheartedly the original audience's pleasure in the humiliation of the enslaved farm manager Olympio and the slave-owner Lysidamus – but we should be able to appreciate the jokes within their cultural contexts. It's ok to laugh where Plautus intended his audience to laugh – but it's also important to notice the assumptions about people's roles in Roman society, and to think about the similarities and differences between mid-republican Rome and our own world.

Fabulae palliatae and Rome

The *Casina* is a type of comedy known as *fabula palliata*, which was a Latin play set in the Greek world but composed for Italian audiences. The actors wore Greek costumes, with the name *fabula palliata* coming from the Latin word *pallium*, referring to a cloak commonly associated with Greek men's clothing. The *fabulae palliatae* were adapted from the plots of plays known as "New Comedy", that had been popular in the Greek world from the early fourth century to at least the mid-third century. The first production of the *Casina* took place about 100 years after the most creative period of Greek New Comedy. As we learn from the prologues of Plautus's *Asinaria*, and of his near-contemporary Terence's plays *Adelphi, Andria,* and *Eunuchus,* it was not just acceptable, but expected and demanded that playwrights re-use Greek plots, rather than write entirely new Latin plays. By Terence's time (his first play was probably produced about two decades after Plautus's death) some sticklers apparently objected to the playwright having used more than one Greek source for his Latin play instead of sticking closely to one, while accusations that he had used a Latin play as a source was a slander that had to be denied (see the prologue of *Eunuchus*).[4] The prologue

---

[2] That is, the actors were meant to be playing Greek characters in a Greek setting.
[3] Lindsay (1903), whose Latin text is used in this volume, changed the spelling of the *matrona*'s name from the original "Cleostrata" to Cleustrata, in order to better reflect what must have been the Latin pronunciation (which is trisyllabic wherever it appears in the text).
[4] Strong objections to originality of plot may have come primarily from the Roman elite, which could explain why Terence (who, unlike Plautus, had elite patrons) mentioned

of the *Casina* reassures the audience of the play's legitimate Greek source: a play by Diphilus called Κληρούμενοι ("The Ones Drawing Lots" or "The Lottery Players"), which Plautus "wrote again in Latin" (31-34).

The *fabulae palliatae*, like the Greek New Comedies on which they were modeled, featured stock characters: personality types played by male actors wearing masks that matched each stock character type so as to make them immediately recognizable to the audience.[5] Among the well-known stock characters were the stern father, the permissive mother, the young man in love, the clever slave who tricks his master (often for the benefit of the master's love-sick son), the wife that gets in the way of her husband's scheming, and others.[6] Audiences knew how each character type was supposed to behave, and this gave the playwright opportunities for playing on the audience's expectations.

The plots of Greek New Comedy tended to center around a heterosexual love affair, often culminating in marriage, and though these plots provide the rough outline for the plays of Plautus, the latter were not simply translations of the Greek originals. Despite the supposedly Greek characters and Greek settings, the plays of Plautus reflect the Graeco-Roman culture of their Italian playwright and audiences. The influence of two other kinds of theatre popular in Italy from his time – the native Italian semi-improvised masked drama that we call Atellan farce, and mime (a Greek import to Italy) – probably explain some of what makes the *palliatae* distinct from Greek New Comedy.[7] The plays were not, at any rate, imported wholesale from

---

such concerns more often than the popular Plautus. See Gowers 2004, however, for a compelling argument that Terence's references to his supposed critics' insistence on authentic Greek plots were part of tongue-in-cheek allusions to the ensuing play and to his own career. Aulus Gellius's disparaging comments about Caecilius's Latin adaptation of a play of Menander are probably indicative of elite sentiment over 300 years later (*Noctes Atticae* 2.23.1-22).

5   The second-century CE rhetorician Julius Pollux (Ἰούλιος Πολυδεύκης) gives us a description of the masks used in New Comedy. There were different masks for the different "grandfather" (πάππος) types, "young man" (νεάνισκος) types, slave (δοῦλος) types, etc. (*Onomasticon* 4.143-154).

6   We get various lists of the stock characters in Greek New Comedy and Roman Comedy: Terence (*Eunuchus* 35-40) includes "the running slave, virtuous wives, the greedy parasite, the boastful soldier, the substitute baby, the old man who is tricked by the slave"; Plautus refers (in *Captivi* 57-58) to "the lying pimp", "the wicked sex worker", and "the boastful soldier"; Terence (*Heauton Timorumenos* 37-39) lists "the running slave, the angry old man, the greedy parasite, the shameless flatterer, and the greedy pimp"; Ovid (*Amores* 1.15.17-18) lists the "trickster slave, harsh father, dishonest procuress and charming sex worker"; Horace (*Epistulae* 2.1.170-173) lists "the young lover, the careful father, the treacherous pimp, [and] voracious parasites"; Apuleius gives us the most complete list with "the lying pimp, the ardent lover, the clever young slave, the teasing girlfriend, the wife that gets in the way, the permissive mother, the stern uncle, the helpful pal, the belligerent soldier, [...] gluttonous parasites, stingy fathers, and sassy sex workers" (*Florida* 16).

7   The influence of Atellan farce and mime on Plautus is also suggested by the playwright's name "Titus Maccius Plautus", which he may have chosen as a deliberate reference to these types of performance. "Maccius" is related to "Maccus", the name of a stock char-

the Greek world of New Comedy, and should therefore be understood as Italian theatre, while the versions that have come down to us were adapted specifically for Roman audiences. This is particularly clear where the plays make topical references to the city of Rome (as, for example, in lines 461-486 in Plautus' *Curculio*), and to recent events in or around Rome (such as to the scandalous Bacchanalian cult stamped out in 186 BCE, referenced in *Amphitruo* 702-707; *Aulularia* 406-412; *Bacchides* 52-53, 368-374; *Menaechmi* 828-39; and *Casina* 979-982). The orator Cicero, admittedly speaking about 100 years after the death of Plautus, claimed that a character from a *palliata*, supposedly Greek and living in the Attic countryside, could be considered very similar to a man one might expect to meet in a field in the town of Veii, not far from Rome (Cic., *Pro Sexto Roscio Amerino* 46-47).[8]

The stock characters in the plays of Plautus, therefore, were an interesting mix of foreign and Italian/Roman. Their Greekness (Greek personal names, and the Greek, usually Athenian, setting), however, allowed Plautus to include plot elements that might not have been acceptable if the actors were supposed to have been playing Roman characters.[9] Indeed, the plays of Plautus are largely unapologetic about the irreverent and potentially subversive depictions of the theoretically less powerful winning over the more powerful. Since the plays were funded by the state for performance at state-sponsored religious festivals, the pretense could be maintained that all this comedic mayhem was not about Rome or Roman values, even though it was not actually very Greek either. Roman audiences could safely laugh at stage authority figures that, in real life, probably irked many of them, while Roman magistrates could allow them to laugh at such an indirect and temporary overturning of accepted Roman social structures.

---

acter in Atellan farce, while "Plautus" ("flat-foot") was probably a nickname for the barefooted actors performing in mime performances. "Titus" was probably slang for "penis", and might refer to the comic phalluses worn in some mime performances (Gratwick 1973: 79-82). Gratwick suggested that his name would have come across to the Romans as "Phallus son of Clown the Mime-actor"; "Dick MacClown the Mime-Guy" and "R. Harpoe Clownshoes III (just call me 'Dick')" are two more recent suggestions (Franko 2001: 149 and Richlin 2005: 10, respectively).

[8] See Leigh on a discussion of this, and of two references to Cicero having stated that comedy imitates life and the daily habits of (presumably) Romans (Leigh 2004: 6-12, citing Cic., *Hort.* fr. 10 Grilli - Donat., *de com.* 5.1, 5.5).

[9] This is implied by the fourth-century CE Aelius Donatus' comment that, in contrast with the *fabulae palliatae*, the comedies performed in Roman dress (the *fabulae togatae*, which do not survive) were not usually allowed to include "slaves wiser than their masters" (*seruos dominis sapientiores* - Donatus, *in Eunuchum Terenti Commentum* 57). The implication is that the *fabulae togatae* were not supposed to upend the proper social order in Rome, while the *palliatae* could, and did.

The Roman Audience

Plautus's Roman audiences were a mixed bunch. There was no charge for admission, and men and women (and even, sometimes, very young babies – Plaut. *Poenulus* 28) of all classes, free, freed, and enslaved,[10] were present, though the final lines of the *Casina* could suggest that a large part of the audience present comprised married men, or that the married men of the audience were deemed the most important ones to appeal to for a good round of applause (1015).

Prior to 195 BCE, the members of the audience may have sat anywhere there was a free seat on a first come, first served basis, though it is likely the wealthy had ways of ensuring they got the best seats (Marshall 2006: 77). Another line from *Poenulus* suggests that enslaved people were expected to stand if there weren't enough seats for free people (Plaut. *Poen.* 23). The *Casina* was probably one of Plautus's last plays, if the reference to there being no more bacchantes at line 980 can be taken as a reference to the senate's crackdown on the Bacchanalian cult in 186 BCE.[11] The version of the play we have, moreover, was from a revival performance several decades later, by which date senators in the audience of the *Casina* would officially have had reserved spaces (Marshall 2006: 77, citing Livy 34.54.3-4, 6-8). Most of the audience probably sat, but there was a short-lived attempt by the senate to ban spectators' sitting in 154 CE (Sear 2006: 55, citing Livy, *Periochae* 48; Valerius Maximus 2.4.2), and this ban on theatre seating could have been in effect for the *Casina*'s revival performance.

When there was seating it would have been on wooden benches, or perhaps the stone steps of a temple, with the temporary stage built in front of the steps. Audiences for the plays were small relative to the much larger size of audiences in Greek theatres. An estimate for the seating area at the Temple of Magna Mater where Plautus's *Pseudolus* was staged in 191 BCE suggests an audience of only 1300-1600 people (Goldberg 1998: 14). By contrast, the first permanent Roman theatre, built in the mid-first century BCE, would have held perhaps 40,000 (Pliny, *Naturalis historia* 36.115). Unlike in Greek theatres, the stage was not very high, and there was no dancing area between the stage and the seats (Vitruvius 5.6.2). The relatively small size of the audience and the spectators' proximity to the actors would have allowed for easy audience engagement (Goldberg 1998: 16).

The prologue of the *Casina* shows that the actor reciting it was simulating a lively interaction with the audience, commiserating with them on their probable financial troubles and their assumed loathing for debt collectors

---

[10] See, however, Brown 2019 for an argument that enslaved persons were excluded from watching performances of the *palliatae*.

[11] The predominance of songs in the play, as well as the increased element of native Italian farce to supplement the borrowed Greek plot, also seem to point to the *Casina* as one of Plautus's last plays (O'Bryhim 1989: 91).

(23-28). He refers to the muttering of some members of the audience in reaction to his reference to slave marriages (67-70), and makes a crude joke about the audience's disappointment when he tells them there won't be any sex scenes (82-86). Plautus regularly "broke the fourth wall" in his plays, disrupting the illusion of the play's reality by having the actors refer to the fact that they were performing a play (as at lines 1005-1006 in this play), or having them appeal directly to the audience for support (as at lines 951-952). Leigh described the edge of the stage in the plays of Plautus as "not an invisible boundary over which the actor must never step but a garden wall across which the actor gossips and flirts with the public as if they were neighbours" (Leigh 2000: 302). When reading the play it is worth keeping in mind how much a role the audience was meant to have in the original performances.

The Plot of the *Casina*

The plot of the *Casina* features the silent and invisible titular[12] character Casina, a sixteen-year-old girl who, after having been rescued from abandonment in infancy, has been brought up by the mistress of the household, Cleustrata. Because of her foundling status, Casina is a slave, but we are told that Cleustrata brought her up as though Casina were her daughter. Casina's teenage attractiveness has aroused the interest of both Lysidamus, the patriarch (what the Romans would have called a *pater familias*) of the family, and of his son, the absent Euthynicus. Lysidamus hopes to get secret access to her by marrying her to his farm manager (or *uilicus*) Olympio, who is loyal to him. Lysidamus's wife Cleustrata, however, plans instead to marry Casina to their son's loyal slave, his former armour-bearer Chalinus, so that Euthynicus will have access to her (due to her supposed enslaved status, a marriage between Casina and Euthynicus is not an option). Casina's wishes in the matter are not mentioned, though we are to assume she would prefer the younger Euthynicus over the older, and married, Lysidamus.

Lysidamus and Cleustrata agree to draw lots about it, and the winning lot is drawn by Olympio. Cleustrata, however, succeeds in undermining her husband's plans to spend the wedding night with Casina himself by, among other tricks, substituting the male slave Chalinus for the bride. Lysidamus and Olympio are humiliated (and Olympio at least is beaten) in their encounter with the unexpectedly male bride, and Lysidamus has to beg his wife for forgiveness. The final plot point, mentioned in a speech by Chalinus, is that Casina will be discovered to be a freeborn citizen, and will marry Euthynicus after all.

---

[12] The play's prologue tells the audience that the Greek source for the play was called Κληρούμενοι (*Clēroumenoe*: "The Lot-Drawers"), and that in Latin the title is (or was) "*Sortientes*". While we know the play as *Casina*, it is possible, as MacCary and Willcock suggest, that the play was titled *Sortientes* by Plautus, and retitled *Casina* in the later rival from which the extant version of the play comes (MacCary and Willcock 1976: 102).

The *Casina* in the Context of Roman Society

Perhaps more important than the plot, however, is how Plautus used the traditional stock characters of Greek New Comedy to play with the norms and rules of the household hierarchy. Only fragments, and the nearly complete text of Menander's *Dyskolos*, remain of Greek New Comedy, but where we have evidence of the Greek source for any of Plautus's plays, we see that Plautus often used the basic plot points, and (with adaptations) the stock characters, of Greek comedy, while creating plays with very different emphases. For instance, the Greek New Comedies tended to centre the plot on the young man's pursuit of the desirable young woman while he negotiated his relationship with his father; the fragments that remain of Menander's Greek New Comedies suggest that his plays generally upheld the traditional values of the family and of the Athenian *polis* (Christenson 2019: 7). The romantic plot line in Plautus, however, is often just a backdrop for Plautus's rowdy and impudent challenging of authority (James 2020: 109-121). The *Casina* is an excellent example of Plautus's choice to de-emphasize the romantic conclusion, and to instead emphasize the successful tricks of the underdog hero (exceptionally, this is primarily the *matrona* Cleustrata in this play). The fragmentary remains of Plautus's Greek model (Diphilos's Κληρούμενοι) are not extensive enough to tell us how important the romantic conclusion was in the Greek original, but they do suggest that the important role of Cleustrata, and the prominent comedic role of the enslaved woman Pardalisca, were Plautus's innovations (Anderson 1993: 57).

The *seruos callidus*

Plautus's plays regularly involve a "clever slave" character (*seruos callidus*) who outwits their master and other characters through deceptions and quick thinking. Scholars of Plautus have wondered whether this shows that the Roman audiences objected at a semi-conscious level to enslavement, or if their sympathy for the *seruos callidus* was a proxy for something else. Stürner suggests that Plautus's *seruos callidus* depictions were not directly about slavery, but rather were about freedom (Stürner 2020: 137). Stürner interprets the plays as "reaffirming the ideal of human freedom against what the philosopher Hans Blumenberg has called the "Absolutism of Reality", and thus that the members of the Roman audiences, whatever their status, interpreted the play's challenging of authority as it might relate to the power structure within which they themselves happened to be.[13] This may indeed be why the Roman elite continued to pay for the productions,[14] and why they

---

[13] Anderson's argument is similar: that every member of the Roman audiences enjoyed watching on stage what those in authority above them considered bad behaviour, and that they thus viewed the character on stage who reveled in "badness" (*malitia*) as heroic (Anderson 1996: 88-106).

[14] While the Roman state treasury supplied some funding for the productions, the aedile or praetor in charge of the festival at which the play was to be performed would have

were so popular with such mixed audiences. Richlin, however, argues that the plays were meant, in part, to appeal to the members the audience who would have endured enslavement themselves, or who would have had friends and family members who had endured it, or for whom their own potential future enslavement was a valid fear (Richlin 2017: 26, 398, 404, 414-415, 478-479 *et passim*). While we'll never know precisely why the Roman audiences loved to see a clever slave outwit his master (the stock *seruos callidus* is typically a man, though enslaved women can occasionally play the role temporarily, as we see with Pardalisca in *Cas.* 621-719), the plays of Plautus make it abundantly clear that they found it hilarious.

In the *Casina*, the enslaved Chalinus is the closest we get to a *seruos callidus*, but though he does help to outwit and dominate his master Lysidamus, he is not the mastermind. The play is unique in that it is not Chalinus's triumph over his master that is the main challenge to authority; rather it is the *matrona* Cleustrata's challenge to the power and status of her husband Lysidamus that carries the plot. The majority of wives in the *palliatae* are either submissive to their husbands or, if they do attempt to interfere in their husband's schemes, are played as unsympathetic. This makes it even more intriguing to ask why Roman audiences might have enjoyed seeing a husband being tricked, humiliated, and dominated by his wife in this play. Understanding the power dynamics of the Roman household with which the Roman audiences of *fabulae palliatae* would have been familiar helps to put the plot into context.

The *senex*

Lysidamus[15] is the stock character known as the *senex*: literally "old man".[16] Italian/Roman audiences would have roughly identified the *senex* with the *pater familias*, or male head of the household, though usually the stage *senex* was a hilariously poor example of one.[17] An essential part of the comedy in the *Casina* is that Lysidamus does not play his *pater familias* role properly.

The power of a Roman *pater familias* over his sons

In Roman law and society, the *pater familias* held extraordinary power over nearly everyone in his household. While the real power that any one *pater fa-*

---

supplemented this amount with his own money in order to ensure the success of the entertainment (Duckworth 1952: 74).

[15] Plautus did not, in fact, give this character a name. The name "Lysidamus" appears in the scene-headings of the Ambrosian Palimpsest (called "A"), which, although it is our earliest extant version, dates to around the 4th century CE. The other extant manuscripts of the play list him simply as "*senex*".

[16] For a discussion of the age at which Romans considered a person to become "old", see Parkin 2003, 16; notes 3-4. Lysidamus has to be old enough to have a grown-up son, and thus would be at least 50, but was probably meant to be older.

[17] Cicero tells us that the *senes* on the Roman stage were usually stupid and gullible – Cic., *De amicitia* 100.

milias might have wielded would have depended on his personality, people-management skills, and economic status, his right to nearly absolute power was enshrined in Roman law. Notoriously, the *XII Tables* (the earliest written laws of the Romans, dating to 451 BCE) stated that a Roman father had the power of life and death over his sons (IV.2a), and the mid-second century CE jurist Gaius commented that few other peoples gave as much power to fathers over their sons as did the Romans (Gaius, *Institutiones* 1.55).[18] This legal power was subsequently limited by various emperors (the emperors Trajan and Hadrian in the early second century CE, for instance, made official rulings against fathers who killed or mistreated their sons, see *Digesta Iustiniani* 48.9.5; 37.12.5), but it was probably rare even during the republic for a *pater familias* to execute his own son. Those who are recorded as having done so are mostly examples of a *pater familias* nobly putting the needs of the Roman state ahead of his fatherly feelings.[19] Nevertheless, a *pater familias* could control his son financially: during the republic, a son in power technically owned nothing of his own, though he was generally allowed to administer his *peculium*, which was money or other assets allocated to his use. Furthermore, a son in power was expected to show respect and obedience to his father.

We see in the *Casina* that Roman society did not necessarily deem it acceptable for a stage *pater familias* to control every aspect of a son's life. In lines 262-265, Cleustrata says to her husband Lysidamus: "we should do what benefits our only son", meaning that they should marry the girl Casina to their son's loyal slave, Chalinus, to which Lysidamus replies: "he may be my only son, but I'm just as much his only father: it's more fair for him to give in to me than for me to give up what I want to him". Given the context, and the tone of these lines, Lysidamus's comments are not meant to reflect the respected right of a *pater familias* to rule his household as he sees fit. Rather, he comes across as selfish and petulant, abusing his authority to try to get what he should not get (access to Casina) at the expense of his son, who

---

[18] The *pater familias*'s power over his daughters was less remarked upon by Roman sources because it was less unusual in the ancient Mediterranean context, but he had not only the legal right to kill his daughter, but the obligation to do so if she were found guilty of a capital crime. This is seen, for instance, in the state's response to the Bacchanalian affair in 186 BCE, when, according to Livy, the guilty women were handed over to be punished by their relatives, or by those in whose power they were (*in quorum manu essent*) (Livy 39.18.4).

[19] Brutus the Liberator, for instance, who had helped to overthrow the last king of Rome, put his treasonous sons to death when they were found to have been conspiring to restore the king to power (Livy 2.3-5). The fathers of Spurius Cassius (late fifth century BCE) and of Aulus Fulvius (who tried to join Catiline's revolt in 63 BCE) were supposed to have used their *potestas vitae necisque* because their sons were likewise a threat to the Roman state (Dionysius of Halicarnassus 8.79.1-2; Valerius Maximus 5.8.5). By contrast, fathers who killed their sons for less patriotic reasons, such as Q. Fabius Maximus Eburnus (consul in 116 BCE) and Tricho (during the time of the emperor Augustus), faced legal consequences (Orosius 5.16.8) and popular outrage (Seneca, *de Clementia* 1.15.1), respectively, which suggests that *patria potestas* was not quite so harsh over adult sons as the law would imply (Gaughan 2010: 44-46).

is considered to have a more legitimate claim on her due to his youth and unmarried state.

The power of a Roman *pater familias* over enslaved persons in his household

The power that a *pater familias* had over the enslaved persons of his household was much more than theoretical, however. Slavery is so embedded in the plays of Plautus that it is essential to know something about how slavery functioned in the Roman world to properly understand the *Casina*. During the Roman republic, there were no legal limits on the abuse of enslaved persons by their masters. They could be beaten, tortured, sexually assaulted, or executed at the will of their owners. In the *Casina*, Lysidamus's sexual pursuit of the enslaved sixteen-year-old Casina has to be thwarted, but not because it was in any way illegal for a *pater familias* to rape an enslaved person of any age or sex in his household, but because it might have disruptive domestic consequences (Marshall 2015: 126). Serious offenses committed by enslaved persons, such as plotting to kill their master, setting fires in the city, or theft of something valuable, were commonly punished with torture and execution (Dowling 2006: 12). The form of execution with which the enslaved characters in Plautus's plays are regularly threatened is crucifixion, considered by Romans to be a shameful, as well as agonizing, way to die. An inscription found in Puteoli (about twenty km south of Rome), dating to the first century BCE or first century CE, lists the price in chilling detail that a slave-owner might pay to have a slave crucified: four sesterces each for the labourers who carried the cross-piece or fork (*patibulum*), for the floggers (*verberatores*), and for the executioner (*carnifex*) (*L'Année épigraphique* 1971, no. 88, II.8-10).[20]

Not all enslaved persons were treated equally badly, and some were highly valued by their masters. The late republican politician Cicero, who certainly considered himself to be a just man, thought he had an excellent relationship with his enslaved secretary Tiro, whom he manumitted, and who apparently continued to be devoted to Cicero's interests (*Epistulae ad Atticum* 6.7.2; 7.2.3). He also expressed grief at the death of another of his slaves, saying that he was more upset than he should be at the death of a slave – showing both that he probably did feel grief, and that Roman society did not approve of such a response (*Att.* 1.12). He was happy about the manumission of certain devoted slaves (*Att.* 4.15), but when another of his freedmen (manumitted slaves) failed to show continued loyalty to Cicero, the latter felt ill-used and vindictive, and wrote to his friend that he was contemplating reversing the manumission by denying he had ever set the man free, there being no official witness at the manumission (*Att.* 7.2.8).

The promise of manumission was more real for the average Roman house-

---

[20] See Cook 2008: 266-272 for details on crucifixion and the other tortures that preceded it.

hold slave[21] than for their Athenian counterparts (Hunt 2018: 134), and this promise appears regularly in the plays of Plautus, including at line 293 of the *Casina* (yet more evidence that the *fabulae palliatae* are meant to be Italian despite the nominal Greek setting and characters). It is not known what percentage of enslaved persons in the Roman world were manumitted, but we do know that manumission was a real possibility for enslaved persons living in the slaveowner's household (Mouritsen 2011: 140). It is important to remember, however, that manumission was part of the system of control of Rome's servile population. Enslaved persons who were in positions of trust were encouraged to accumulate a *peculium* (see page 9 above), with which the enslaved person could eventually buy his or her[22] freedom. This benefited the slave-owner because it encouraged the enslaved person to try to win the master's good favour, and give the master the most productive years of the slave's life. It ended, moreover, with the slave exchanging his or her own freedom for the price of a younger replacement.[23]

The examples of viciously cruel slave-owners are far more numerous (Wiedemann 1994: 167-187). Roman law and society supported slave-owners' abusive control of their slaves because the state had an interest in keeping the vast numbers of enslaved persons in too vulnerable a position to mount an effective resistance. Fifty years after the death of Plautus there occurred the first of the Roman world's three major slave uprisings; all were ultimately crushed.

Given this context, how do we interpret comments like those of Chalinus at line 293 in this play, where, in response to Lysidamus's offer to free him if he will give up his claim to marry Casina, Chalinus says "if I were free, I'd be living at my own expense. As it is, I live at your expense"? Did the Roman audience really believe that slavery was better than freedom for some people? No doubt many did, if we can extrapolate from the attitudes of modern slave-owners (see, for example, Fitzhugh 1857 *passim*). If we are to take the line seriously at all, however (seriously, that is, within the logic of the comic plot), it's more likely that Chalinus simply doesn't trust Lysidamus to uphold his side of the bargain. Furthermore, in his role as the *seruos callidus*, he has to refuse to be manipulated by the master and to succeed in manipulating the master instead.

---

[21] As opposed to those who worked as agricultural labourers on large rural estates, or those who worked in the mines, whose chance at freedom was small.
[22] The *Digest* makes it clear that an enslaved woman could also have a *peculium* (15.1.27 *pr.*).
[23] The *peculium* as part of a slave-owner's manipulative strategy for getting the most labour and financial gain from the enslaved person is only one part of a larger strategy of exploitation, including informal manumission, which left the informally freed person still striving to win full formal freedom and Roman citizenship. See Roth on the advantages to slave-owners of granting informal citizenship (which, in the early empire, was given the specific legal status of Junian Latin status) (Roth 2010: 110-111 *et passim*).

The vilicus (*uilicus*)

Olympio, who shares in the humiliation meted out to Lysidamus in the play, is a vilicus (spelled *uilicus* in the Latin text of this play, and translated as "farm manager"). A vilicus was usually enslaved, but was in a position of authority over the other labourers on the master's villa, or farm. Olympio's status as vilicus places him into a similar category as Lysidamus: he holds potentially abusive power over others, and therefore, in the logic of the play, deserves his downfall.

Columella, the first century CE author of a treatise on agriculture, advised absentee landowners on how to run their estates profitably, and he gives us a description of the role and responsibilities of a vilicus. His job was to ensure that the other enslaved labourers on the farm worked hard, and, according to Columella, he was more likely to be effective at this if he was older than the other slaves (*De re rustica* 1.8.3) and was not too friendly with them (1.8.5). He was in charge of ensuring they had adequate but not attractive clothing so that bad weather would not be an excuse for them not to work (1.8.9), and to make them work hard enough to want only rest and sleep at the end of the day, instead of pleasure (1.8.11). He was to carry out the landowner's orders as to which slave was to be put in chains or released from them (1.8.16). He was to exercise his authority over the other slaves so they would be afraid of his strictness (1.8.10). This last remark appears in the context of Columella's advice that a landowner not allow his vilicus to behave with cruelty towards the other slaves, and at 1.8.18 Columella advises the landowner to check up on whether the vilicus has been giving the slaves substandard food and drink, giving them inadequate clothing, or otherwise treating them cruelly.

Depending on how personally involved the landowner was in the day-to-day running of his villa (farm), a vilicus might function nearly autonomously as business manager and overseer of the agricultural slaves under his power (Aubert 1994: 169-175). From the point of view of the average rural slave, the vilicus wielded almost unlimited authority. In the opening scene of the *Casina*, Olympio tells Chalinus of his plan to get the latter under his authority at the villa, where he plans to torment him both physically and psychologically (117-142). A real-life Chalinus would have had good reason to fear his slave overseer, though the stage Chalinus, being a *seruos callidus* (the stock "clever slave"), naturally manages to turn the tables on the stage vilicus. If any of the Roman spectators had had a vilicus – or someone with similarly arbitrary power – in authority over them at one time, they must have found it vindicating and funny to see the vilicus humiliated on stage by the household slave Chalinus.

The women

The female characters in the *Casina* include two *matronae*, or free married women (Cleustrata and Myrrhina), the enslaved older woman (Pardalisca), and, if we can count a silent invisible character, the enslaved young woman (Casina). The ways in which these characters reflect, to some extent, Roman social norms make the play particularly interesting for the study of gender roles in republican Rome. The silence and invisibility of Casina, as well as her supposed objection to her impending marriage to Olympio, frame her as the ideal citizen bride she is ultimately proved to be. The way Cleustrata ends up taking over the role of master manipulator and star of the play, on the other hand, is truly unexpected.

Casina as unconsenting bride

The Roman audiences would not have expected Casina, whether she was enslaved or freeborn, to have any choice in the matter of her marriage. An enslaved woman's placement in a marriage-like relationship with a man of her master's choosing would have been a common enough occurrence in the Roman world. Columella (whose advice on choosing a good vilicus is mentioned on page 12) advises absentee landowners to assign a *contubernalis mulier* – that is, a female bed mate or sex partner – to the vilicus, to keep him in check and to help him with some of his responsibilities (1.8.5). Columella does not, of course, mention asking the consent of either the vilicus or the *contubernalis mulier* for this arrangement, since their consent was irrelevant to the slave-owning class.

Her consent was likely also irrelevant to the enslaved man to whom she was given as a sex partner. A woman called Aurelia Philematium, commemorated on a first century BCE funerary inscription, was described by her husband (called Lucius Aurelius Hermia) as a devoted, faithful, and dutiful wife (*Corpus Inscriptionum Latinarum* 6.9499 = *CIL* 1.1221). She had originally been enslaved in the same household as her future husband Hermia, who had also been enslaved. The inscription tells us that the two first met when she was seven years old, when Hermia received her in his lap (*gremio ipse recepit*) as more than a parent (*plus superaque parens*). The bland praise of the inscription gives no hint that Aurelia Philematium could have been anything other than compliant and grateful for the probable sexual relationship with her "parental" fellow-slave while she was a child, nor that she may have had few other options than to consent to her eventual marriage to him.[24]

Casina, of course, is not actually a slave in the play, as the audience learns from the prologue. Furthermore, the audience is explicitly told that Casina was brought up by Cleustrata "very carefully, just as though the girl were

---

[24] See Jeppesen-Wigelsworth (2023) for a lengthy discussion of this inscription and its implications.

her own daughter" (*era fecit, educauit magna industria / quasi si esset ex se nata, non multo secus* 45-46). This is an important statement, since it tells the audience that Casina has been brought up with the modesty and sexual inhibitions of a citizen girl, and that her virginity has been protected. This is what makes it feasible for her to turn out to be of free birth, since, in the world of Plautus, young women are only worthy of marriage to citizen men if they have not already had sexual relationships with anyone else.

When we view Casina as a freeborn Roman girl, her submissive compliance is part of what makes her an ideal bride, according to Roman expectations. A key plot point, however, is the lie told by Pardalisca to Lysidamus in act III, scene v (lines 621-719) that Casina is wielding swords and threatening to "kill any man that shared her bed tonight" (670-671), and that "the only way she'll put the swords down is if she knows she won't be married off to the farm manager" (698-699). While Casina's supposed homicidal response to her impending marriage probably does not strike the modern reader as so unlikely a response in a teenaged girl being forced into a sexual relationship with a much older man, let alone with two older men, it is interesting to consider how the Roman audiences would have interpreted it. Lysidamus's terrified response is played for laughs, of course, but it may be that her falsely-reported plan to prevent her impending marriage, extreme though it was, would have been seen as evidence for her freeborn girlish modesty – exaggerated, of course, for the comic stage.

Romans considered it natural for a young bride to be unwilling. It is not clear whether or not a bride had to legally consent to her marriage in Plautus's time, though we know that her consent was required by the late second century CE (*Digesta Iustiniani* 23.2.2). We also know that, in the late republic, Tullia's very fond father Cicero had no expectation that he would be able to overrule her disinclination to marry a man of whom he approved (Cic., *Epistulae ad Atticum* 5.4.1). Tullia, however, was in her late twenties and had been married twice already. For Roman girls and women, at least for those of the elite whose lives are more accessible to us, any freedom they may have had in choosing their own husband probably did not begin with their first marriage, which could legally have taken place when they were as young as twelve (*Codex Iustinianus* 5.4.24).

Catullus's wedding song (62), dating to the mid-first century BCE, suggests that a first-time bride was expected to fear her wedding night: lines 20-24 involve a chorus singing that giving a girl in marriage is crueler than what an enemy does to a captured city. In the late first or early second century CE, Plutarch suggests that a Roman bride was supposed to be unwilling, and that she had to be coerced – at least, that is his explanation for the Roman wedding ritual of carrying the bride over the threshold of her new husband's house (Plut. *Quaestiones Romanae* 29).

Catullus' poem continues with a chorus singing that the girl should not fight with her new husband, since her virginity is only one-third her own; the other two-thirds belong to her parents, who have the right to give it to the husband they have chosen for her (59-65). The lives of as yet unmarried girls, at least, among the Roman elite, were geared almost exclusively towards providing a man with a proven virgin who would be childlike enough to be guided by her considerably older husband (Caldwell 2015: 105-106). Her objections (whether ritual or, as in the *Casina*, fictional) would have been seen as evidence for her sexual inexperience and thus as proof of her qualification as citzen bride.

Marriage with and without *manus*

Despite the Roman social norm that an as-yet-unmarried citizen girl be silent and biddable, older married women were not necessarily without a certain amount of independence and power. While the Roman *pater familias* had theoretical power of life and death over his children and slaves, he did not necessarily have a similar legal power over his wife.

One kind of Roman marriage (marriage *cum manu*) involved the transfer of power over the bride from her original *pater familias* to her husband, who now became her new *pater familias*.[25] A husband's power over his *in manu* wife – that is, over his wife who had been married to him *cum manu* – was certainly limited by the mid-second century CE, when she could divorce him unilaterally (Gaius, *Institutiones* 1.137a), but an *in manu* wife probably did not have this right during Plautus's time (Treggiari 1991: 459). She would legally have been under her husband's financial control, as he controlled any property she brought into the marriage (Treggiari 1991: 324). An *in manu* wife, who had brought a wealthy dowry into the marriage, might have held more financial power than the law implied. Certainly there are enough comic complaints by husbands in Plautus's plays about the unfair financial power that their well-dowered wives (*dotatae uxores*) hold over them (Treggiari 1991: 329-330). These complaints are, however, difficult to evaluate, since it is rarely clear whether or not the marriages in Plautus are supposed to be *cum manu*.

Marriage without *manus* (*sine manu*) involved no transfer of power from the bride's father to her husband. In such a marriage, the wife remained in her original *pater familias*'s power, or, if he had died, in her own power (*sui iuris*).[26] Marriage *sine manu* was becoming increasingly popular by Plautus's day, and became the most common type of marriage by the late republic.

---

[25] Unless his own *pater familias* was still living, in which case her husband's *pater familias* would also become hers.

[26] A Roman woman whose *pater famlias* had died did not acquire the same independent status as her brothers did, since she was required to have a male guardian (*tutor*) for any financial transactions. The *tutor*'s power over her was, however, much more limited than that of her *pater familias* while he lived.

It is unclear what kind of marriage was meant to exist between Lysidamus and Cleustrata in the play, and given the pretended Greek setting, Plautus may not have intended to depict a plausible Roman marriage at all. Act II, scene ii suggests that their marriage could have been recognized as *cum manu*, since their neighbour Myrrhina says to Cleustrata:

> a good wife shouldn't have any private property apart from her husband. If she does, she can't have come by it honestly, since either she's stolen it from her husband or she's received it from a lover. In my opinion everything you own is your husband's. (199-201)

It is equally possible that Roman patriarchal culture was trending, when the *Casina* was first produced, against wives' independence from their husbands, and that significant portions of Plautus's Roman audience would have approved of Myrrhina's opinions on marriage regardless of the legal norms.[27] This interchange between Cleustrata and Myrrhina has, indeed, been interpreted as a debate on the principles of *sine manu* vs. *cum manu* marriage (Christenson 2019: 44). A few lines later Myrrhina cautions Cleustrata not to behave in any way that might prompt her husband to want to divorce her (208-211), as though only he, and not she, had the right to unilaterally initiate divorce. This again suggests a marriage *cum manu* – or a cultural expectation that wives would be financially and socially disadvantaged by divorce.

Regardless of whether or not Lysidamus' and Cleustrata's marriage was meant to look like a legal Roman marriage, the right of a *pater familias* to have financial and moral authority over his wife is an important element in the play. The fact that Lysidamus tries to exercise his authority over his wife, but that she undermines his plans and ultimately wins in their battle of wills, is the core to the play's comic plot. Lysidamus's inability to dominate his wife effectively is partly why, in the play, he is meant to deserve his humiliation.

The *matrona* Cleustrata

We now come to the most interesting element of the *Casina*: that the *matrona* Cleustrata should be the star whose triumph dominates the plot. As mentioned earlier on page 7, Plautus's audiences enjoyed seeing a clever slave outwit his master. It is surprising, however, that on this occasion they also

---

[27] For an interesting analysis of Myrrhina's apparent inconsistency in first advising Cleustrata against interfering in her husband's sexual pursuit of Casina, and later helping Cleustrata to trick and humiliate him, see Feltovitch 2015. She argues that Myrrhina's initial advice reflects a woman's sensible caution around challenging the legally powerful husband openly, while her subsequently taking part in Lysidamus's humiliation reflects the reality that married women were more likely to achieve their ends by working against their husbands indirectly.

enjoyed seeing a clever wife outwit her husband because this seemingly conflicts with the stock character roles with which his plays were populated.

At the beginning of the play, Cleustrata seems to represent the stock character that Apuleius named as the *uxor inhibens* ("the wife that gets in the way" – *Florida* 16) though, as Franko points out, the lyric verses that comprise her opening lines are unusual for the "traditional nagging matron" who normally speaks in plainer metres (Franko 2001: 173). McCarthy defined her also as the *uxor dotata* – a wife whose money gives her unfair power over the husband (McCarthy 2000: 81, 86; see also James 2015: 124 n. 12).[28] It was unusual in the *fabulae palliatae* for a *matrona* to have a sympathetic rapport with the audience. Some of Plautus's *matronae*, as Moore points out, are objects of hostility to their stage husbands (*Trinummus* 42, 58-65; *Menaechmi* 127-134, 159; *Epidicus* 178-179, *Cistellaria* 175), wives in general are described as punishment (*Miles gloriosus* 681-700; *Aulularia* 154-157), and wives with dowries are "imperious agelasts" – that is, they are ruiners of comic fun (Moore 1998: 158-159). By contrast, the sympathetic wives in Plautus, Moore points out, are "comfortably and emphatically under the control of their husbands" (150).

Moore argues that the *Casina* "represents an undermining of conservative views on contemporary controversies about marriage" (Moore 1998: 6). At the beginning of the play Cleustrata seems to be true to type: she wants to interfere in her husband Lysidamus's sexual pursuit of Casina, and he makes hostile comments about his wife when he thinks she can't hear (*Cas.* 275). As the play continues, however, Cleustrata's rapport with the audience is built, partly through her and her ally Chalinus's successful eavesdropping on Lysidamus and Olympio, which causes the audience to side with her and against Lysidamus (Moore 1998: 170-179). Though the audience would have initially viewed Cleustrata as "an unsympathetic stock *matrona*", and would have agreed with Myrrhina's first lines about the obligation for a good wife to submit to her husband, the spectators, like Myrrhina, become Cleustrata's ally by the end of the play (Moore 1998: 180).

Moore further points out that the *Casina* was first produced at a time when continual warfare had changed the traditional legal and social status of wives (160). The lengthy absences, or warfare-related deaths, of their husbands, and the fact that women from wealthy families were increasingly inheriting considerable fortunes, had made many women financially independent. The Oppian Law limiting women's expenditures (Livy 34.1.3) had been passed in 215 BCE, and was repealed (against Cato the Elder's opposition) in 195 BCE. Meanwhile the cult of Bacchus, which included visible and socially disruptive roles for women (*Amphitruo* 702-707; *Aulularia* 406-412; *Bacchides* 52-53, 368-374; *Menaechmi* 828-39; *Casina* 979-982), had an increasing

---

[28] As Christenson points out, however, there is no mention of Cleustrata's dowry in the play (Christenson 2019: 27).

presence in late second century Italy until it was crushed by the Roman senate probably a year before the *Casina*'s first production (*Inscriptiones Latinae Liberae Rei Republicae* 511). There was a climate of male hostility to women's increasing power and independence – and Plautus's *Casina* played on, and overturned, the audience's expectations by making them enjoy Cleustrata's victory over her husband. Cleustrata, in fact, becomes the poet who stage-manages the action, and indeed concludes it neatly by agreeing to forgive her husband (1004-1006).[29]

As mentioned at the start of this introduction, the *Casina* was not revolutionary. McCarthy, in fact, argues that Cleustrata's punishment and subsequent forgiveness of Lysidamus results in a return to the status quo of comic marital hierarchy, with Lysidamus in the role of rebel trying to get around his "dour, rich, and unattractive wife" while Cleustrata "must revert to being a *matrona*, enforcer of decorum" (102). Even if Cleustrata and her allies are imagined to settle back into their traditional roles, however, their moment of power supplies the climax of the comic plot.

Sexuality and status

While Cleustrata's revenge presents us with a puzzle about Roman attitudes around women having power over men, what she and her allies actually do to Lysidamus and Olympio gives us insight into the Roman spectators' anxieties about male dominance and sexuality. After Cleustrata's comical undermining of Lysidamus's and Alcesimus's confidence in each other (at lines 541-562 and 577-590, in act III, scenes ii-iii), it becomes clear that Myrrhina and Pardalisca have enthusiastically allied themselves to Cleustrata. They frustrate Lysidamus and Olympio first by denying them food (772-777), and then by denying them their planned sexual encounter with Casina. Indeed, the men's inability to get their dinner foreshadows their eventual sexual frustration (Slater 1987: 87). Cleustrata and her allies, exploiting another of the traditional female household responsibilities (that of preparing a bride for her wedding), substitute the male slave Chalinus for the intended bride Casina. They dress him in a bride's wedding dress, and lead him out to Olympio and Lysidamus in order to turn the sexual tables on the would-be bridegrooms. Pardalisca recites a parody of what must have been a traditional ritual speech to a new bride: she tells "her" to lift her feet carefully over the threshold[30] in order to ensure a propitious marriage, the goal of which, she says, is to achieve dominance over her husband and (if we interpret *superstes* as referring to the wife's surviving her husband) an early widowhood (815-824). McCarthy interprets the speech as "the manifesto of the clever slave instead of advice of submission to the bride" (McCarthy 2000: 99).

---

[29] See Slater 1987: 84 on Cleostrata (Cleustrata) as *poeta*.
[30] This was a known element of Roman wedding ritual (Plutarch, *Quaestiones Romanae* 29), though it ought to have been the threshold of the bride's new home, not of the home she was leaving (Williams 1958: 17).

When Olympio, and subsequently Lysidamus, try to have sex with the person they suppose to be Casina, Chalinus sexually assaults them instead (lines 875-962, act V, scenes ii-iii). The text is fragmentary at this point, so we don't know exactly what Olympio and Lysidamus were so horrified by, but it involved at least an unexpected encounter with Chalinus's erect penis combined with a physical assault upon Olympio and possibly Lysidamus, though it stopped short of involving "what a husband normally does to his new bride" (1011).[31] Within the logic of the play, this is a just and deserved revenge, but not perhaps in the way we might think. We may see that Olympio and Lysidamus suffer a form of what they had intended to do to Casina: sexual assault. The Roman audience, however, was more likely to see the men's punishment as a serious loss of status.

Roman attitudes around sexuality focused on the phallus, and who sexually penetrated whom. As Kamen and Levin-Richardson put it, "penetrating was associated with freeborn status, masculinity, and social dominance, whereas being penetrated was associated with servility, femininity, and social inferiority" (2014: 449). A bride could not lose status by being sexually penetrated by her husband, therefore, however traumatic her experience might be. She, being already female, was merely playing her expected social role, and being forced to have sex with her husband was considered by the Romans to be neither a loss of status nor a sexual crime. It was very different for men to be put into what the Romans considered to be a female, and thus dishonourable, role. The loss of Lysidamus's staff (line 975) may be meant to represent a loss of his phallic/sexual power, and it certainly represents his loss of authority; the fact that he only gets the staff back because his wife allows it makes it clear that his authority is conditional (Heil 2012: 485-486; see also Gold 2003: 344).

Enslaved men also risked loss of status if they were known to have been sexually penetrated, though freeborn men had more status to lose. Earlier in the play there is another reference to sex between men. In act II, scene viii, Chalinus eavesdrops, and comments aloud, on a conversation between Lysidamus and Olympio. Lysidamus in this scene is using Olympio as a prop in an imaginary conversation with Casina, but Chalinus, and perhaps Olympio as well, interpret his remarks as referring to a sexual relationship between Lysidamus and Olympio. Lysidamus says, apparently talking to Olympio: "I can hardly keep my lips from kissing you [...] my sweet!" (452-453). Chalinus the eavesdropper is presumably reflecting the expected reactions of the Roman audience when he comments in an aside to the audience: "What? Kissing? What's going on? What 'sweet' is he talking about? By Hercules, I think he wants to explore the farm manager's interior" (*quid, deosculere? quae res? quae uoluptas tua? / credo hercle ecfodere hic uolt uesicam*

---

[31] McCarthy interprets this line as proving that "nothing happened", meaning that nothing irremediable has been done to Lysidamus's status as an inviolable man (*uir*) (McCarthy 2000: 104, 110).

uilico 454-455).³² Chalinus then suggests that Olympio must have acquired his job as vilicus in payment for, or reward for, having allowed Lysidamus to sexually penetrate him.

A male Roman slave-owner had every legal right to have sex with the enslaved persons, male or female, in his power³³ and, provided that the slave-owner did the penetrating and was not himself penetrated, he suffered no loss of status. The enslaved person's lack of legal protection from unwanted sexual advances by the master did not, however, absolve a male slave that was known to have had sex with his master from ridicule and contempt. Chalinus claims that he too had been offered a position of authority (in his case, head household slave, or *atriensis*),³⁴ in exchange for complying with Lysidamus's sexual desires (462); since he is not Lysidamus's *atriensis*, we are to assume that Chalinus turned Lysidamus down. The play, thus, implies that an enslaved man had the choice not to be sexually used by his master, and that Olympio was offered such a choice and chose wrongly. Lines 811-813 (IV.iii) may imply that Olympio has not had sex with Lysidamus after all, but Olympio's claim (*di melius faciant!* – "may the gods grant a better outcome!") could also simply be Olympio's attempt to pretend nothing like that had ever happened between him and Lysidamus (because of the loss of status such an admission would bring him).

The ending

Olympio's punishment at the end of the play may have been supposed to be deserved because of his possible former sexual relationship with Lysidamus, but more obviously he deserves his punishment because he abuses his power (his abusive plans for Chalinus make up the bulk of the first scene of the play – lines 89-141). Lysidamus, on the other hand, is punished with loss of sexual status partly for his planned marital infidelity, but mostly because, in the world of Plautus, old men are not supposed to fall in love with much younger women. Roman morality deemed it no crime for a husband to cheat on his wife (though a wife who cheated on her husband was guilty of adultery), but in Plautus, love is for the young (Anderson 1993: 79-80); furthermore, while wives may have had no legal recourse when their husbands cheated on them, they might nevertheless object on personal grounds. Lysidamus's love-smitten song at lines 217-228 (II.iii), and his inept attempts to lie to his wife about the cologne he's wearing, make him look foolish and out of control.

---

[32] Literally, Chalinus says that he thinks Lysidamus wants to "dig out the vilicus's bladder/vagina".

[33] A female slave-owner might effectively have this same right, but Roman law and custom restricted women's sexual behaviour far more than it restricted men's sexual behaviour.

[34] In Plautus's time, the *atriensis* had a parallel status to the vilicus, in that he oversaw the household slaves (with the potential for treating them like his own personal slaves), as well as managing his master's business transactions with others including handling money (Carlsen 1994: 143-144).

Cleustrata's temporary overturning of the domestic patriarchy in her household may have been interpreted by the Roman spectators as a generalized fantasy for an overturning of the power structures that irked them. It is also possible, however, that the spectators enjoyed seeing a wronged wife take on the *seruos callidus*'s role in the *Casina*. How the modern readers of the play will interpret the various plot points depends to some extent on how they understand the social context of the play. The modern reader is likely to find some of Plautus's jokes and comic situations funny, and some decidedly unfunny. It may horrify us that Plautus could make comedy about the kinds of social injustice that prevailed in ancient Rome, but it is also worth remembering that, as T. G. A. Nelson wrote, "a heightened sensitivity to the potential dreadfulness of the universe seems to be characteristic of those who know how to make others laugh" (Nelson 1990: 34). It is important to read the plays of Plautus (or watch them performed) if we want to understand mid-republican Rome. The comedy we now enjoy says a lot about us, and not all of it good; the same is true for the comedy of mid-republican Rome.

Helpful Information for Reading the Latin Text

Plautine Latin

The Latin of Plautus is called "Early Latin", and it therefore looks a bit different from the Classical Latin that is taught in most beginners' textbooks. The following spelling and grammar variants, which had mostly disappeared from Latin prose by the time of Cicero and Caesar, will enable those who want to read the Latin text of the *Casina* to master the most obvious characteristics of Plautine Latin as they appear in this play.

1. **The letter *u*/V:** When writing, the Romans did not distinguish between the vowel *u* and the semivowel that was later written as "v" (which was pronounced like our "w"). The Latin text of the play used in this volume (which is Lindsay's edition from 1903) therefore uses the letter *u* for both the vowel and the semivowel. When written in upper case both the vowel and the semivowel are written like a capital V, following Lindsay's practice.
   For example, in the word *uirtute* (in the last line of the prologue), the first *u-* is a semivowel, while the second *-u-* is a vowel, and it would consequently be spelled *virtute* in most Latin textbooks (like its English derivative "virtue"). The reason introductory Latin textbooks distinguish between the two is because it is believed to help beginners learn how to pronounce Latin correctly. Those whose Latin skills have reached the point where they can read this play should have no real trouble distinguishing the vowel *u* from the semivowel *u*.

2. **Removal of final *-s*:** Lindsay's Latin text removes a final *-s* after a short vowel when the metre requires that vowel to be scanned as short despite the following word beginning with a consonant. Hence we see *fori', magi', nimi', priu', sali', seruo's, tribu'*, etc. (instead of *foris, magis, nimis, prius, salis, seruos es, tribus*, etc.).

3. **Interrogative particle *-n* where you might expect *-ne*/*-sne*:** The interrogatory suffix *-ne* can, in Plautus, be shortened to *-n* even when followed by a word beginning with a consonant. When the suffix is added to a word ending in *-s*, the *-s* can be dropped out. In this play we see *ain, compressan, iussin, men, potin, satin, scin, seruin, tuaen, uin,* etc. (instead of *aisne, compressane, iussine, mene, potisne, satisne, scisne, seruine, tuaene, uisne,* etc.).

©2025 Catherine Tracy, CC BY-NC-ND 4.0   https://doi.org/10.11647/OBP.0482.02

4. **Avoidance of -*uu*-:** A spelling change took place between Archaic Latin and Classical Latin, such that final syllables -*od*, -*os*, -*om*, and -*ont* were changed to -*ud*, -*us*, -*um*, and -*unt* (Weiss 2009: 140). This change was still mid-process in Early Latin, such that the Archaic spelling (-*od*, -*os*, -*om*, and -*ont*) was still used when that final syllable followed a letter -*u*-. That is, Early Latin avoided the letter combination -*uu*-, regardless of whether or not they were a paired vowel and semivowel. For this reason we find that *seruus* (nominative singular) and *seruum* (accusative singular) in Plautus are spelled *seruos* and *seruom*, respectively. Similarly in this play we see the Early Latin spellings *aequom*, *coquos*, *fugitiuos*, *mortuos*, *nouom*, *restinguont*, *suom*, *tuom*, *uiuont*, *uolt*, etc. (instead of the Classical Latin spellings of these words: *aequuum*, *coquus*, *fugitiuus*, *mortuus*, *nouum*, *restinguunt*, *suum*, *tuum*, *uiuunt*, *uult*, etc.).

5. ***Quo-/qu-* where you might expect *cu-*:** the conjunction that was later spelled *cum* was spelled *quom* in Early Latin (though the same was not normally true for the preposition *cum*, which Lindsay thus spells throughout as *cum*). In this play we also see *quoi*, *quoidam*, *quoiuis*, *quoius*, *qur*, and *ubiquomque*, etc. (instead of the Classical Latin *cui*, *cuidam*, *cuiuis*, *cuius*, *cur*, and *ubicumque*).

6. **Non-assimilation of prepositional compounds:** where a preposition has become the prefix of a word, this Latin text preserves the original, non-assimilated spelling, so that we see *adlegauit*, *adpone*, *ecfer*, *ecfexis*, *ecfodere*, *ecfugerit*, *inprobus*, and *inpudens*, etc. (instead of the regressive assimilation of these words that we usually find in Classical Latin: *allegauit*, *appone*, *effer*, *effexis*, *effodere*, *effugerit*, *improbus*, and *impudens*.)

7. **Early forms of prepositions/prefixes:** The preposition *a* (short for *ab*) before a word beginning with *t-* (most commonly the pronoun *te*) was usually *aps* in the time of Plautus. Prepositional compounds that in Classical Latin would begin with *ab(s)* are spelled, in Early Latin, *ap(s)-*; thus we see *apscede*, *apsentes*, and *apstine*, etc. (instead of the Classical Latin *abscede*, *absentes*, and *abstine*).
Words that, in Classical Latin, begin with the prefix *ob-*, in Early Latin may begin instead with *op-*. In the *Casina* we see *optinere*, *optunso*, *opsaeptum*, *opsecro*, *opsignate*, *opsonato*, etc. (instead of the Classical Latin *obtinere*, *obtunso*, *obsaeptum*, *obsecro*, *obsignate*, *obsonato*).
We also see, in this play, the forms *supsilit* and *suptus*, instead of the Classical Latin *subsilit* and *subtus*.

8. **Superlative adjectives/adverbs ending in -*umus* instead of -*imus*, etc.:** in Early Latin the superlative forms of adjectives and adverbs were often spelled with a -*u*- for the penultimate vowel instead of the -*i*- that was standard in Classical Latin. Hence in this play we see the forms *aequissumum*, *maxume*, *miserrumum*, *optume*, *pessuma*, *proxumum*,

etc. (instead of the Classical Latin spellings *aequissimum, maxime, miserrimum, optime, pessima, proximum*).

(a) **Other words spelled with *u* where you might expect *i***: you will also find *lubens, magnufice, manufesta*, etc. which in Classical Latin are *libens, magnifice, manifesta* (see Weiss 2009: 118 for an explanation of this vowel change).

9. **The syllable *uo-* where you might expect *ue-***: words that, in Classical Latin, included the syllable *ue-*, in Early Latin retained the earlier form *uo-* when followed by a dental (*d, t, th, n, l, r, s, z*). In this play we find the forms *uostro, uotat, aduorsum, obuortam, peruortunt, reuortar, uorsabere, uorsuti*, etc. (instead of the Classical Latin *uestro, uetat, aduersum, obuertam, peruertunt, reuertar, uersabere, uersuti*).

10. ***Sis* instead of *si uis***: The phrase *si uis* was often contracted to *sis* in Plautus as well as in some later writers, and meant "please" when paired with an imperative.

11. **Fourth declension genitive singular in *-i***: the genitive singular of fourth declension nouns in Plautus almost always ends in *-i*; hence in this play we get *senati, sumpti*, and *tumulti* (instead of the Classical Latin *senatūs, sumptūs*, and *tumultūs*).

12. **Variant forms of pronouns/adjectives**:

    - ***Illaec, istac*, etc.**: The final *-c* (originally *-ce*), that in Classical Latin appears in half of the demonstrative pronoun/adjective *hic, haec, hoc* could also be added, in Early Latin, to forms of *ille* and *iste*. In this play we get *illaec, illic, illisce, illuc, istāc, istaec, istanc, istuc,* and *istunc* (instead of the Classical Latin *illa/illae, illi, illis, illud, istā, ista, istam, istud,* and *istum*).

        – ***Hisce***: We also see two forms of *hic, haec, hoc* that don't, in Classical Latin, include the *-c/-ce* suffix, but do in this play: the masculine dative plural at line 434, and the masculine nominative plural at line 744 are both spelled *hisce*, but in Classical Latin would be spelled *his*, and *hi*, respectively.

    - ***Eccam, eccum*, etc.**: the interjection *ecce* combines with accusative forms of (probably) the pronoun *hic, haec, hoc*, hence in this play we get *eccam* and *eccum* in place of *ecce hanc* and *ecce hunc*. Similarly, we get *eccere* (instead of, probably, *ecce rem*).

    - ***Eiius* and *huiius***: Lindsay chose to use archaic spelling for the Classical Latin genitives singular *eius* (< *is, ea, id*) and *huius* (< *hic, haec, hoc*) in order to make it clearer that the first syllable of these words is long.

    - **Ablative *qui***: the old ablative form of the relative/interrogative pronoun/adjective *qui* appears in Plautus, often with an adverbial sense. In this play we also see *quiqui* and *quicum* (instead of the Classical Latin *quoquo* and *quocum*).

- **Med and ted instead of *me* and *te*:** Plautus sometimes used the older ablative/accusative forms of the personal pronouns *med* and *ted*, though the forms *me* and *te* occur more frequently.

- *Eapse* **where you might expect** *ipsa*: The pronoun/adjective *ipse, ipsa, ipsum* had, in Early Latin, some forms where -*pse* functioned as a suffix tacked onto a word that declined like *is, ea, id* (Weiss 2009: 346). Hence in this play we get *eapse* (instead of the Classical Latin *ipsa*).

- *Ipsus*: Plautus used both *ipse*, familiar in Classical Latin, and a form that later fell out of use: *ipsus*, for the nominative masculine singular of *ipse, ipsa, ipsum*.

13. **Variant verb forms:**

    - **Shortening of verb forms *es, est* to -'s, -'st:** Lindsay's Latin text frequently includes spelling that reflects the loss of the initial *e*- of the 2nd and 3rd person singular present tense of *esse* (*es* and *est*) after words that end in a vowel, an -*m*, or a short vowel + -*s*. In this play we see *abiegnast, amarumst, conspicatust, dignu's, factost, necessumst, opust, totast*, etc. (instead of *abiegna est, amarum est, conspicatus est, dignus es, facto est, necessum est, opus est, tota est*, etc.).

    - **Present passive/deponent infinitive in -*ier*:** Plautus sometimes used an alternate form of the present passive infinitive that ended in -*er*, so that in this play we see *amicirier, commemorarier, contarier, depugnarier, fungier, morarier, subblandirier,* and *utier* (instead of the Classical Latin *amiciri, commemorari, contari, depugnari, fungi, morari, subblandiri,* and *uti*). The -*ier* infinitives usually appear at the end of a line, for metrical reasons (de Melo 2023: 104).

    - **Present subjunctive of *sum*:** Plautus often used the older forms *siem, sies, siet,* and *sient* that were in the process of being replaced by the Classical Latin *sim, sis, sit,* and *sint*. The *siem*, etc. forms usually appear at the end of a line for metrical reasons (de Melo 2023: 102). In this play, only *sies* and *siet* appear.

    - **Sigmatic forms:** some verbs in Early Latin had forms that functioned as future indicative or future perfect with the endings -(s)sō, -(s)sĭs, -(s)sĭt, -(s)sĭmus, -(s)sĭtis, -(s)sĭnt (or -xō, -xĭs, -xĭt, etc. with verb stems ending in -*c* or -*g*); hence in this play we find *amasso, decolassit, effexis, faxit, occepso,* and *peccassit*, which function as the Classical Latin future perfects *amauero, decolauerit, ef-*

feceris, fecerit, occepero, and *peccauerit*. We also find an instance of the sigmatic future *faxo* (< *facere*), but this has the specific meaning of "I'll make [it happen]", "I promise", "definitely".
Sigmatic verb forms with the slightly different endings -(s)sĭm, -(s)sīs, -(s)sĭt, -(s)sīmus, -(s)sītis, -(s)sĭnt (or -xĭm, -xīs, -xĭt, etc.) function as subjunctives; hence in this play we find *empsim, faxit, obiexis*, and *seruassint*, instead of the perfect subjunctives *emerim, fecerit, obieceris*, and *seruauerint* (or present subjunctive – see de Melo 2007: 199-209 regarding the time reference of the sigmatic subjunctive).
This play also has a sigmatic future active infinitive form: *impetrassere*, instead of the Classical Latin *impetraturum esse*.

- **Fourth conjugation verb forms with -*bo***: the future tense signifier -*bo*, -*bis*, etc. which in Classical Latin is used only for the first and second conjugations and in the verb *eo*, can also appear in Early Latin in verbs of the fourth conjugation, and in the third conjugation verb *reddo*, so that in this play we see *conuenibo, scibis*, and *reddibo* (instead of the Classical Latin *conueniam, scies*, and *reddam*).

- **Indeclinable future active infinitive:** Plautus occasionally used an old non-inflected future active infinitive that did not agree with its subject accusative. In this play we see two instances of *occisurum*, where the accusative subject is feminine (instead of the Classical Latin *occisuram esse*).

- **Perfect system forms of *sum* in perfect passive tenses:** perfect passive forms of verbs that in Classical Latin use *sum, eram*, or *ero* (indicative) or *sim, essem* (subjunctive) sometimes use instead the perfect system forms *fui, fueram, fuero* (indicative) and *fuerim, fuissem* (subjunctive). We see this once in this play with *oblitus fui* (instead of the Classical Latin *oblitus sum*).

The Rhythm of Plautus

The plays of Plautus were musical. While the tunes have been lost, what remains in the text is a wide variety of metres. "Metre" (also spelled "meter") refers to the rhythmic structure of a line of poetry, and different metres in Latin poetry involve different numbers and combinations of long and short syllables. Different metres inspire different feelings and reactions, and were used, by Plautus, to differentiate between dialogue and song, and to mark different characters and elements of the plot. While English metres, unlike Latin, emphasize the stress accent more than quantity (syllable length), we can nevertheless see the importance of metre in English by contrasting, for instance, the rhythm of a sonnet (try reading the opening lines of Percy Bysshe Shelley's "Ozymadias" aloud) from the rhythm of a limerick, or by contrasting the rhythm of a danceable pop song with the rhythm of a sad country music song.

The metres of Plautus can be categorized into three types:

1. *Deverbia* (or *diverbia*): spoken dialogue in a metre called iambic senarius, performed without music,

2. Polymetric *cantica*: songs performed to musical accompaniment in a mix of different metres, and

3. Recitative: sung passages performed to musical accompaniment, involving long lines of usually iambic or trochaic metre (these passages are also considered *cantica*, but they do not use the many mixed metres of the polymetric *cantica*).

Different sections of the plays of Plautus can be identified by their "musical arcs", that begin with a passage of iambic senarii (*deverbia*) and end with a passage of "recitative", with or without polymetric *cantica* in between (Marshall 2006: 207-208). These musical arcs are the real divisions within the plays, since the act and scene divisions are not original to Plautus. Being able to identify the different metres is, therefore, important in fully understanding the play. Gellar-Goad's article "Music and Meter in Plautus" is an excellent discussion of how our awareness and understanding of Plautine metre can add immensely to our appreciation of the plays, and suggests an approach to identifying metrical structure and meaning in the plays that doesn't require one to be an expert (Gellar-Goad 2020).

Reading a line of Latin verse in metre requires knowing the length (quantity) of each syllable of each word, and that depends both on how the Romans normally pronounced the word in question (i.e., whether the vowel was pronounced as long or short), and on how the pronunciation may be affected by the letters following the vowel, the word that follows a final syllable, or sometimes by the word that comes before an initial syllable. Learning to scan a line of Latin poetry – that is, learning to identify the metrical structure – is best done by regular practice, with the help of an instructor and/or one of the excellent introductory guides to Latin metre.

For beginners, I suggest getting a copy of Raven's *Latin Metre: An Introduction* (1967),[1] which explains the elements of scansion (scansion is the practice of "scanning" lines of poetry to detect its metre). Chapter 2 of Raven's book gives a helpful explanation of how to identify the "quantity" of a syllable (that is, whether it counts as "long" or "short", and what that means for scansion), what combinations of letters and/or syllables can then change how a syllable should be scanned (synizesis, elision, hiatus, iambic shortening/*brevis brevians*, etc.), and what the basic rhythms of Latin poetry are. Chapter 4 then explains the two most common rhythms in Plautus: iambic and trochaic verse. Chapter 4 is divided between what Raven calls the "type A" and "type B" rules of iambic and trochaic verse, placed on facing pages, with "type B" (the type found in Plautus) appearing on the right-hand pages.

A short but excellent discussion of Plautine metre specifically (as opposed to Latin metre generally) can be found in Christenson's edition of Plautus's *Amphitruo* (Christenson 2000: 56-71), and in his edition of Plautus's *Pseudolus* (Christenson 2020: 52-63). Appendix 1 of MacCary and Willcock's edition of *Casina* contains a useful guide to the metres found in this play specifically, though be warned that their discussion of the *ictus* (beat) does not agree with current thinking about Plautine metre (MacCary and Willcock 1976: 211-232). Those who read Italian should consult Questa's 1967 *Introduzione alla metrica di Plauto*.

Below is a simplified explanation of the two most common metres of Plautus: the **trochaic septenarius** (used in the *Casina* for the "recitative" passages that were sung to the music of a woodwind instrument called a *tibia*), and the **iambic senarius**, which was used for the *deverbia*, or spoken dialogue sections.

The Two Most Common Metres in Plautus

In the following explanation:

– a horizontal bar represents a long syllable.

∪ a semi-circular or U-shaped mark represents a short syllable.

× an X-shape represents an anceps, where a syllable may be either long or short.

---

[1] Raven's *Latin Metre* is currently freely available for download at https://archive.org/details/raven-d.-latin-metre-1965

Trochaic Septenarii

A trochaic septenarius is a line theoretically made up of seven trochees plus an additional long syllable at the end.[2] A basic trochee is a long syllable followed by a short syllable ($-\smile$), but in Plautus, the "short" syllable in any of the first six trochees can be either long or short (anceps). We can visualize a trochaic septenarius line as follows (the double vertical bar marks where a diaeresis, i.e. where a word and the metrical foot end in the same place, is commonly found):[3]

$$-\times \quad -\times \quad -\times \quad -\times \parallel -\times \quad -\times \quad -\smile \quad -$$

Potentially any of the first six trochees may be:

- a true trochee ($-\smile$), where the anceps turns out to be a short syllable, or

- a spondee ($--$), where the anceps turns out to be a long syllable.

Furthermore, since the important thing about syllable length in Latin metre is literally how long it took to pronounce, two short syllables can replace a long syllable (or, in other words, a long syllable can be resolved into two shorts),[4] allowing a so-called trochee to potentially be replaced by:

- a dactyl ($-\smile\smile$), where the anceps has theoretically turned out to be long, but that long is resolved into two shorts (i.e., two shorts are substituted for that theoretical long),

- an anapaest ($\smile\smile -$), where the normally long syllable is resolved into two short syllables, and the anceps turns out to be long,

- a tribrach ($\smile\smile\smile$), where the normally long syllable is resolved into two short syllables, and the anceps turns out to be short,

- a proceleusmatic ($\smile\smile\smile\smile$), where the normally long syllable is resolved into two short syllables, and a theoretically long anceps is also resolved into two shorts (rare in trochaic verse).

That so many variations are possible may sound anarchic, but with enough practice it is possible to get a sense of the unifying rhythm that makes passages of trochaic septenarii distinct from the other metres in the play.

---

[2] Such an analysis interprets the line in terms of metrical "feet"; another way to interpret it is in terms of "metra", which are made up of two feet or partial feet, in which case we would say that a trochaic septenarius is a line theoretically made up of 3 pairs of trochees ($-\smile-\smile$) plus a trochee and half trochee ($-\smile-$).

[3] Note that the final syllable counts as long regardless of that syllable's normal length. It is called *brevis in longo* when a short syllable appears where a long syllable would be expected. *Brevis in longo* is common at the end of a line.

[4] Note that, while the final long syllable in the trochaic senarius may be replaced by a short syllable (see *brevis in longo* in note 3 above), it cannot be resolved into two short syllables.

The first passage of trochaic septenarii in the *Casina* is at lines 252-308. We can visualize the scansion of line 252 as follows:

sēd quĭd | aīs? iām | dŏmŭīs- | -t$_i$ ănĭmūm, ‖ pŏtĭŭs | ūt quōd | uīr uĕ- | -līt

NOTE:
- The foot divisions are marked with vertical bars: |
- The double vertical bar: ‖ marks where a diaeresis (where a word and the metrical foot both end in the same place) coincides with a pause in the sense of the line. In this metre this diaeresis usually appears after the fourth foot, and is one of the distinct aspects of a trochaic septenarius.
- The final -*i* of *domuisti*, printed in subscript, was pronounced so subtly, due to the next word beginning with a vowel, that it doesn't count as a syllable within the metre (this is called elision).

The following lines of the *Casina* are in trochaic septenarii: 252-308; 353-423; 515-562; 963-1018.

Iambic Senarii

An iambic senarius is theoretically made up of six iambs.[5] A basic iamb is a short syllable followed by a long ($\smile$ –), but the "short" syllable of the iamb in Roman comedy is an anceps (i.e. it can be either long or short) in all but the last foot. As in the trochaic septarius, the final syllable counts as long regardless of that syllable's normal length (see note 3 above). We can visualize this as follows:

$$\times - \quad \times - \quad \times \,\|\, - \quad \times - \quad \times - \quad \smile -$$

The same possible substitutions as seen above in the trochaic septenarius exist for the iambic senarius: a long syllable, or an anceps syllable that turns out to be long, can be replaced with two short syllables (except for the final syllable in an iambic senarius).

The prologue of the *Casina* is in iambic senarii. We can visualize the scansion of line 1 as follows:

Sālŭē- | -rĕ iŭbĕ- | -ō ‖ spēc- | -tātō- | -rēs ōp- | -tŭmōs

---

[5] That is, six "feet," each comprising the equivalent of an iamb; we could also describe it as three "metra," each comprising two iambs.

NOTE:

- The prominent caesura is here marked with the same notation (a double vertical bar) as for the diaeresis in the trochaic septenarius above. A caesura is the ending of a word in the middle of a foot; in Plautus an iambic senarius usually has a prominent caesura (where a pause in the sense of the line coincides with a caesura) in the third or fourth foot.

The following lines of the *Casina* are in iambic senarii: 1-143; 309-352; 424-514; 563-620, and the *argumentum* (placed at the end of this volume on page 220).

When you can't make the line scan properly, it will probably be because you have missed an elision/prodelision, hiatus, iambic shortening (also known as *brevis brevians*) or one of the other characteristic changes to pronunciation in Plautine verse, and you should consult one of the sources on Latin metre mentioned above.[6] The Latin text in this volume reproduces Lindsay's accent marks (what he called *apices* – Lindsay 1903: vii) placed over a long syllable, or over the first short of a resolved long, where he considered that the metre might otherwise be obscure.

For example, in line 2 of the play (*Fidem qui facitis maxumí, – et uos Fides*) the accent mark over the *-í* of *maxumí* indicates that the *-í* is not elided despite the initial vowel of *et* that follows (i.e. the accent indicates that there is a hiatus after *maxumí*). In line 18 (*ea témpestate flos poetarum fuit*) the accent mark over the *-é-* of *témpestate* indicates that the *-é-* is the long syllable of the iambic foot, despite the fact that the *-a-* of the preceding word *ea* would normally be long (because it is ablative). The *-a-* of *ea* is short in this line because of iambic shortening (*brevis brevians*) (see Raven 1965: 26-27).

The more you practice reading in metre, the easier it will get. Readers who are reasonably familiar with trochaic septenarii and iambic senarii will enjoy practicing on the polymetric cantica of the play. Caesar Questa's Latin edition of the *Casina* lists the metres of each line of the play (Questa 2001: 105-110). This allows the reader to practice reading a line in metre, working out the long and short syllables, and any elision or other pronunciation changes, within the restrictions of that known metre. Especially helpful for reading the more complicated metres is Questa's 1995 edition of the Plautine *cantica*, where he has written out the scansion, in terms of long and short syllables, for all the polymetric *cantica* in each of the plays of Plautus. Be ad-

---

[6] Specifically Raven 1965: 26-28 (sections 14-15), MacCary and Willcock 1976: 214-217, Christenson 2000: 61-65, or Christenson 2020: 52-57.

vised that Questa's Latin text occasionally differs from the Latin text in this volume, since the plays of Plautus were preserved via hand-written copies (manuscripts), and copying errors crept in over the centuries which editors have attempted to correct. Questa's metrical analysis applies to his version of the Latin text, which includes some emendations done since Lindsay produced his text of the play.

Casina (Annotated Latin Text)

©2025 Catherine Tracy, CC BY-NC-ND 4.0   https://doi.org/10.11647/OBP.0482.03

PERSONAE

OLYMPIO: SERVOS (Lysidamus's loyal *uilicus*, or farm manager; enslaved)

CHALINVS: SERVOS (loyal servant to the son of Lysidamus and Cleustrata; enslaved)

CLEVSTRATA: MATRONA (wife of Lysidamus; free)

PARDALISCA: ANCILLA (Cleustrata's elderly servant; enslaved)

MYRRHINA: MATRONA (wife of Alcesimus, and Cleustrata's friend and neighbour; free)

LYSIDAMVS: SENEX (the head of the household, and husband of Cleustrata; free)

ALCESIMVS: SENEX (Myrrhina's husband, neighbour to Cleustrata and Lysidamus; free)

CHYTRIO: COCVS (the hired cook; probably enslaved)

Notes:

- For the acrostic *argumentum* (plot summary) that was added to the play perhaps around 150 CE, see page 220.
- A guide to the pronunciation of the characters' names in English can be found on page 167.
- In the vocabulary and grammar notes for the Latin text of the play, there are frequent references to the Latin grammar books of Bennett and of Allen and Greenough. These can be found online at:
  https://www.thelatinlibrary.com/bennett.html
  https://dcc.dickinson.edu/grammar/latin/credits-and-reuse

PROLOGVS (1-88)

Prologue summary: *The actor speaking the prologue refers to the fact that some of the older members of the current audience may remember the play from when it was first produced, about thirty years before. He encourages the audience to forget about their worries and to enjoy this revival of a play from the past, which was based on a Greek comedy called "The Lottery Players". He gives a brief plot summary, which involves a planned wedding between two slaves, and reassures his audience that, though enslaved people can't marry in Rome, it's possible in Greece, where the play is set. He concludes with a coarse joke about the sexual availability of the actor playing Casina to anyone who will pay money after the show (which will turn out to be a joke on the audience – see note 14 on page 171).*

Saluere iubeo[1] spectatores optumos,[2]

Fidem[3] qui[4] facitis maxumí,[5] – et uos Fides.[6]

si uerum[7] dixi, signum[8] clarum[9] date mihi,

ut uos mi[10] esse aequos[11] iam inde a principio[12] sciam.

qui[13] utuntur[14] uino uetere[15] sapientis[16] puto[17]   5

et qui lubenter[18] ueteres spectant fabulas;[19]

---

[1] *saluere iubeo*: "welcome", "I welcome you".
[2] *optumos = optimos*.
[3] *Fides, Fidei* (f.): "good faith", "honesty", "sincerity" (here personified as the goddess of good faith, etc.).
[4] *qui*: "you, who…".
[5] *maxumi = maximi* (genitive of indefinite value; see Bennett 203.3); translate as "of the greatest value".
[6] *et uos Fides = et uos Fides facit maxumi*.
[7] *uerum, -i* (n.): "the truth".
[8] *signum, -i* (n.): "sign", "indication".
[9] *clarus, -a, -um*: "clear".
[10] *mi = mihi*.
[11] *aequus, -a, -um*: "fair", "friendly".
[12] *iam inde a principio*: "(right/now) from the beginning".
[13] *qui*: "those who…".
[14] *utuntur* (< *utor, uti, usus sum* + ablative): "use", "enjoy".
[15] *uetus, ueteris* (adjective): "old", "aged".
[16] *sapientis = sapientes* (accusative plural < *sapiens, sapientis*: "wise", "having good judgment").
[17] *puto* introduces indirect discourse (the accusative-infinitive construction comprises an implied *eos* (antecedent of *qui*) and an implied *esse*).
[18] *lubenter = libenter* (adverb): "willingly", "gladly".
[19] *fabula, -ae* (f.): "play".

anticua[20] opera[21] et uerba quom[22] uobis placent,[23]

aequom[24] est placere ante[25] <alias>[26] ueteres fabulas:

nam nunc nouae quae prodeunt[27] comoediae[28]

multo[29] sunt nequiores[30] quam nummi[31] noui.   10

nos postquam[32] populi[33] rumore[34] intelleximus[35]

studiose[36] expetere[37] uos Plautinas[38] fabulas,[39]

anticuam[40] eiius[41] edimus[42] comoediam,[43]

quam uos probastis[44] qui estis in senioribus;[45]

nam[46] iuniorum[47] qui sunt non norunt,[48] scio;   15

uerum[49] ut cognoscant[50] dabimus operam[51] sedulo.[52]

---

[20] *anticua = antiqua < antiquus, -a, -um*: "ancient", "old".
[21] *opus, operis* (n.): "work (of literature, art, etc.)".
[22] *quom = cum* (conjunction).
[23] *placeo, -ere, placui, placitum*: "please (+ dative)", "give pleasure to (+ dative)".
[24] *aequom = aequum*.
[25] *ante* (preposition): "before".
[26] *alius, -a, -ud*: "other".
[27] *prodeo, -ire, -iui/-ii, -itum*: "come out", "be produced".
[28] *comoedia, -ae* (f.): "comedy", "comedy as a form of drama or literature".
[29] *multo* (adverb < *multus, -a, -um*): "much".
[30] *nequior, nequioris* (comparative adjective < indeclinable adjective *nequam*): "more worthless".
[31] *nummus, -i* (m.): "coin" (often referring to a sestertius); translate here in plural as "coinage". The "new coinage" was, presumably, of debased value.
[32] *postquam*: "after", "when".
[33] *populus, -i* (m.): "people", "the crowd".
[34] *rumor, -oris* (m.): "rumour", "hearsay"; ablative of source.
[35] *intellego, -ere, -exi, -ectum*: "understand", "perceive", "find out".
[36] *studiose* (< *studiosus, -a, -um*): "eagerly".
[37] *expeto, -ere, -iui, -itum*: "ask for", "look for"; "demand", "want", "desire", "be eager for".
[38] *Plautinus, -a, -um*: "Plautine", "of the playwright Plautus".
[39] *fabulas* (see note 19 on the previous page at line 6, prologue).
[40] *anticuam = antiquam* (see note 20 at line 7, prologue).
[41] *eiius = eius < is, ea, id*.
[42] *edo, -ere, edidi, editum*: "bring forth", "produce", "perform".
[43] *comoediam* (see note 28 at line 9, prologue).
[44] *probastis = probauistis < probo, -are, -aui, -atus*: "approve (of)", "think well done".
[45] *senior, -oris* (comparative of *senex, senis*): "older".
[46] *nam* (conjunction): "for"; translate here "now", "obviously".
[47] *iuniorum* (partitive genitive) < *iunior, iunioris* (comparative of *iuuenis, -is*): "younger".
[48] *norunt = nouerunt < nosco, noscere, novi, notus*: "know", "get to know", "be acquainted with".
[49] *uerum* (conjunction): "but".
[50] *cognosco, -ere, cognoui, cognitus*: "become acquainted with".
[51] *opera, -ae* (f.): "service", "activity", "effort"; *operam dare*: "take care", "give attention".
[52] *sedulo* (adverb): "industriously", "enthusiastically".

haec quom[53] primum[54] acta est,[55] uicit omnis[56] fabulas.[57]

ea témpestate[58] flos[59] poetarum fuit,

qui nunc abierunt[60] hinc[61] in communem[62] locum.

sed tamen[63] apsentes[64] prosunt[65] <pro>[66] praesentibus.[67] 20

uos omnis[68] opere magno[69] esse oratos[70] uolo

benigne[71] ut operam detis[72] ad nostrum gregem.[73]

eicite[74] ex animo[75] curam[76] atque alienum[77] aes[78] *,

ne quis[79] formidet[80] flagitatorem[81] suom:

ludi[82] sunt, ludus datus est[83] argentariis;[84] 25

---

[53] *quom* = *cum*.
[54] *primum* (adverb): "first".
[55] *acta est* < *ago, -ere, egi, actum*: "act", "perform".
[56] *omnis* = *omnes*.
[57] *fabulas* (see note 19 on page 37 at line 6, prologue).
[58] *tempestas, -atis*: (f.): "season", "time"; *ea tempestate* is ablative of time when; see Bennett 230.
[59] *flos, floris* (m.): "flower"; "prime", "glory days".
[60] *abeo, -ire, -iui/-ii, -itum*: "go away", "depart".
[61] *hinc* (adverb): "from this place".
[62] *communis, -is*: "common to all".
[63] *tamen* (adverb): "nevertheless", "still".
[64] *apsentes* = *absentes* < *absum, abesse, afui, afuturus*: "be absent".
[65] *prosum, prodesse, profui, profuturus*: "benefit".
[66] *pro* (preposition + ablative): "as if", "in the same way as".
[67] *praesens, praesentis*: "present", "at hand".
[68] *omnis* = *omnes*.
[69] *opere magno*: "particularly", "especially".
[70] *oro, -are, -aui, -atum*: "ask", "beg"; *esse oratos*: "to have been asked", "to consider yourselves asked" (+ *ut*).
[71] *benigne* (adverb): "kindly", "generously".
[72] *operam dare* (see note 51 on the preceding page at line 16, prologue).
[73] *grex, gregis* (m.): "company", "troop" (of actors).
[74] *eicio, -ere, eieci, eiectum*: "cast/drive out".
[75] *animus, -i* (m.): "mind".
[76] *cura, -ae* (f.): "care", "worry".
[77] *alienus, -a, -um*: "belonging to another".
[78] *aes, aeris* (n.): "money"; *alienum aes*: "debt" (literally: "another's money").
[79] *quis, quid*: "anyone".
[80] *formido, -are, -aui, -atum*: "be afraid of".
[81] *flagitator, -oris* (m.): "creditor", "debt collector".
[82] *ludus, -i* (m.): "game", "sport"; (plural): "festival", "public spectacles".
[83] *ludum dare* (+ dative): "allow (someone) to enjoy themselves"; "make (someone) ridiculous", "play tricks on (someone)"; *ludus datus est argentariis* is a pun, meaning "money-lenders are allowed some fun too" and/or "money-lenders are outwitted" (Franko suggests, for this line: "it's the *ludi*, the bankers are e-luded" – Franko 2001: 160).
[84] *argentarius, -i* (m.): "banker", "money-lender".

tranquillum[85] est, Alcedonia[86] sunt circum[87] forum:[88]
ratione[89] utuntur,[90] ludis[91] poscunt[92] neminem,[93]
secundum[94] ludos reddunt[95] autem[96] nemini.
aures uociuae[97] si sunt, animum aduortite:[98]
comoediai[99] nomen dare uobis uolo.   30
Κληρούμενοι[100] uocatur haec comoedia
graece,[101] latine[102] Sortientes.[103] Diphilus[104]
hanc graece scripsit, postid[105] rusum[106] denuo[107]
latine Plautus cum latranti[108] nomine.[109]

---

[85] *tranquillus, -a, -um*: "quiet", "calm".
[86] *Alcedonia, -orum* (n.): "halcyon days" (the two-week period on either side of the Winter solstice when the seas were supposed to be calm enough for the halcyon (kingfisher) to lay its eggs on a floating nest on the sea – see Ovid, *Metamorphoses* 11.645-6).
[87] *circum* (preposition): "around", "in the vicinity of".
[88] *forum, -i* (n.): "forum" (the forum was a big open area, the bustling economic and political centre of Rome).
[89] *ratio, rationis* (f.): "reason", "judgment", "prudence".
[90] *utor, uti, usus sum* (see note 14 on page 37 at line 5, prologue).
[91] *ludis* (ablative of time when): "during the festival".
[92] *posco, -ere, poposci, –*: "ask", "demand"; translate here: "ask (no one) to pay their debts".
[93] *nemo, neminis* (m./f.): "no one"
[94] *secundum* (preposition): "after", "following".
[95] *reddo, -ere, reddidi, redditum*: "return", "repay" (+ dative of person repaid); "render", "make or cause to be".
[96] *autem* (conjunction): "on the other hand", "however".
[97] *uociuus, -a, -um* = *uacuus, -a, -um*: "empty"; translate here: "ready to listen".
[98] *aduortite* = *aduertite* < *aduerto, -ere, aduerti, aduersum*: "turn/direct (a thing) towards"); *animum aduortite*: "pay attention".
[99] *cōmoedĭāī* (= *comoediae*). The older disyllabic genitive singular ending "-*āī*" implies a more formal tone (de Melo 2023: 110).
[100] Κληρούμενοι = *Clēroumenoe*: "The Lot-Drawers", "The Lottery Players".
[101] *graece* (adverb): "in Greek".
[102] *latine* (adverb): "in Latin".
[103] *Sortientes* (present active participle) < *sortior, sortiri, sortitus sum*: "draw lots".
[104] Diphilus was a writer of Greek New Comedy who wrote during the late fourth and early third centuries BCE.
[105] *postid* = *post id*.
[106] *rusum* = *rursum* (adverb): "again"
[107] *denuo* (adverb): "once more", "again".
[108] *latro, -are, -aui, -atum*: "bark".
[109] *cum latranti nomine*: "with the barking name" (*plautus* meant "flat", hence, according to the second century CE grammarian Festus, the name "Plautus" was often used as a name for dogs with broad flat ears that hung down – Paul. Fest. p. 231 M).

senex[110] híc[111] maritus[112] itat;[113] ei[114] est filius,   35

is una[115] cum patre ín illisce[116] itat aedibus.[117]

est ei[118] quidam[119] seruos[120] qui in morbo[121] cubat,[122]

immo[123] hercle[124] uero[125] in lecto,[126] ne quid[127] mentiar;[128]

is seruos,[129] sed abhinc[130] annos factum est[131] sedecim[132]

quom[133] conspicatust[134] primulo[135] crepusculo[136]   40

puellam exponi.[137] adit[138] extemplo[139] ad mulierem[140]

quae illam exponebat, orat[141] ut eam det sibi:

---

[110] *senex, senis* (m.): "old man".
[111] *hīc* (adverb): "here".
[112] *maritus, -a, -um*: "married".
[113] *ito, -are, -aui, -atum*: "live", "dwell".
[114] *ei* (dative of possession, see Bennett 190) < *is, ea, id*.
[115] *unā* (adverb): "together"
[116] *illisce = illis*.
[117] *aedis/aedes, -is* (f.): "building", "house" (often used in the plural, as here).
[118] *ei* (dative of possession, referring to the *senex*).
[119] *quidam, quaedam, quoddam*: "a certain".
[120] *seruos = seruus*.
[121] *morbus, -i* (m.): "sickness".
[122] *cubo, -are, cubui, cubitum*: "lie down", "be in bed", "lie down to sleep".
[123] *immo* (adverb): "no, really", "in fact".
[124] *hercle* (exclamation): "by Hercules". In Plautus, the oath *"hercle"* (or sometimes *"mehercle"*) was commonly used by men as mild Latin swear words, referring to the most popular hero of both Greek and Latin mythology. Both men and women also swore by the divine hero Pollux (*"pol"* or *"edepol"* in Latin), whereas only women swore by the hero Castor (mortal twin brother of Pollux), usually with the Latin form *"mecastor"* or *"ecastor"*. We know this from the second century CE author Aulus Gellius, who wrote: "In the ancient authors women do not swear by Hercules, and men do not swear by Castor. [...] 'Edepol' however, which means to swear 'by Pollux', is used by men and women" (Gell. Noctes Atticae 11.6.1; 4).
[125] *uero* (adverb): "truly", "certainly".
[126] *lectus, -i* (m.): "bed".
[127] *quid* (object of *mentiar*) < *quis, quid*: "anyone / anything".
[128] *mentior, -iri, mentitus sum*: "lie (about)", "tell a lie (about)".
[129] *seruos = seruus*.
[130] *adhinc* (adverb): "ago" (translate with the accusative of duration of time: *annos sedecim*).
[131] *factum est* (< *facio, -ere, feci, factum*): "it happened".
[132] *sedecim* (cardinal number; indeclinable): "sixteen".
[133] *quom = cum*.
[134] *conspicatust = conspicatus est* < *conspicor, -ari, -atus sum*: "catch sight of", "notice", "see".
[135] *primulus, -a, -um*: "first".
[136] *crepusculum, -i* (n.): "twilight", "dusk"; *primulo crepusculo* is ablative of time when.
[137] *expono, -ere, -posui, -positum*: "expose", "abandon".
[138] *adeo, -ire, -iui/-ii, -itum*: "go to", "approach".
[139] *extemplo* (adverb): "immediately".
[140] *mulier, mulieris* (f.): "woman".
[141] *oro, -are, -aui, -atum* (see note 70 on page 39 at line 21, prologue).

exorat,¹⁴² aufert;¹⁴³ detulit¹⁴⁴ recta¹⁴⁵ domum,¹⁴⁶
dat erae¹⁴⁷ suae, orat ut eam curet,¹⁴⁸ educet.¹⁴⁹
era fecit, educauit magna industria,¹⁵⁰   45
quasi si¹⁵¹ esset ex se nata,¹⁵² non multo secus.¹⁵³
postquam¹⁵⁴ ea adoleuit¹⁵⁵ ad eam aetatem¹⁵⁶ út uiris
placere¹⁵⁷ posset, eam puellam híc senex
amat ecflictim,¹⁵⁸ ét item¹⁵⁹ contra¹⁶⁰ filius.
nunc sibi¹⁶¹ utérque¹⁶² contra legiones parat,¹⁶³   50
paterque filiusque, clam¹⁶⁴ alter alterum:¹⁶⁵
pater adlegauit¹⁶⁶ uilicum¹⁶⁷ qui¹⁶⁸ posceret¹⁶⁹
sibi istánc¹⁷⁰ uxorem:¹⁷¹ is sperat,¹⁷² si ei¹⁷³ sit data,

---

¹⁴² *exoro, -are, -aui, -atum*: "persuade", "plead".
¹⁴³ *aufero, -ferre, abstuli, ablatum*: "take away", "carry off".
¹⁴⁴ *defero, -ferre, detuli, delatum*: "bring away", "carry away".
¹⁴⁵ *recta* (adverb): "directly".
¹⁴⁶ *domus, -us/-i* (f.): "home", "house".
¹⁴⁷ *era, -ae* (f.): "mistress (of the house; of the household slaves)".
¹⁴⁸ *curo, -are, -aui, -atum*: "care for".
¹⁴⁹ *educo, -are, -aui, -atum*: "raise (a child)", "bring up", "educate".
¹⁵⁰ *industria, -ae* (f.): "diligence", "care".
¹⁵¹ *quasi si*: "just as if", "as though".
¹⁵² *nascor, nasci, natus sum*: "be born".
¹⁵³ *non multo secus*: "not much differently".
¹⁵⁴ *postquam*: see note 32 on page 38 at line 11, prologue.
¹⁵⁵ *adolesco, -ere, adoleui, adultum*: "grow up", "reach maturity".
¹⁵⁶ *aetas, aetatis* (f.): "age", "stage of life", "life".
¹⁵⁷ *placeo, -ere, placui, placitum*: "be pleasing to" (+ dative).
¹⁵⁸ *ecflictim = efflictim* (adverb): "passionately", "desperately".
¹⁵⁹ *item* (adverb): "likewise", "besides".
¹⁶⁰ *contra* (adverb): "in opposition (to him)", "on the other side".
¹⁶¹ *sibi* (dative of reference): "for himself".
¹⁶² *uterque, utraque, utrumque*: "each" (of two); "both".
¹⁶³ *paro, -are, -aui, -atum*: "prepare"; *legiones parat*: "recruits their legions/armies".
¹⁶⁴ *clam* (adverb): "secretly (from)", "unknown to" (+ accusative).
¹⁶⁵ *alter alterum*: "the one (secretly from) the other".
¹⁶⁶ *adlego < allego, -are, -aui, -atum*: "employ (someone) as an agent", "use (someone) as a proxy", "delegate".
¹⁶⁷ *uilicus, -i* (m.): "slave-overseer", "(enslaved) farm manager".
¹⁶⁸ *qui* introduces a relative clause of purpose (see Bennett 282.2).
¹⁶⁹ *posco, -ere, poposci, –*: "ask", "demand".
¹⁷⁰ *istanc = istam*.
¹⁷¹ *uxor, uxoris* (f.): "wife".
¹⁷² *spero, -are, -aui, -atum*: "hope".
¹⁷³ *ei* (refers to the *uilicus*, Olympio).

sibi fore[174] paratas[175] clam[176] uxorem excubias[177] foris;[178]

filius is autem armigerum[179] adlegauit suom[180]

qui[181] sibi eam uxorem poscat: scit, si id impetret,[182] 55

futurum[183] quod amat intra[184] praesepis[185] suas.

senis[186] uxor sensit[187] uirum amóri[188] operam dare,[189]

propterea[190] úna[191] consentit[192] cum filio.

ille autem postquam filium sensit suom 60

eandem[193] illam amare et esse impedimento[194] sibi,

hinc[195] adulescentem[196] peregre[197] ablegauit[198] pater;

sciens[199] ei[200] mater dat operam apsenti[201] tamen.[202]

---

[174] *fore* = *futurum esse*: "(that) there will be".
[175] *paratas* (see note 163 on the preceding page at line 50, prologue).
[176] *clam* (see note 164 on the facing page at line 51, prologue).
[177] *excubia, -ae* (f.): "night quarters" (normally a military term, referring to soldiers keeping night watch, but here referring to the *senex* Lysidamus's hope for extra-marital sex).
[178] *foris*: "out of doors", "away from home".
[179] *armiger, armigeri* (m.): "armour-bearer", "shield-bearer" (a slave/servant assistant to a soldier).
[180] *suom* = *suum* (modifies an implied *seruom*).
[181] *qui* (see note 168 on the preceding page at line 52, prologue).
[182] *impretro, -are, -aui, -atum*: "obtain", "succeed (at)".
[183] *futurum* (supply *esse*): "there there will be".
[184] *intra* (preposition + accusative): "within".
[185] *praesepīs* = *praesepēs* < *praesepes, praesepis* (f.): "house", "dwelling" (often used in the plural, as here).
[186] *senex, senis* (see note 110 on page 41 at line 35, prologue).
[187] *sentio, -ire, sensi, sensum*: "perceive", "understand", "realize".
[188] *amor, amoris* (m.): "love", "love affair".
[189] *operam dare* (see note 51 on page 38 at line 16, prologue).
[190] *propterea* (adverb): "therefore", "because of this/that".
[191] *unā* (adverb): "together".
[192] *consentio, -ire, -sensi, -sensum*: "agree".
[193] *idem, eadem, idem* (adjective): "the same".
[194] *impedimentum, -i* (n.): "hindrance", "obstacle", "interference"; *impedimento* is dative of purpose or tendency (see Bennett 191.2); translate *esse impedimento sibi*: "(that he) was an obstacle to him".
[195] *hinc* (see note 61 on page 39 at line 19, prologue).
[196] *adulescens, adulescentis* (m./f.): "young man", "young woman".
[197] *peregre* (adverb): "abroad", "out of the country".
[198] *ablego, -are, -aui, -atum*: "send away".
[199] *sciens*: present active participle < *scio, scire, sciui/scii, scitum*.
[200] *ei* refers to the *adulescens*.
[201] *apsenti* = *absenti* < *absens, absentis*: "absent", "(being) away".
[202] *tamen* (adverb): "nevertheless", "still".

is,[203] ne exspectetis,[204] hodie[205] in hac comoedia
in urbem non redibit:[206] Plautus noluit,[207] 65
pontem[208] interrupit,[209] qui erat ei[210] in itinere.[211]
sunt hic[212] inter[213] se quos nunc credo dicere:
'quaeso[214] hercle,[215] quíd istuc[216] est? seruiles[217] nuptiae?[218]
seruin[219] uxorem ducent[220] aut poscent[221] sibi?
nouom[222] attulerunt,[223] quod fit[224] nusquam[225] gentium.'[226] 70
at ego aiio[227] id fieri in Graecia et Carthagini,[228]
et hic[229] in nostra terra in <terra> Apulia;[230]
maioreque opere[231] ibi seruiles nuptiae

---

[203] *is* refers to the *adulescens*.
[204] *exspecto, -are, -aui, -atum*: "look out for", "expect".
[205] *hodie* (adverb): "today".
[206] *redeo, -ire, -iui/-ii, -itum*: "return", "come back".
[207] *nolo, nolle, nolui, –*: "not... wish", "not... want".
[208] *pons, pontis* (m.): "bridge".
[209] *interrumpo, -ere, interrupi, interruptum*: "break up", "destroy".
[210] *ei* (dative of reference) refers to the *adulescens*.
[211] *iter, itineris* (n.): "journey", "route".
[212] *hīc* (adverb).
[213] *inter* (preposition + accusative): "between", "among".
[214] *quaeso*: "I beg", "please" (< *quaeso, -ere, -iui/-ii*: "seek", "beg").
[215] *hercle* (see note 124 on page 41 at line 38, prologue).
[216] *istuc* = *istud* < *iste, ista, istud*: "that of yours", "that" (implying contempt).
[217] *seruilis, -is*: "servile", "relating to enslaved persons".
[218] *nuptiae, -arum* (f. pl.): "marriage", "wedding", "wedding festivities / rituals".
[219] *seruin* = *serui* + *ne*.
[220] *uxorem ducere*: "to marry".
[221] *posco, -ere, poposci, –*: "ask", "demand".
[222] *nouom* = *nouum*.
[223] *affero, afferre, attuli, allatum*: "bring in", "introduce" (the actors are the subject of *attulerunt*).
[224] *fio, fieri, factus sum*: "be done", "be made", "happen", "take place".
[225] *nusquam* (adverb): "nowhere", "in no place".
[226] *gens, gentis* (f.): "people", "nation"; *gentium* is a partitive genitive, or genitive of the whole; see Bennett 201.
[227] *aiio* = *aio* (defective verb): "say"; "say yes", "affirm".
[228] *Carthagini* = *Carthagine* (locative case) < *Carthago, Carthaginis* (f.): "Carthage" (city in North Africa).
[229] *hīc* (adverb).
[230] *Apulia, -ae* (f.): "Apulia" (a region in south-eastern Italy).
[231] *maioreque opere* (comparative form of *magno opere*): "even more seriously", "with more enthusiasm".

quam liberales[232] etiam curari[233] solent;[234]

id ni fit,[235] mecum pignus[236] si quis[237] uolt[238] dato[239]   75

in urnam[240] mulsi,[241] Poenus[242] dum[243] iudex[244] siet[245]

uel Graecus adeo,[246] uel mea caussa[247] Apulus.[248]

quid nunc? nihil agitis?[249] sentio,[250] nemo[251] sitit.[252]

reuortar[253] ad illam puellam éxpositiciam:[254]

quam serui summa[255] ui[256] sibi uxorem expetunt,[257]   80

ea inuenietur[258] et pudica[259] et libera,[260]

ingenua[261] Atheniensis,[262] neque quicquam[263] stupri[264]

---

[232] *liberalis, -is*: "free-born".
[233] *curo, -are, -aui, -atum*: "arrange", "manage".
[234] *soleo, -ere, – , solitus sum*: "be accustomed", "tend" (+ infinitive).
[235] *id ni fit*: "if that isn't so", "if it's not true".
[236] *pignus, pignoris* (n.): "pledge", "bet".
[237] *quis, quid*: "anyone / anything".
[238] *uolt = uult < uolo, uelle, uolui, –*.
[239] *dato* (3rd person singular future imperative active < *do, dare, dedi, datum*).
[240] *urna, -ae* (f.): "urn", "jar".
[241] *mulsum, -i* (n.): "honeyed wine"; *mecum pignus dato in urnam mulsum*: "let him make a bet with me for a jar of honeyed wine".
[242] *Poenus, -a, -um*: "Carthaginian", "Punic".
[243] *dum* (+ subjunctive): "provided that".
[244] *iudex, iudicis* (m.): "judge".
[245] *siet = sit < sum, esse, fui, futurus*.
[246] *adeo* (adverb): "even", "as well".
[247] *caussā = causā; meā caussā*: "for all I care".
[248] *Apulus, -a, -um*: "Apulian", "from Apulia".
[249] *ago, -ere, egi, actum*: "do", "act"; *nihil agitis*: "you aren't interested?", "you're not biting?"
[250] *sentio, -ire, sensi, sensum* (see note 187 on page 43 at line 58, prologue).
[251] *nemo, neminis* (see note 93 on page 40 at line 27, prologue).
[252] *sitio, -ire, sitiui, –*: "be thirsty".
[253] *reuortar = reuertar < reuertor, reuerti, reuersus sum*: "return", "go back".
[254] *expositicius, -a, -um*: "exposed", "foundling".
[255] *summus, -a, -um*: "highest", "greatest".
[256] *uis, uis* (f.): "power", "might".
[257] *expeto, -ere, -iui, -itum* (see note 37 on page 38 at line 12, prologue).
[258] *inuenio, -ire, inueni, inuentum*: "find", "discover".
[259] *pudicus, -a, -um*: "sexually pure", "virtuous", "chaste".
[260] *liber, libera, liberum*: "free", "free-born".
[261] *ingenuus, -a, -um*: "free-born", "native".
[262] *Atheniensis, -is* (m./f.): "Athenian", "Athenian citizen".
[263] *quisquam, quaequam, quicquam*: "any(one) / any(thing)", "whoever / whatever".
[264] *stuprum, -i* (n.): "lewdness", "inappropriate sexual behaviour", "debauchery"; *stupri* is a partitive genitive, or genitive of the whole (see Bennett 201.2).

faciet[265] profecto[266] in hac quidem[267] comoedia.
mox[268] hercle uero,[269] post transactam[270] fabulam,[271]
argentum[272] si quis[273] dederit, ut[274] ego suspicor,[275]   85
ultro[276] ibit nuptum,[277] non manebit[278] auspices.[279]
tantum est.[280] ualete,[281] bene rem gerite,[282] [et] uincite[283]
uirtute uera, quod fecistis antidhac.[284]

---

[265] *neque quicquam stupri faciet*: "and she won't do anything indecent", "and she won't be having sex at all".
[266] *profecto* (adverb): "certainly".
[267] *quidem* (adverb): "at least".
[268] *mox* (adverb): "soon".
[269] *uero* (see note 125 on page 41 at line 38, prologue).
[270] *transigo, -ere, transegi, transactum*: "finish", "perform".
[271] *fabula, -ae* (see note 19 on page 37 at line 6, prologue).
[272] *argentum, -i* (n.): "silver", "money".
[273] *quis, quid* (see note 237 on the previous page at line 75, prologue).
[274] *ut*: "as".
[275] *suspicor, -ari, -atus sum*: "suspect", "suppose".
[276] *ultro* (adverb): "of his/her own accord", "on his/her own initiative" (the subject is the male actor who played Casina).
[277] *nuptum* (supine < *nubo, -ere, -nupsi, nuptum*: "marry", "be married"); *ibit nuptum*: "he/she will do a bit of marrying".
[278] *maneo, -ere, mansi, mansus*: "stay", "wait for".
[279] *auspex, auspicis* (m./f.): "priest who interprets omens given by birds", "augur", "soothsayer".
[280] *tantum est*: "that's all", "that's it".
[281] *ualete*: "fare well", "so long".
[282] *bene rem gerite*: "manage things well", "be successful (in your endeavours)".
[283] *uinco, -ere, uici, uictum*: "conquer".
[284] *antidhac* (adverb): "before", "formerly".

ACTVS I

The play is supposed to take place in the Greek city of Athens. The opening scene takes place in front of two neighbouring houses, one belonging to Lysidamus and his wife Cleustrata, the other belonging to their neighbours Alcesimus and his wife Myrrhina. The exit at stage left leads to the forum; the exit at stage right leads to the countryside.

I.i OLYMPIO, CHALINVS (89-143)

Scene summary: *Olympio (Lysidamus's enslaved farm manager) and Chalinus (also a slave in Lysidamus's household, but one who served his son in the army and is loyal to this son) exchange insults over their shared desire to be married to the pretty young Casina. Olympio taunts Chalinus with his plan to have Chalinus put under his authority on the farm. He says he'll force Chalinus to work at a tediously pointless job, and that he'll make him spend the night where he'll have to overhear Olympio's wedding night with Casina.*

Olympio: Non mihi licere[1] meam rem me[2] solum,[3] ut[4] uolo,

loqui[5] atque cogitare[6] sine ted[7] arbitro?[8]   90

quid[9] tu, malum,[10] me sequere?[11] **Chalinus:** quia certum[12] est mihi,

quasi[13] umbra,[14] quoquo[15] tu ibis, te semper sequi;[16]

---

[1] *licere* (exclamatory infinitive) < *licet, licere, licuit, licitum est*: "be allowed", "be permitted" (+ dative of person to whom the thing is (not) allowed).
[2] *me* is the accusative subject of the infinitives *loqui* and *cogitare*.
[3] *solus, -a, -um*: "alone".
[4] *ut*: "as".
[5] *loquo, loqui, locutus sum*: "speak", "talk" (about).
[6] *cogito, -are, -aui, -atum*: "think".
[7] *ted = te*.
[8] *arbiter, arbitri* (m.): "judge", "onlooker"; translate here "eavesdropper".
[9] *quid*: "why?".
[10] *malum, -i* (n.): "misfortune", "misery" (used here as a term of abuse).
[11] *sequere* (2nd person singular present indicative < *sequor, sequi, secutus sum*: "follow").
[12] *certus, -a, -um*: "certain", "settled", "resolved".
[13] *quasi* (adverb): "as if", "just like".
[14] *umbra, -ae* (f.): "shadow", "ghost".
[15] *quoquo* (adverb): "(to) wherever".
[16] *certum est mihi ... te semper sequi*: "it's certain that I'll always follow you", "I'll certainly always follow you".

quin[17] edepol[18] etiam si in crucem[19] uis[20] pergere,[21]

sequi decretumst.[22] dehinc[23] conicito[24] ceterum,[25]

possisne necne[26] clam[27] me sutelis[28] tuis   95

praeripere[29] Casinam uxorem, proinde ut[30] postulas.[31]

Olympio: quid tibi negotist[32] mecum? **Chalinus:** quid ais,[33] inpudens?[34]

quid in urbe reptas,[35] uilice hau[36] magni preti?[37]

Olympio: lubet.[38] **Chalinus:** quin[39] ruri[40] es in praefectura[41] tua?

---

[17] *quin*: "no, really", "I mean!"; "actually", "in fact", "but"; "why... not?"
[18] *edepol*: "by Pollux!" (see note 124 on page 41 at line 38, prologue).
[19] *crux, crucis* (f.): "cross" (referring to the torture device used in crucifixion, which was the most extreme punishment given to slaves).

References to crucifixion occur quite casually in Plautus, as though they weren't meant literally, though crucifixion was a real punishment that presumably the slaves in Plautus's audience knew and feared. Jokes that were obviously funny to Plautus's audience but that we don't find funny now are a useful reminder of how much we don't understand about mid-republican Roman society.

[20] *uis* < *uolo, uelle, uolui,* –.
[21] *pergo, -ere, perrexi, perrectum*: "go", "proceed".
[22] *decretumst* = *decretum est* < *decerno, -ere, decreui, decretum*: "decide", "determine", "decree"; *sequi decretumst* means essentially the same as *certum est mihi... te... sequi*.
[23] *dehinc* (adverb): "henceforth", "from now on".
[24] *conicito* (2nd person singular future imperative active < *conicio, -ere, conieci, coniectum*: "bring together", "infer", "conclude".
[25] *ceterum* (adverb): "else", "besides", "for the rest".
[26] *possisne necne*: "whether or not you could...".
[27] *clam* (adverb): "secretly (from)", "unknown to" (+ accusative).
[28] *sutela, -ae* (f.): "trick", "machination".
[29] *praeripio, -ere, praeripui, praereptum*: "snatch away", "grab".
[30] *proinde ut*: "just as", "like".
[31] *postulo, -are, -aui, -atum*: "ask", "desire", "claim".
[32] *negotist* = *negotii est*; *negotium, -ii* (n.): "business"; *tibi* is a dative of reference and *negotii* is a partitive genitive; translate *quid tibi negotist mecum* as "what business do you have with me?" or "what business is it of yours?".
[33] *ais* (2nd person singular present indicative active < *aio*: "say"; "say yes", "affirm").
[34] *inpudens* = *impudens* (adjective): "shameless", "impudent".
[35] *repto, -are, -aui, -atum*: "creep", "crawl".
[36] *hau* = *haud*: "not at all".
[37] *preti* = *pretii* < *pretium, -i* (n.): "value", "price", "worth"; (*hau*) *magni preti* (genitive of quality, see Bennett 203): "of (no) great value".
[38] *lubet* = *libet* < *libet, libuit, libitus est* (impersonal verb): "it is pleasing"; translate here: "because I want to".
[39] *quin*: "no, really", "I mean!"; "actually", "in fact", "but"; "why... not?"
[40] *ruri* = *rure* (locative case) < *rus, ruris* (n.): "the country", "the farm".
[41] *praefectura, -ae* (f.): "district", "area of control/authority" (*praefectura* normally referred to the area over which a provincial or municipal governor had authority).

quin potius[42] quod legatum[43] est tibi negotium, 100
id curas[44] atque urbanis[45] rebus[46] te apstines?[47]
huc[48] mihi uenisti sponsam[49] praereptum[50] meam:
abi[51] rús,[52] abi díerectus[53] tuam in prouinciam.[54]
Olympio: Chaline, non sum oblitus[55] officium[56] meum:
praefeci[57] ruri recte[58] qui[59] curet tamen.[60] 105
ego huc quod[61] ueni in urbem[62] si impetrauero,[63]
uxorem ut istam ducam[64] quam tu deperis,[65]
bellam et tenellam[66] Casinam, conseruam[67] tuam,
quando ego eam mecum rus[68] uxorem abduxero,[69]
ruri[70] incubabo[71] usque[72] in praefectura[73] mea. 110

---

[42] *potius* (comparative adverb): "rather", "instead".
[43] *lego, -are, -aui, -atum*: "entrust", "commit".
[44] *curo, -are, -aui, -atum*: "take care of", "look after", "arrange", "make sure".
[45] *urbanus, -a, -um*: "urban", "relating to the city", "sophisticated".
[46] *res, rei* (f.): "thing", "circumstance", "situation", "matter", concern".
[47] *apstines = abstines < abstineo, -ere, -ui, abstentum*: "keep away", "abstain" (from).
[48] *huc* (adverb): "to this place".
[49] *sponsa, -ae* (f.): "bride".
[50] *praereptum* (supine < *praeripio, -ere, -ripui, -reptum*: "take away", "carry off"; the supine here expresses purpose, with *sponsam... meam* as its direct object, see Bennett 340).
[51] *abi* (2nd person singular present imperative active < *abeo, -ire, -ii/-iui, -itum*: "go away".
[52] *rus* here is the accusative of limit of motion, see Bennett 182).
[53] *dierectus* (adverb): "directly", "immediately".
[54] *prouincia, -ae* (f.): "province", "business", "area of authority".
[55] *obliuiscor, -i, oblitus sum*: "forget".
[56] *officium, -ii* (n.): "duty", "job".
[57] *praeficio, -ere, -feci, -fectum*: "put in charge", "appoint".
[58] *recte* (adverb): "properly", "correctly".
[59] *qui* introduces a relative clause of purpose (see Bennett 282.2); translate *praefeci... qui curet tamen* as "I put someone in charge to look after (things), anyway".
[60] *tamen* (adverb): "nevertheless", "still".
[61] *quod*: "because", "the fact that"; translate here: "the reason why".
[62] *ego huc quod ueni in urbem*: "what I came to the city for".
[63] *impetrauero* (1st person singular future perfect indicative active) < *impetro, -are, -aui, -atum*: "obtain", "succeed".
[64] *uxorem ducere*: "to marry".
[65] *depereo, -ire, -iui/-ii, -itum*: "die", "be lost", "be desperately in love with (+ accusative)".
[66] *tenellus, -a, -um*: "tender", "delicate".
[67] *conserva, -ae* (f.): "fellow (female) slave", "(female) slave of the same household".
[68] *rus* (accusative of limit of motion).
[69] *abduco, -ere, -duxi, -ductum*: "lead away", "bring back".
[70] *ruri = rure* (locative case).
[71] *incubo, -are, -aui, -atum*: "bed down"; translate here: "sleep every night".
[72] *usque* (adverb): "continuously", "constantly", "without interruption".
[73] *praefectura* (see note 41 on the preceding page at line 102, I.i).

Chalinus: tun[74] illam ducas?[75] hercle[76] me suspendio[77]

quam[78] tú eius potior[79] fias[80] satiust[81] mortuom.[82]

Olympio: mea praedast[83] illa: proin[84] tu te in laqueum[85] induas.[86]

Chalinus: ex sterculino[87] ecfosse,[88] túa illaec[89] praeda sit?

Olympio: scies hóc ita esse. **Chalinus:** uae tibi![90] **Olympio:** quot[91] te modis,[92]   115

si uiuo, ebo in nuptiis[93] miserum[94] meis!

Chalinus: quid tu mihi facies? **Olympio:** egone[95] quid faciam tibi?

primum omnium huic lucebis[96] nouae nuptae facem;[97]

postilla[98] ut semper inprobus[99] nihilique[100] sis,[101]

---

[74] *tun = tune*.
[75] *ducas* (deliberative subjunctive) = *uxorem ducas*.
[76] *hercle* (see note 124 on page 41 at line 38, prologue).
[77] *suspendium, -ii* (n.): "hanging".
[78] *quam* (relative adverb): "than".
[79] *potior, potius* (comparative adjective): "better entitled to", "having greater control over" (+ genitive).
[80] *quam tu eius potior fias*: "than that you become more entitled to her", "than that you get more rights over her".
[81] *satiust= satius est*: "it is better", "it is preferable".
[82] *me suspendio... satiust mortuom*: "it's better I be dead from hanging", "it would be better for me to be hanged".
[83] *praedast = praeda est; praeda, -ae* (f.): "booty", "prize", "spoils of war".
[84] *proin* (adverb): "accordingly", "therefore".
[85] *laqueus, -i* (m.): "noose".
[86] *induo, -ere, indui, indutum*: "put on", "clothe oneself in".
[87] *sterculinum, -i* (n.): "dung heap", "midden".
[88] *ecfosse* (perfect passive participle masculine vocative singular) = *effosse < effodio, -ere, -odi, -ossum*: "dig out"; *ex sterculino ecfosse*: "you thing, dug out of a dung heap!", "you piece of shit!".
[89] *illaec = illa*.
[90] *uae tibi*: "woe to you!", "just go and die!".
[91] *quot* (adverb): "how many".
[92] *modus, -i* (m.): "way".
[93] *nuptiae, -arum* (f. pl.): "marriage", "wedding", "wedding festivities / rituals".
[94] *te... ebo miserum*: "I'll make you miserable".
[95] The affirmative particle *-ne* here acts to underline the pronoun *ego*.
[96] *luceo, -ere, luxi, –*: "shine", "cause to shine".
[97] *fax, facis* (f.): "torch".
[98] *postilla* (adverb): "afterwards".
[99] *inprobus = improbus < improbus, -a, -um*: "shameless", "wicked".
[100] *nihili* (genitive of indefinite value; see Bennett 203.3); translate as "of no account", "worthless".
[101] *ut semper inprobus nihilique sis*: "so that you'll always be shameless and worthless".

postid[102] locorum[103] quando ad uillam[104] ueneris,　　　　　　　　120
dabitur tibi amphora[105] una et una semita,[106]
fons[107] unus, unum ahenum[108] et octo[109] dolia:[110]
quae nisi erunt semper plena,[111] ego té implebo[112] flagris.[113]
ita te aggerunda[114] curuom[115] aqua faciam probe[116]
ut postilena[117] possit ex te fieri.[118]　　　　　　　　　　　　　　125
post autem ruri nisi tu áceruom[119] ederis[120]
aut quasi[121] lumbricus[122] terram, quod[123] te[124] postules[125]
gustare[126] quicquam,[127] numquam edepol ieiunium[128]
ieiunumst[129] aeque atque[130] ego te ruri reddibo.[131]

---

[102] *postid* (adverb): "afterwards", "then".
[103] *locus, -i* (m.): "place", "spot", "topic", "point"; *locorum* is a partitive genitive; translate *post locorum* "the next point".
[104] *uilla, -ae* (f.): "farm", "country estate".
[105] *amphora, -ae* (f.): "earthenware pitcher / jar".
[106] *semita, -ae* (f.): "path".
[107] *fons, fontis* (m.): "fountain", "spring".
[108] *ahenum, -i* (n.): "bronze pot / kettle".
[109] *octo* (indeclinable cardinal numeral): "eight".
[110] *dolium, -ii* (n.): "wide-mouthed earthenware jar" (a *dolium* was much larger than an *amphora*).
[111] *plenus, -a, -um*: "full".
[112] *impleo, -ere, -pleui, -pletum*: "fill up".
[113] *flagrum, -i* (n.): "whip", "scourge".
[114] *aggerundā* (gerundive) < *aggero, -ere, aggessi, aggestum*: "carry", "bring".
[115] *curuom = curuum* < *curuus, -a, -um*: "bent", "bent over".
[116] *prope* (adverb): "properly".
[117] *postilena, -ae* (f.): "crupper" (a piece of horse tack consisting of a loop that goes under the horse's tail to stop the saddle from slipping forward). *Postilena* may be a play on the name *Chalinus*, which refers to another piece of horse tack: "bridle" (Franko 1999: 11, note 28).
[118] *fio, fieri, factus sum*: "be done", "be made", "happen", "take place".
[119] *aceruom = aceruum* < *aceruus, -i* (m.): "heap", "pile"; translate here "pile of hay", "heap of cattle fodder".
[120] *ederis* (2nd person singular perfect subjunctive active) < *edo, -ere, edi, esum*: "eat".
[121] *quasi* (see note 13 on page 47 at line 92, I.i).
[122] *lumbricus, -i* (m.): "earth worm".
[123] *quod*: "because"; "the reason why", "the fact that", "as for".
[124] *te* is the accusative subject of the infinitive *gustare* (indirect discourse introduced by *postules*).
[125] *postulo, -are, -aui, -atum* (see note 31 on page 48 at line 96, I.i).
[126] *gusto, -are, -aui, -atum*: "taste", "enjoy".
[127] *quisquam, quaequam, quicquam*: "any(one) / any(thing)", "whoever / whatever".
[128] *ieiunium, -ii* (n.): "hunger".
[129] *ieiunumst = ieiunum est* < *ieiunus, -a, -um*: "hungry".
[130] *aeque atque*: "as... as", "as much as".
[131] *reddibo = reddam* < *reddo, -ere, reddidi, redditum*: "return", "repay" (+ dative of person repaid); translate here: "render", "make or cause to be".

postid,¹³² quom¹³³ lassus¹³⁴ fueris et famelicus,¹³⁵   130

noctu¹³⁶ ut¹³⁷ condigne¹³⁸ te cubes¹³⁹ curabitur.¹⁴⁰

Chalinus: quid facies? **Olympio:** concludere¹⁴¹ in fenstram¹⁴² firmiter,¹⁴³

unde auscultare¹⁴⁴ possis quóm ego illam ausculer:¹⁴⁵

quom mihi illa dicet 'mi animule,¹⁴⁶ mi Olympio,

mea uita, mea mellilla,¹⁴⁷ mea festiuitas,¹⁴⁸   135

sine tuos ocellos¹⁴⁹ deosculer,¹⁵⁰ uoluptas¹⁵¹ mea,

sine¹⁵² amabo¹⁵³ ted¹⁵⁴ amari, meu'¹⁵⁵ festus¹⁵⁶ dies,¹⁵⁷

meu' pullus¹⁵⁸ passer,¹⁵⁹ mea columba,¹⁶⁰ mi lepus',¹⁶¹

---

[132] *postid* (see note 102 on the previous page at line 120, I.i).
[133] *quom = cum*.
[134] *lassus, -a, -um*: "tired".
[135] *famelicus, -a, -um*: "starving", "hungry", "famished".
[136] *noctu* (adverb): "by night".
[137] *ut*: "as".
[138] *condigne* (adverb < *condignus, -a, -um*): "worthily", "deservedly" (+ ablative); *condigne te*: "the way you deserve".
[139] *cubo, -are, cubui, cubitum*: "lie down", "be in bed", "lie down to sleep".
[140] *curo, -are, -aui, -atum* (see note 44 on page 49 at line 101, I.i).
[141] *concludere* (2nd person singular future indicative passive < *concludo, -ere, conclusi, concludum*: "confine", "shut up", "conceal").
[142] *fenstram = fenestram < fenestra, -ae*: "window".
[143] *firmiter = firme* (adverb): "firmly", "securely".
[144] *ausculto, -are, -aui, -atum*: "hear", "listen".
[145] *ausculer = osculer* (1st person singular present subjunctive passive < *osculor, -ari, -atus sum*: "kiss").
[146] *animulus, -i* (m.): "darling", "heart" (term of endearment).
[147] *mellilla, -ae* (f.): "little honey", "sweetheart".
[148] *festiuitas, -atis* (f.): "celebration", "joy".
[149] *ocellus, -i* (m.): "dear little eye".
[150] *deosculor, -ari, -atus sum*: "kiss", "shower kisses on".
[151] *uoluptas, -atis* (f.): "pleasure", "delight".
[152] *sine < sino, -ere, -siui, situm*: "allow", "let".
[153] *amabo*: "please", "I beg" (< *amo, -are, -aui, -atum*).
[154] *ted = te*.
[155] *meu' = meus*.
[156] *festus, -a, -um*: "festive", "joyous".
[157] *meu' festus dies, meu' pullus passer, mea columba, mi lepus* are all vocative in meaning, despite the nominative forms of *meu' festus dies* and *meu' pullus*.
[158] *pullus, -i* (m.): "chick".
[159] *passer, -eris* (m.): "sparrow" (either interpret *passer* as the possessive genitive *passeris*, or reuse *meu'* to modify *passer*).
[160] *columba, -ae* (f.): "dove".
[161] *lepus, leporis* (m.): "hare".

quom mihi haec dicentur dicta,[162] tum tu, furcifer,[163]
quasi mus,[164] in medio[165] parieti[166] uorsabere.[167]   140
nunc ne tu te mihi respondere postules,[168]
abeo[169] intro.[170] taedet[171] tui sermonis.[172] — **Chalinus:** te sequor.
hic[173] quidem[174] pol[175] certo[176] nil[177] ages[178] síne med[179] arbitro.[180] —

---

[162]   *dictum, -i* (n.): "word", "expression".
[163]   *furcifer, furciferi* (m.): literally a *furcifer* was one who deserved to be punished with a *furca*, or two-pronged fork or yoke to which an enslaved person might be tied as a form of punishment that probably also included whipping; "worthless loser", "good-for-nothing".
[164]   *mus, muris* (m./f.): "mouse".
[165]   *medius, -a, -um*: "in the middle of".
[166]   *paries, parietis* (m.): "wall", "house wall"; *in medio parieti*: "in the middle of the wall".
[167]   *uorsabere = uersabere* (2nd person singular future indicative passive) < *uerso, -are, -aui, -atum*: "turn about", "twist/squirm about".
[168]   *ne tu te mihi respondere postules* (negative purpose clause + indirect discourse): "so you won't claim to answer me", "so you won't try to answer me back".
[169]   *abeo, -ire, -iui/-ii, -itum* (see note 51 on page 49 at line 103, I.i).
[170]   *intro* (adverb): "inside", "into the house".
[171]   *taedet, taedere, taedui, taesus est* (impersonal verb): "it's tiring", "it's tedious" (+ accusative of the thing that is tiring/tedious).
[172]   *sermo, sermonis* (m.): "conversation".
[173]   *hīc* (adverb).
[174]   *quidem* (adverb): "indeed", "in fact".
[175]   *pol = edepol*.
[176]   *certo* (adverb): "certainly", "really".
[177]   *nil = nihil*.
[178]   *ago, -ere, egi, actum*: "do", "act", "perform".
[179]   *med = me*.
[180]   *arbiter, arbitri* (m.): "judge", "watcher", "witness".

ACTVS II

II.i CLEVSTRATA, PARDALISCA (144-164)

Scene summary: *Cleustrata tells Pardalisca (an older enslaved woman who serves her) that she's going to see her next-door neighbour. Pardalisca reminds her that Cleustrata's husband, Lysidamus, has asked for a meal to be prepared, but Cleustrata insists she won't make any food for him because she's so angry about his plan to cheat on her with Casina.*

Cleustrata: Opsignate[1] cellas,[2] referte[3] anulum[4] ad me:

ego huc[5] transeo in proxumum[6] ad meam uicinam.[7]   145

uir si quid uolet me,[8] facite hinc[9] accersatis.[10]

Pardalisca: prandium[11] iusserat[12] senex sibi parari.[13]

Cleustrata: st!

tace[14] atque abi; neque paro neque hodie coquetur,[15]   149-50

quando is mi[16] et filio áduorsatur[17] suo

animi amorisque caussa[18] sui,   152-4

flagitium[19] illud hominis![20] ego illum fame,[21] ego illum siti,[22]   155

---

[1] *opsignate = obsignate < obsigno, -are, -aui, -atum*: "seal up", "close with a seal".
[2] *cella, -ae* (f.): "storeroom", "larder".
[3] *refero, referre, rettuli, relatum*: "bring back".
[4] *anulus, -i* (m.): "ring", "signet ring".
[5] *huc* (adverb): "to this place".
[6] *in proxumum = in proximum*: "next-door".
[7] *uicina, -ae* (f.): "(female) neighbour".
[8] *uir si quid uolet me*: "if my husband wants me for anything".
[9] *hinc* (adverb): "from this place".
[10] *arcesso/accerso, -ere, -iui, -itum*: "send for", "fetch"; *facite... accersatis* involves a substantive clause of result (see Bennett 297.1).
[11] *prandium, -ii* (n.): "lunch".
[12] *iubeo, -ere, iussi, iussum*: "order", "tell".
[13] *paro, -are, -aui, -atum*: "prepare".
[14] *taceo, -ere, tacui, tacitum*: "be silent", "be quiet".
[15] *coquo, -ere, coxi, coctum*: "cook"; *neque... coquetur*: "nothing will be cooked".
[16] *mi = mihi*.
[17] *aduorsatur = aduersatur < aduersor, -ari, -atus sum*: "act against the interests of", "oppose" (+ dative).
[18] *caussā = causā*: "for the sake of" (+ preceeding genitive); *animi... caussā* : "for (his own) gratification".
[19] *flagitium, -ii/-i* (n.): "shameful act"; "disgrace".
[20] *hominis* is a partitive genitive.
[21] *fames, famis* (f.): "hunger".
[22] *siti* (ablative) *< sitis, -is* (f.): "thirst".

maledictis,[23] malefactis amatorem[24] ulciscar,[25]

ego pól illum probe[26] incommodis[27] dictis angam,[28]

faciam uti[29] proinde ut est dignus[30] uitam colat,[31]

Accheruntis[32] pabulum,[33]

flagiti persequen-   160

tem,[34] stabulum[35] nequitiae.[36]

nunc huc[37] meas fortunas[38] eo questum[39] ad uicinam.[40]

sed fori'[41] concrepuit,[42] atque eapse[43] eccam[44] egreditur![45]

non pol per tempus[46] iter[47] huc mi[48] incepi.[49]

---

[23]   *maledictum, -i* (n.): "curse", "insult".
[24]   *amator, -oris* (m.): "lover", "loverboy", "a man in love", "womanizer".
[25]   *ulciscor, -i, ultus sum*: "punish", "take revenge on".
[26]   *prope* (adverb): "properly".
[27]   *incommodus, -a, -um*: "disagreeable", "unsuitable".
[28]   *ango, -ere, anxi, anctum*: "choke".
[29]   *uti = ut*.
[30]   *proinde ut est dignus*: "just like he deserves".
[31]   *colo, -ere, colui, cultum*: "cultivate", "init"; translate here "live", "live out".
[32]   *Accheruntis = Acheruntis < Acheruns, -untis* (m.): "Acheron" (river that leads to the underworld).
[33]   *pabulum, -i* (n.): "food", "fodder".
[34]   *persequor, -i, persecutus sum*: "pursue", "accomplish"; *flagiti persequentem*: "pursuer of disgrace".
[35]   *stabulum, -i* (n.): "stable", "den".
[36]   *nequitia, -ae* (f.): "wickedness", "worthlessness".
[37]   *huc* (see note 5 on the facing page at line 145, II.i).
[38]   *fortuna, -ae* (f.): "luck", "fate", " bad luck".
[39]   *questum* (supine) *< queror, -i, questus sum*: "complain" (for the supine see Bennett 340).
[40]   *uicina, -ae* (f.): "(female) neighbour".
[41]   *fori' = foris < foris, -is* (f.): "door", "gate".
[42]   *concrepo, -are, concrepui, concrepitum*: "creak".
[43]   *eapse* here may *= ea ipsa*; it may also be an old form of the nominative feminine singular of *ipse*.
[44]   *eccam = ecce + eam*, or perhaps *+ ham* (*= hanc*); *ecce* usually means "look!", "behold", and frequently refers to someone off stage.
[45]   *egredior, egredi, egressus sum*: "come out", "go out".
[46]   *per tempus*: "at the right time", "in time".
[47]   *iter, itineris* (n.): "journey", "route".
[48]   *mi = mihi* (dative of reference).
[49]   *incipio, -ere, -cepi, -ceptum*: "begin", "start".

II.ii MYRRHINA, CLEVSTRATA (165-216)

Scene summary: *Cleustrata and her next-door neighbour Myrrhina meet, having each headed over to visit the other at the same time. Cleustrata complains to Myrrhina about her husband's disrespectful treatment of her, saying that Lysidamus plans to marry Casina to his loyal farm manager Olympio so that Lysidamus will have easy access to Casina himself. Myrrhina says that anything a wife owns (by which she means the enslaved Casina) really belongs to her husband, and urges Cleustrata not to fight with Lysidamus for fear he'll divorce her.*

Myrrhina: Sequimini,[1] comites,[2] in proxumum[3] me huc.[4] heus[5] uos, ecquis[6] haec quae loquor audit?	165-6
ego hic ero, uir si aut quispiam[7] quaeret.[8]	
nam ubi domi[9] sola sum, sopor[10] manus caluitur.[11]	168-9
iussin[12] colum[13] ferri mihi? **Cleustrata:** Myrrhina, salue.[14]	170-1
Myrrhina: salue mecastor.[15] sed quid[16] tu es tristis, amabo?[17]	172-3
Cleustrata: ita solent[18] omnes quae sunt male nuptae:[19]	174-5
domi et foris[20] aegre[21] quod siet[22] sati'[23] semper est.[24]	176-7

---

[1] *sequimini* (2nd plural present imperative passive < *sequor, -i, secutus sum*).
[2] *comes, comitis* (m./f.): "companion"; translate here: "attendant" (referring to the slaves that accompany her).
[3] *in proxumum = in proximum*: "next-door".
[4] *huc* (adverb): "to this place".
[5] *heus*: "hey!", "listen!" (used to try to get someone's attention).
[6] *ecquis, ecquid* (interrogative pronoun): "is there anyone who / anything which".
[7] *quispiam, quaepiam, quodpiam / quidpiam / quippiam* (indefinite pronoun): "anyone/anything".
[8] *quaero, -ere, quaesiui, quaesitum*: "ask", "inquire", "seek".
[9] *domi* (locative case).
[10] *sopor, soporis* (m.): "sleep".
[11] *caluor, -i, –, –*: "deceive"; translate here: "get in the way of", "hinder".
[12] *iussin = iussine < iubeo, -ere, iussi, iussum*: "order", "tell".
[13] *colus, -i* (m.): "distaff" (a stick or small staff used for holding flax or other raw fibers before spinning).
[14] *salue* (salutation): "hello".
[15] *mecastor* (see note 124 on page 41 at line 38, prologue).
[16] *quid*: "why?".
[17] *amabo* (see note 153 on page 52 at line 137, I.i).
[18] *soleo, -ere, –, solitus sum*: "be accustomed", "tend" (+ infinitive).
[19] *sunt... nuptae < nubo, -ere, nupsi, nuptum*: "marry", "be married".
[20] *foris*: "out of doors", "away from home".
[21] *aegre esse*: "to be disagreeable/displeasing to"
[22] *siet = sit*.
[23] *sati' = satis*.
[24] *aegre quod siet sati' semper est*: "there is always enough that is disagreeable".

nam ego ibam ad te. **Myrrhina:** et pol ego isto[25] ad te.

sed quid est quod tuo nunc animo aegrest?[26]

nam quód tíbi est aégré, idem[27] mist[28] diuidiae.[29]   180-1

Cleustrata: credo, ecastor, nam uicinam neminem[30] amo merito[31] magi'[32] quam te

nec qua in[33] plura[34] sunt

mihi quae ego uelim.   183a

Myrrhina: amo te, atque istuc[35] expeto[36] scire quid sit.

Cleustrata: pessumis[37] me modis despicatur[38] domi.   185-6

Myrrhina: hem,[39] quid est? dic idem (nam pol hau[40] sati'[41] meo

corde[42] accepi querellas[43] tuas), opsecro.[44]

Cleustrata: uir me et pessumis despicatam[45] modis,

nec mihi ius meum óptinendi[46] optio[47] est.   190

---

[25] *isto* (adverb): "there", "to that place" (here implying a reference to Cleustrata's house).
[26] *aegrest = aegre est*: "is upsetting" (+ dative of person being upset).
[27] *idem, eadem, idem*: "the same"; "likewise".
[28] *mist = mihi est*.
[29] *diuidia, -ae*: "trouble", "sadness"; *diuidiae* is dative of purpose or tendency (see Bennett 191.2).
[30] *nemo, neminis* (m./f.): "no one".
[31] *merito* (adverb): "deservedly".
[32] *magi' = magis*: "rather", "more".
[33] *quā in = in quā*.
[34] *plura* can be translated here as "more good qualities" or "more sympathetic feelings".
[35] *istuc = istud < iste, ista, istud*: "that of yours"; translate here: "what's wrong".
[36] *expeto, -ere, -iui, -itum*: "ask for", "look for"; "demand", "want", "desire", "be eager for".
[37] *pessumis = pessimis*.
[38] *despicor, -ari, -atus sum*: "despise", "disrespect" (+ accusative of person disrespected).
[39] *hem* (expression of surprise and/or concern): "oh no!".
[40] *hau = haud*.
[41] *sati' = satis*.
[42] *cor, cordis* (n.): "heart", "mind".
[43] *querella, -ae* (f.): "complaint", "grievance".
[44] *opsecro = obsecro < obsecro, -are, -aui, -atum*: "beg", "implore"; *opsecro* (interjection): "please!".
[45] *despicatam < despicor, -ari, -atus sum*: "despise", "disrespect" (the perfect participle of deponents can sometimes have a passive meaning).
[46] *optinendi = obtinendi* (gerund < *obtineo, -ere, -tinui, -tentum*: "obtain", "maintain", "assert").
[47] *optio, optionis* (f.): "choice", "option"; *nec mihi ius meum optinendi optio est*: "and I've no option to assert my right(s)".

Myrrhina: mira sunt,[48] uera si praedicas,[49] nam uiri
ius suom ad[50] mulieres[51] optinere hau queunt.[52]
Cleustrata: quin[53] mihi[54] ancillulam[55] ingratiis[56] postulat,
quae mea est, quae meo educta[57] sumptu[58] siet,[59]
uilico[60] suo se dare,[61]   195
sed ipsus[62] eam amat. **Myrrhina:** opsecro,   195a
tace.[63] **Cleustrata:** nam hic nunc licet[64] dicere:
nos sumus.[65] **Myrrhina:** ita est. unde[66] ea tibi[67] est?   197-8
nam peculi[68] probam[69] nil ere addecet[70]
clam[71] uirum, ét quae et, partum[72] ei[73] hau commode[74] est,   200

---

[48] *mirus, -a, -um*: "astonishing" (the neuter plural *mira* modifies the things said by Cleustrata).
[49] *praedico, -are, -aui, -atum*: "proclaim", "say".
[50] *ad* (preposition + accusative): "to", "towards"; translate here: "in front of", "before" (the implication being that the *mulieres* are like judges, before which the husbands never receive justice).
[51] *mulier, mulieris* (f.): "woman".
[52] *queo, quire, quiui/quii, quitum*: "be able".
[53] *quin*: "no, really", "I mean!"; "actually", "in fact", "but"; "why... not?"
[54] *mihi* (dative of reference).
[55] *ancillula, -ae* (f.): "young slave girl", "little slave girl" ("little" means teen-aged here).
[56] *ingratiis* (adverb): "against (my) will".
[57] *educo, -ere, -duxi, -ductum*: "lead out"; "bring up", "rear".
[58] *sumptus, -ūs* (m.): "expense".
[59] *siet = sit*; *educta siet* is probably a concessive subjunctive (see Bennett 278) as suggested by MacCary and Willcock 1976, citing Ussing 1887; translate *quae meo educta sumptu siet* as "although she was brought up at my expense".
[60] *uilicus, -i* (m.): "slave-overseer", "(enslaved) farm manager".
[61] *postulat... se dare*: "he wants to give" (*se dare* is the accusative-infinitive construction after *postulat* (line 193).
[62] *ipsus = ipse*.
[63] *taceo, -ere, tacui, tacitum*: "be silent", "be quiet". Lindsay's text has *dice* instead of *tace*; see note 6 on page 176 (lines 196-198) in the English translation regarding changes from Lindsay's Latin text.
[64] *licet, licere, licuit, licitum est*: "be allowed", "be permitted".
[65] *nos sumus*: "we are the only ones here", "it's just us here".
[66] *unde*: "from where", "from what cause"; translate here: "in what way".
[67] *tibi* is dative of possession (see Bennett 190).
[68] *peculium, -ii/-i* (n.): "private savings", "personal property"; *peculi* is partitive genitive after *nil*.
[69] *probus, -a, -um*: "good", "honest", "proper"; translate here: "a good wife".
[70] *addecet, addecere* (impersonal verb): "it is fitting", "it is appropriate" (+ accusative + infinitive).
[71] *clam* (adverb): "secretly (from)", "unknown to" (+ accusative).
[72] *pario, parere, peperi, paritum/partum*: "bring forth", "produce"; translate here: "acquire".
[73] *ei* (dative of reference).
[74] *commode* (adverb): "properly".

quin[75] uiro aut suptrahat[76] aut stupro[77] inuenerit.[78]

hoc uiri[79] censeo[80] esse omne quidquid[81] tuom[82] est.

Cleustrata: tu quidem[83] aduorsum[84] tuam amicam omnia loqueris.[85] **Myrrhina:** tace sis,[86]

stulta,[87] et mi[88] ausculta.[89] noli[90]

sis tu illic[91] aduorsari,[92]   205

sine[93] amet, sine quod lubet[94] id faciat, quando tibi nil[95]   206-7
domi[96] delicuom[97] est.

Cleustrata: satin[98] sana[99] es? nam tuquidem[100] aduorsus   208-9
tuam istaec[101] rem[102] loquere.[103] **Myrrhina:** insipiens,[104]

---

[75]   *quin* (+ subjunctive): "except", "not without", "so that... not".
[76]   *suptrahat* = *subtrahat* < *subtraho, -ere, -traxi, -tractum*: "take away from", "steal from" (+ dative).
[77]   *stuprum, -i* (n.): "inappropriate sexual behaviour"; translate here: "cheating".
[78]   *inuenerit* (3rd person singular perfect subjunctive active < *inuenio, -ire, -ueni, -uentum*: "find"; translate here: "acquire", "get").
[79]   *uiri* (possessive genitive).
[80]   *censeo, -ere, censui, censitum*: "think", "suppose", "recommend".
[81]   *quisquis, quidquid* (indefinite relative): "whoever / whatever".
[82]   *tuom* = *tuum*.
[83]   *quidem* (adverb): "indeed", "in fact".
[84]   *aduorsum* = *aduersum* (preposition): "against", "in opposition to" (+ accusative).
[85]   *loqueris*: (2nd person singular present indicative passive) < *loquor, -i, locutus sum*.
[86]   *sis* = *si uis*; translate here: "please".
[87]   *stultus, -a, -um*: "stupid", "silly".
[88]   *mi* = *mihi*.
[89]   *ausculto, -are, -aui, -atum*: "hear", "pay attention".
[90]   *noli* (2nd person singular present imperative active) < *nolo, nolle, nolui, –*: "not... want"; *noli* + an infinitive makes a negative command.
[91]   *illic* = *illi* (dative singular).
[92]   *aduorsari* = *aduersari* < *aduersor, -ari, -atus sum*: "oppose", "set oneself against" (+ dative).
[93]   *sine* < *sino, -ere, -siui, situm*: "allow", "let" (+ subjunctive here).
[94]   *lubet* = *libet* < *libet, libuit, libitus est* (impersonal verb): "it is pleasing"; *quod lubet id*: "what he wants".
[95]   *nil* = *nihil*.
[96]   *domi* (locative case).
[97]   *delicuom* = *deliquus, -a, -um*: "lacking".
[98]   *satin* = *satisne*; *satis* (adverb): "enough", "sufficiently".
[99]   *sanus, -a, -um*: "sane", "in one's right mind".
[100]   *tuquodem* = *tu quidem*.
[101]   *istaec* = *ista* (accusative neuter plural).
[102]   *res, rei* (f.): "thing", "circumstance", "situation", "matter", concern"; translate here: "interest".
[103]   *loquere* (2nd person singular present indicative) < *loquor, -i, locutus sum*.
[104]   *insipiens, insipientis*: "foolish".

semper tu huic uerbo uitato[105] aps[106] tuo uiro. **Cleustrata:** quoi[107] uerbo? **Myrrhina:** i foras,[108] mulier.   210-2

Cleustrata: st! tace. **Myrrhina:** quid est? **Cleustrata:** em![109] **Myrrhina:** quis est, quem uides? **Cleustrata:** uir eccum[110] it.

intro[111] abi, adpropera,[112] age[113] amabo.[114] **Myrrhina:** ímpetras,[115] abeo.

Cleustrata: mox[116] magis[117] quom[118] otium[119] <ét> mihi et tibi erit,   215

igitur[120] tecum loquar. nunc uale.[121] **Myrrhina:** ualeas. —

---

[105] *uitato* (2nd person singular future active imperative) < *uito, -are, -aui, -atum*: "avoid" (+ dative).
[106] *aps = ab*.
[107] *quoi = cui*.
[108] *foras* (adverb): "out of doors", "out of the house"; *i foras, mulier* seems to have been a formulaic expression used when a husband divorced his wife.
[109] *em*: "here/there you are!", "look!".
[110] *eccum = ecce + eum* or *ecce + hum* (= *hunc*) (*ecce* usually means "look!", "behold", and frequently refers to someone off stage).
[111] *intro* (adverb): "inside", "into the house".
[112] *adpropero, -are, -aui, -atum*: "hurry", "go quickly".
[113] *age* (< *ago, -ere, egi, actum*): "come on", "go on".
[114] *amabo*: "please", "I beg" (< *amo, -are, -aui, -atum*).
[115] *impetras*: "all right", "I'll do what you ask" (< *impetro, -are, -aui, -atum*: "accomplish", "get").
[116] *mox* (adverb): "soon".
[117] *magis* (adverb): "more," "rather", "instead".
[118] *quom = cum*.
[119] *otium, -ii* (n.): "leisure", "free time".
[120] *igitur* (conjunction): "therefore"; translate here: "then".
[121] *uale*: "good bye" (< *ualeo, -ere, ualui, ualitum*: "be well").

II.iii LYSIDAMVS, CLEVSTRATA (217-278)

Scene summary: *Lysidamus arrives, singing about the delights of being in love with Casina and talking about all the cologne he's been buying to make himself more attractive to her. He pretends to be happy to see his wife Cleustrata, while muttering to himself that he wishes she were dead. Cleustrata asks him why he smells of cologne, and Lysidamus claims he has been helping a friend buy some. They exchange hostile words, and then Lysidamus asks Cleustrata if she's going to agree to marry Casina to his farm manager Olympio, rather than to the younger slave Chalinus. Cleustrata argues that the slave girls should be her responsibility, not his, and that marrying Casina to Chalinus would benefit their son. Lysidamus argues that his son should do what benefits his father, instead. They finally agree that, if either of them can persuade Olympio or Chalinus to give up the opportunity to marry Casina, this will decide the matter.*

Lysidamus: Omnibu'[1] rebus ego amorem credo et nitoribu'[2] nitidis[3]

anteuenire[4] nec potis[5] 217a

quicquam[6] commemorari<er>[7] quod plus sali'[8] plusq'[9] leporis[10] hodie

eat; coquos[11] equidem[12] nimi'[13] demiror,[14] qui utuntur[15] condimentis,[16]

eos[17] eo condimento uno <non> utier,[18] omnibu' quod praestat.[19] 220

---

[1] *omnibu'* = *omnibus*.
[2] *nitoribu'* = *nitoribus* < *nitor, -oris* (m.): "brightness", "splendour".
[3] *nitidus, -a, -um*: "shining", "bright".
[4] *anteuenio, -ire, -ueni, -uentum*: "come before", "surpass" (+ dative).
[5] *potis* = *potis est*: "(it) is able", "(it) can't".
[6] *quisquam, quaequam, quicquam / quidquid* (indefinite pronoun): "any(one) / any(thing)", "whoever / whatever".
[7] *commemorarier* = *commemorari* < *commemoro, -are, -aui, -atum*: "remember", "keep in mind", "mention".
[8] *sali'* = *salis* < *sal, salis* (m.): "salt"; translate here: "spice", "wit".
[9] *plusqu'* = *plusque*.
[10] *lepor, -oris* (m.): "charm", "pleasantness".
[11] *coquus, -i* (m.): "cook" (usually an enslaved person, and often hired for special feasts).
[12] *equidem*: "indeed", "truly".
[13] *nimi'* = *nimis* (adverb): "too much", "excessively".
[14] *demiror, -ari, -atus sum*: "wonder", "be amazed at".
[15] *utor, uti, usus sum*: "use", "enjoy" (+ ablative).
[16] *condimentum, -i* (n.): "spice", "seasoning".
[17] *eos* refers to the *coquos* of the previous line.
[18] *utier* = *uti* < *utor, uti, usus sum*; *coquos* is the accusative subject of *utier* in indirect discourse after *demiror*.
[19] *praesto, -are, -stiti, -stitum*: "stand before", "surpass".

nam ubi amor condimentum inierit,[20] quoiuis[21] placituram[22] <escam>[23] credo;

neque salsum[24] neque suaue[25] esse potest quicquam, ubi amor non admiscetur:[26]

fel[27] quod amarumst,[28] id[29] mel[30] faciet,[31] hominem ex tristi[32] lepidum[33] et lenem.[34]

hanc ego de me[35] coniecturam[36] domi[37] facio magi'[38] quam ex auditis;[39]

qui quóm[40] amo Casinam magi'[41] niteo,[42] munditiis   225
Munditiam[43] antideo:[44]

myropolas[45] omnis[46] sollicitó,[47] ubiquomque[48] est lepidum unguentum,[49] unguor,[50]

---

[20] *inierit* < *ineo, -ire, -iui/-ii, -itum*: "go in", "enter".
[21] *quoiuis* = *cuiuis* (genitive) < *quiuis, quaeuis, quoduis*: "anyone/anything that you please", "no matter who/what".
[22] *placeo, -ere, placui, placitum*: "please", "be pleasing to" (+ dative).
[23] *esca, -ae* (f.): "dish", "food".
[24] *salsus, -a, -um*: "salty"; "witty".
[25] *suauis, -is*: "sweet", "agreeable".
[26] *admisceo, -ere, -ui, -mixtum*: "mix in", "add (as an ingredient)".
[27] *fel, fellis* (n.): "gall", "bile" (gall, or bile, is a fluid produced by the liver).
[28] *amarumst* = *amarum est*; *amarus, -a, -um*: "bitter".
[29] *id* refers to the *fel*.
[30] *mel, mellis* (n.): "honey".
[31] *amor* serves as the subject of *faciet*, which has as direct objects first *fel* and *id*, and then *hominem lepidum et lenem*.
[32] *ex tristi*: "out of a gloomy man".
[33] *lepidus, -a, -um*: "charming", "witty".
[34] *lenis, -is*: "gentle", "moderate", "mild".
[35] *de me*: "from my own situation".
[36] *coniectura, -ae* (f.): "reasoning", "inference", "prophesy".
[37] *domi* (locative case).
[38] *magi'* = *magis* (adverb): "more," "rather", "instead".
[39] *ex auditis*: "from what I've heard", "from hearsay".
[40] *quom* = *cum*.
[41] *magi'* = *magis*.
[42] *niteo, -ere, nitui, –*: "shine", "look good".
[43] *munditia, -ae* (f.): "elegance of appearance".
[44] *antideo, antidire, antidiui/-ii, antiditum*: "go before", "surpass".
[45] *myropola, -ae* (f.): "perfume seller".
[46] *omnis* = *omnes*.
[47] *sollicito, -are, -aui, -atum*: "stir up", "harass".
[48] *ubiquomque* = *ubicumque* (adverb): "wherever".
[49] *unguentum, -i* (n.): "ointment", "perfume", "cologne".
[50] *unguo, -ere, unxi, unctum*: "smear with oil/grease", "anoint with unguents, perfumes".

ut illi placeam; et placeo, ut uideor.⁵¹ sed uxor⁵² me excruciat,⁵³ quia uiuit.

tristem⁵⁴ astare⁵⁵ aspicio.⁵⁶ blande⁵⁷ haec mihi⁵⁸ mala res⁵⁹ appellanda est.⁶⁰

uxor mea meaque amoenitas,⁶¹ quid tu agis?⁶² **Cleustrata:** abi atque apstine⁶³ manum.

Lysidamus: heia,⁶⁴ mea Iuno,⁶⁵ non decet⁶⁶ esse te tam tristem tuo Ioui.⁶⁷   230

quo⁶⁸ nunc abis? **Cleustrata:** mitte⁶⁹ me. **Lysidamus:** mane.⁷⁰ **Cleustrata:** non maneo. **Lysidamus:** at pol ego te sequar.

Cleustrata: opsecro,⁷¹ sanun⁷² es? **Lysidamus:** sanus. quam⁷³ ted⁷⁴ amo.

Cleustrata: nolo ames.⁷⁵ **Lysidamus:** non potes impetrare.⁷⁶ **Cleustrata:** enicas.⁷⁷

---

51   *ut videor*: "as it seems to me", "in my opinion".
52   *uxor, uxoris* (f.): "wife".
53   *excrucio, -are, -aui, -atum*: "torture", "torment".
54   *tristis, -e*: "sad"; translate here: "upset", "grumpy".
55   *asto, astare, astiti, –*: "stand nearby".
56   *aspicio, -ere, aspexi, aspectum*: "look at", "see".
57   *blande* (adverb): "sweetly", "flatteringly", "charmingly".
58   *mihi* (dative of agent with the gerundive, see Bennett 189).
59   *mala res*: "the evil thing", "the old hag" (referring to his wife).
60   *appello, -are, -aui, -atum*: "call", "address", "solicit", "beseech".
61   *amoenitas, -atis* (f.): "delight", "pleasantness", "charm".
62   *quid tu agis*: "how are you?".
63   *apstine = abstine < abstineo, -ere, -ui, abstentum*: "keep away", "abstain" (from).
64   *heia* (exclamation, here implying pretended pleasure at seeing her): "ah!"
65   *Iuno, Iunonis* (f.): "Juno" (powerful patron goddess of Rome, and wife of Jupiter; she was equated to the Greek goddess Hera).
66   *decet, decuit* (impersonal verb): "it is fitting", "it is appropriate".
67   *Iuppiter, Iouis* (m.): "Jupiter" (Roman sky god and ruler of the other gods, and husband of Juno; he was equated to the Greek god Zeus).
68   *quo* (adverb): "where", "why".
69   *mitto, -ere, misi, missum*: "send"; translate here: "let go", "release".
70   *maneo, -ere, mansi, mansum*: "remain", "stay".
71   *opsecro = obsecro < obsecro, -are, -aui, -atum*: "beg", "implore"; *opsecro* (interjection): "please!".
72   *sanun = sanusne < sanus, -a, -um*: "sane", "in one's right mind".
73   *quam* (adverb): "how", "how much".
74   *ted = te*.
75   *nolo ames* (substantive clause without *ut*, see Bennett 296.2a) = *nolo ut ames*.
76   *impetro, -are, -aui, -atum*: "accomplish", "get", "succeed", "be granted"; "to succeed in one's request (that)" (+ *ut*) + subjunctive.
77   *enicas = enecas < eneco, -are, -aui, -atum*: "kill off", "torment", "wear out", "exhaust"; translate *enicas* here: "you're tiring me to death".

Lysidamus: uera dicas uelim.[78] **Cleustrata:** credo ego istuc[79] tibi.[80]

Lysidamus: respice,[81] o mi lepos.[82] **Cleustrata:** nempe[83] ita[84]   235
ut[85] tu mihi es.[86]

unde[87] hic,[88] amabo,[89] unguenta olent?[90] **Lysidamus:** oh perii![91]

manufesto[92] miser teneor.[93] cesso[94] caput pallio[95] detergere.[96]

ut[97] te bonu'[98] Mercurius[99] perdat,[100] myropola,[101] quia haec mihi dedisti.

Cleustrata: eho[102] tu nihili,[103] cana[104] culex,[105] uix[106] teneor quin[107] quae decent te[108] dicam,[109]

---

[78] *dicas uelim* (substantive clause without *ut*) = *uelim ut dicas*.
[79] *istuc* = *istud* < *iste, ista, istud*: "that", "that of which you speak".
[80] *tibi* (dative of reference); translate *credo ego istuc tibi*: "I believe you mean that".
[81] *respicio, -ere, respexi, respectum*: "look back".
[82] *lepos, leporis* (m.): "charm", "grace".
[83] *nempe* (adverb): "surely", "of course".
[84] *ita*: "in this way", "so", "thus"; translate here: "just like".
[85] *ut*: "as".
[86] *nempe ita ut tu mihi es*: "naturally, just as you are my 'charm'".
[87] *unde*: "from where", "from what cause".
[88] *hīc* (adverb).
[89] *amabo*: "please", "I beg" (< *amo, -are, -aui, -atum*).
[90] *oleo, -ere, olui, –*: "emit a smell", "smell", "smell of".
[91] *pereo, -ire, periui/-ii, peritum*: "die"; "be ruined"; "be lost".
[92] *manufesto* = *manifesto* (adverb): "undeniably", "evidently"; "red-handed", "in the act".
[93] *teneo, -ere, tenui, tentum*: "hold", "keep"; "comprehend"; translate *teneor* here: "I'm trapped".
[94] *cesso, -are, -aui, -atum*: "be remiss"; "delay", "cease from".
[95] *pallium, -i* (n.): "cloak" (specifically a Greek cloak worn by most actors in the *fabulae palliatae*, hence the name of this type of drama).
[96] *detergeo, -ere, detersi, detersum*: "wipe off", "wipe clean"; translate *cesso... detergere* here: "I didn't clean off...".
[97] *ut* = *utinam* (+ optative subjunctive; see Allen & Greenough 442a).
[98] *bonu'* = *bonus*.
[99] *Merciurius, -ii* (m.): "Mercury" (the Roman god of buying and selling, messages, travelers, and trickery).
[100] *perdo, -ere, perdidi, perditum*: "ruin", "destroy"; "lose".
[101] *myropola, -ae* (see note 45 on page 62 at line 226, II.iii).
[102] *eho* (exclamation of disgust/anger).
[103] *nihili* (genitive of indefinite value; see Bennett 203.3); translate as "worthless", "nothing" (as an insult).
[104] *canus, -a, -um*: "white", "white-haired"; "old".
[105] *culex, culicis* (f.): "gnat".
[106] *uix* (adverb): "scarcely", "barely".
[107] *quin* (conjunction + subjunctive): "so as to prevent", "so that... not".
[108] *quae decent te*: "what you deserve".
[109] *teneor quin quae decent te dicam*: "I'm barely keeping myself from calling you what you deserve".

senectan[110] aetate[111] unguentatus[112] per uias, ignaue,[113]   240
incedis?[114]

Lysidamus: pol ego amico dedi quoidam[115] operam,[116] dum[117] emit[118] unguenta. **Cleustrata:** ut cito[119] commentust![120]

ecquid[121] te pudet?[122] **Lysidamus:** omnia quae tu uis. **Cleustrata:** ubi in[123] lustra[124] iacuisti?[125]

Lysidamus: egone in lustra? **Cleustrata:** scio plus quam tu me[126] arbitrare.[127] **Lysidamus:** quid id est? quid [tu] scis?

Cleustrata: te sene[128] omnium senem[129] <hominem> neminem[130] esse[131] ignauiorem.[132]

unde is,[133] nihili?[134] ubi fuisti? úbi lustratu's?[135] ubi   245
bibisti?[136]

---

[110] *senectān = senectāne < senectus, -a, -um*: "old", "senile".
[111] *aetas, aetatis* (f.): "age", "stage of life", "life".
[112] *unguentatus -a, -um*: "perfumed", "anointed with perfume/cologne".
[113] *ignauus, -a, -um*: "lazy", "cowardly", "deadbeat".
[114] *incedo, -ere, -cessi, -cessum*: "walk", "proceed".
[115] *quoidam = cuidam < quidam, quaedam, quoddam*: "a certain".
[116] *opera, -ae* (f.): "service", "activity", "effort"; *operam* dare: "take care", "give attention"; "help" (+ dative).
[117] *dum* (conjunction): "while".
[118] *emit* (present indicative) < *emo, -ere, emi, emptum*: "buy".
[119] *cito* (adverb): "quickly".
[120] *commentust = commentus est < cominiscor, -i, commentus sum*: "invent", "come up with (a story / lie)".
[121] *ecquis, ecquid* (interrogative pronoun): "is there anyone who? / is there anything that".
[122] *pudet, pudēre, pudit / puditum est* (usually impersonal): "make ashamed", "cause shame".
[123] In Classical Latin this meaning of *in* would be followed by the ablative (*lustris*), but here we have the accusative (*lustra*).
[124] *lustrum, -i* (n.): "den", "swamp"; "brothel".
[125] *iaceo, -ere, iacui, iacitum*: "lie", "lie down".
[126] *me* + an implied *scire* is indirect discourse after *arbitrare*.
[127] *arbitror, -ari, -atus sum*: "think".
[128] *senex, senis* (adjective and noun): "old"; "old man".
[129] *senem* has been emended to *senum* in some editions, which works better, though *senem* is still possible.
[130] *nemo, neminis* (m./f.): "no one"; translate here as an adjective: "no", "not a...".
[131] *esse* is indirect discourse, after *scio* in line 243: [*scio*]... *senem <hominem> neminem esse*...: "[I know] that there is no old man...".
[132] *ignauior, -orius* (comparative adjective < *ignauus, -a, -um*).
[133] *is < eo, ire, iui/ii, itum*; translate here: "come".
[134] *nihili* (see note 103 on the preceding page at line 239, II.iii).
[135] *lustratu's = lustratus es < lustror, -ari, -atus sum*: "going to a brothel".
[136] *bibo, -ere, bibi, bibitum*: "drink".

mades[137] mecastor:[138] uide palliolum[139] ut[140] rugat![141]
Lysidamus: di me et te infelicent,[142]

sí ego in os[143] meum hodie uini[144] guttam[145] indidi.[146]

Cleustrata: immo[147] age ut lubet[148] bibe, es,[149] disperde[150] rem.[151]

Lysidamus: ohe,[152] iam satis uxor[153] est; comprime[154] te; nimium[155] tinnis,[156]   249-50

relinque[157] aliquantum[158] orationis,[159] cras[160] quod mecum litiges.[161]

sed quid ais?[162] iam domuisti[163] animum, potius[164] ut quod uir uelit

fieri id facias quam aduorsere[165] contra?[166] **Cleustrata:** qua de re? **Lysidamus:** rogas?

---

[137] *madeo, -ere, madui, –*: "be wet"; "be drunk".
[138] *mecastor* (see note 124 on page 41 at line 38, prologue).
[139] *palliolum, -i* (diminutive of *pallium, -ii*).
[140] *ut*: "how".
[141] *rugo, -are, -aui, -atum*: "wrinkle"; "become wrinkled".
[142] *infelico, -are*: "grant bad luck"
[143] *os, oris* (n.): "mouth", "face".
[144] *uinum, -i* (n.): "wine".
[145] *gutta, -ae* (f.): "drop".
[146] *indo, indere, indidi, inditum*: "put into".
[147] *immo*: "by all means", "indeed"; "on the contrary", "by no means".
[148] *lubet = libet < libet, libuit, libitus est* (impersonal verb): "it is pleasing"; *age ut lubet*: "do as you like".
[149] *es* (2nd person singular present imperative active) *< edo, esse, edi, esum/essum*: "eat".
[150] *disperdo, -ere, -didi, -ditum*: "spoil", "ruin".
[151] *res, rei* (f.): "matter", "circumstance", "situation", "interest"; translate here: "property", "patrimony".
[152] *ohe* (exclamation): "stop".
[153] *uxor* (vocative).
[154] *comprimo, -ere, -pressi, -pressum*: "press together", "restrain", "control".
[155] *nimium* (adverb): "too much", "excessively".
[156] *tinnio, -ire, -iui, -itum*: "ring"; "make a high-pitched noise", "be shrill".
[157] *relinquo, -ere, reliqui, relictum*: "leave behind", "leave".
[158] *aliquantus, -a, -um*: "some".
[159] *oratio, -onis* (f.): "speech", "eloquence",
[160] *cras* (adverb): "tomorrow".
[161] *litigo, -are, -aui, -atum*: "quarrel".
[162] *ais* (2nd person singular present indicative active *< aio*: "say"; "say yes", "affirm"); *quid ais*: "what do you say?".
[163] *domo, -are, domui, domitum*: "subdue", "tame".
[164] *potius* (comparative adverb): "rather", "instead".
[165] *aduersere = aduersere < aduersor, -ari, -atus sum*: "oppose", "set oneself against" (+ dative).
[166] *contra* (adverb): "in opposition".

super[167] ancilla[168] Casina, ut detur nuptum[169] nostro uilico,[170]

seruo frugi[171] atque ubi[172] illi[173] bene sit ligno,[174] aqua calida,[175] cibo,[176]   255

uestimentis,[177] ubique educat[178] pueros quos pariat[179] <sibi>,[180]

quam[181] illi seruo nequam[182] des, armigero[183] nili[184] atque inprobo,[185]

quoi[186] hominí hodie peculi[187] nummus[188] non est plumbeus.[189]

Cleustrata: mirum[190] ecastor te senecta[191] aétate[192] officium[193] tuom[194]

---

[167] *super* (preposition + ablative): "about", "concerning", "with regard to".
[168] *ancilla, -ae* (f.): "enslaved woman/girl" (often used instead of *serva*).
[169] *nuptum* (supine < *nubo, -ere, -nupsi, nuptum*: "marry", "be married"); *detur nuptum*: "she'll be given in marriage".
[170] *uilicus, -i* (m.): "slave-overseer", "(enslaved) farm manager".
[171] *frugi* < *frugi bonae* (predicate dative used as adjectival phrase): "honest", "virtuous", "thrifty" (this is an attribute often applied to slaves who thriftily save up money in their *peculia* in order that they might eventually buy their own freedom).
[172] *ubi*: "where" (here implying "in which marriage").
[173] *illi* (refers to Casina).
[174] *lignum, -i* (n.): "wood", "firewood".
[175] *calidus, -a, -um*: "hot".
[176] *cibus, -i* (m.): "food".
[177] *uestimentum, -i* (n.): "clothing"; *bene sit ligno, aquā calidā, cibo, uestimentis*: "she'd be well off with (plenty of) firewood, hot water, food, clothing".
[178] *educo, -ere, eduxi, eductum*: "lead out"; "bring up", "rear".
[179] *pario, -ere, peperi, partum*: "bear", "give birth to".
[180] *sibi* (a suggested emendation to fill in a gap in the text as it has come down to us) is a dative of reference.
[181] *quam* (relative pronoun whose antecedent is Casina).
[182] *nequam* (indeclinable adjective): "worthless", "useless".
[183] *armiger, armigeri* (m.): "armour-bearer", "shield-bearer" (a soldier's assistant, usually enslaved).
[184] *nili = nihili* (genitive of indefinite value; see Bennett 203.3); translate as "worthless", "nothing" (as an insult).
[185] *inprobo = improbo < improbus, -a, -um*: "shameless", "wicked".
[186] *quoi = cui*.
[187] *peculium, -ii/-i* (n.): "private savings", "personal property".
[188] *nummus, -i* (m.): "coin" (often referring to a *sestertius*).
[189] *plumbeus, -a, -um*: "made of lead"; "worthless".
[190] *mirum = mirum est; mirus, -a, -um*: "wonderful", "strange", "amazing".
[191] *senectus, -a, -um* (see note 110 on page 65 at line 240, II.iii).
[192] *aetas, aetatis* (see note 111 on page 65 at line 240, II.iii).
[193] *officium, -ii* (n.): "duty", "obligation".
[194] *tuom = tuum*.

non meminisse.[195] **Lysidamus:** quid iam?[196] **Cleustrata:** 260
quia, si facias recte[197] aut commode,[198]

me sinas[199] curare[200] ancillas, quae mea est curatio.[201]

Lysidamus: qui,[202] malum,[203] homini scutigerulo[204] dare
lubet? **Cleustrata:** quia enim[205] filio

nos oportet[206] opitulari[207] único.[208] **Lysidamus:** at
quamquam[209] unicust,[210]

nihilo magis[211] ille unicust mihi filius quam ego illi pater:

illum mi[212] aequiust[213] quam mé illi quae uolo concedere.[214] 265

Cleustrata: tu ecastor tibi, homo, malam rem quaeris.[215]
Lysidamus: subolet,[216] sentio.[217]

egone? **Cleustrata:** tu. nam quid friguttis?[218] quid[219] istuc[220]
tam cupide[221] cupis?[222]

---

[195] *memini, meminisse, –:* "remember", "keep in mind".
[196] *qui iam:* "what's the matter now?", "what do you mean?"
[197] *recte* (adverb): "rightly", "correctly".
[198] *commode* (adverb): "properly", "conveniently".
[199] *sino, -ere, -siui, situm:* "allow", "let".
[200] *curo, -are, -aui, -atum:* "take care of", "look after", "arrange", "make sure".
[201] *curatio, -onis* (f.): "concern", "object of care".
[202] *qui* (an old ablative): "why?".
[203] *malum, -i* (n.): "misfortune", "misery"; here used as an expression of frustration/anger.
[204] *scutigerulus, -i* (m.): "shield-bearer".
[205] *enim* (conjunction): "in fact".
[206] *oportet, oportere, oportuit, –* (impersonal verb): "it is right", "it is fitting"; translate here: "we ought".
[207] *opitulor, -ari, -atus sum:* "bring aid to", "help", "be of service to" (+ dative).
[208] *unicus, -a, -um:* "only", "sole".
[209] *quamquam:* "although".
[210] *unicust = unicus est.*
[211] *nihilo magis:* "no more", "in no way more".
[212] *mi = mihi.*
[213] *aequiust = aequius est; aequius* (comparative adjective): "more fair", "more just".
[214] *concedo, -ere, concessi, concessum:* "give up", "submit" (+ dative of person submitted to).
[215] *quaero, -ere, quaesiui, quaesitum:* "ask", "inquire", "seek".
[216] *subolet* (impersonal + accusative of thing suspected + dative of person detecting): "there is a suspicion"; translate *subolet* here: "she's suspects", "she smells a rat".
[217] *sentio, -ire, sensi, sensum:* "perceive", "think", "realize".
[218] *friguttio, -ire, – , –:* "stammer".
[219] *quid:* "why?".
[220] *istuc = istud.*
[221] *cupide* (adverb): "eagerly".
[222] *cupio, -ere, -iui, -itum:* "want", "desire".

Lysidamus: ut²²³ enim frugi seruo detur potius²²⁴ quam seruo inprobo.

Cleustrata: quid si ego impetro²²⁵ atque exoro²²⁶ a uilico caussa²²⁷ mea

ut eam illi permittat?²²⁸ **Lysidamus:** quid si ego autem ab armigero impetro   270

eam illí permittat? atque hóc credo impetrassere.²²⁹

Cleustrata: conuenit.²³⁰ uis²³¹ tuis Chalinum huc²³² euocem²³³ uerbis²³⁴ foras?²³⁵

tú eum orato,²³⁶ ego autem orabo uilicum. **Lysidamus:** sane uolo.²³⁷

Cleustrata: iam²³⁸ hic erit. nunc experiemur²³⁹ nostrum²⁴⁰ uter²⁴¹ sit blandior.²⁴² —

Lysidamus: Hercules dique istam perdant,²⁴³ quod nunc   275
liceat²⁴⁴ dicere.

---

223 *ut... detur* is a substantive clause after an implied *cupio* (see Bennett 296 and Allen & Greenough 563b).
224 *potius* (see note 164 on page 66 at line 252, II.iii).
225 *impetro, -are* (see note 76 on page 63 at line 233, II.iii).
226 *exoro, -are, -aui, -atum*: "persuade", "plead".
227 *caussā = causā*.
228 *permitto, -ere, -misi, -missum*: "permit", "allow", "relinquish"; translate here: "give (her) up to him".
229 *impetrassere = impetraturum esse*; *hoc credo impetrassere* (indirect discourse with the accusative subject *me* implied): "I believe that I'll succeed in this".
230 *conuenit* (impersonal): "it's agreed".
231 *uis < uolo, uelle, uolui, –*.
232 *huc* (adverb): "to this place".
233 *euoco, -are, -aui, -atum*: "call out", "summon"; *uis... euocem* is a substantive clause without *ut* (see Bennett 296a).
234 *tuis... uerbis*: "on your instructions".
235 *foras* (adverb): "out of doors", "out of the house".
236 *orato* (2nd person singular future imperative active < *oro, -are, -aui, -atum*: "ask", "beg").
237 *sane uolo*: "by all means", "certainly".
238 *iam* (when paired with future tense): "soon".
239 *experior, -iri, expertus sum*: "test", "put to the test", "find out (by experience)".
240 *nostrum* (genitive < *nos*).
241 *uter, utra, utrum*: "which (of two)".
242 *blandior < blandus, -a, -um*: "flattering", "persuasive".
243 *perdo, -ere, perdidi, perditum* (see note 100 on page 64 at line 238, II.iii).
244 *licet, licere, licuit, licitum est*: "be allowed", "be permitted".

ego discrucior[245] miser amore, illa autem quasi[246] ob industriam[247]

mi[248] aduorsatur.[249] subolet[250] hoc iam uxori quod ego machinor:[251]

propter eam rem[252] magis[253] armigero dat operam[254] de industria.

---

[245] *discrucio, -are, -aui, -atum*: "torture" (see note 53 on page 63 at line 227, II.iii).
[246] *quasi* (adverb): "as if", "just like".
[247] *industria, -ae* (f.): "activity", "industry", "purposefulness"; *ob industriam*: "on purpose".
[248] *mi* = *mihi*.
[249] *aduorsatur* = *aduersatur* < *aduersor, -ari, -atus sum* (see note 165 on page 66 at line 252, II.iii).
[250] *subolet* (see note 216 on page 68 at line 266, II.iii).
[251] *machinor, -ari, -atus sum*: "devise", "plot", "invent".
[252] *propter eam rem*: "because of this" (referring to her detection of his plot).
[253] *magis* (see note 38 on page 62 at line 224, II.iii).
[254] *operam dare* (see note 116 on page 65 at line 241, II.iii).

II.iv LYSIDAMVS, CHALINVS (279-308)

Scene summary: *Lysidamus offers to grant Chalinus his freedom if he will give up Casina to Olympio. Chalinus insists that Cleustrata promised Casina to him, and claims that he'd rather remain enslaved and be married to Casina. Lysidamus loses his temper, and calls for a water jar and lottery tokens so that Casina's future husband can be chosen by the gods. Lysidamus hopes that Cleustrata has not, meanwhile, persuaded Olympio to give up Casina.*

Lysidamus: Qui[1] illum[2] di omnes deaeque perdant![3]
Chalinus: te[4] uxor aiebat[5] tua –

me uocare. **Lysidamus:** ego enim uocari[6] iussi.[7] **Chalinus:** 280
eloquere[8] quid uelis.

Lysidamus: primum ego te porrectiore[9] fronte[10] uolo mecum loqui;

stultitia[11] est ei[12] te esse tristem quoius[13] potestas plus potest.[14]

probum[15] et frugi[16] hominem iam pridem[17] esse árbitror.[18]
Chalinus: intellego.

---

[1] *qui* (adverb, here used like *utinam*): "I wish", "if only".
[2] *illum* (refers to Chalinus).
[3] *perdo, -ere, perdidi, perditum*: "ruin", "destroy"; "lose".
[4] *te uxor aiebat tua*: Chalinus probably wants Lysidamus to interpret the first half of his sentence to mean that his wife was cursing him (Lysidamus). As Chalinus continues his sentence with a more innocent object, however ("... that you were calling for me"), he makes it difficult for Lysidamus to know whether or not Chalinus had intended to be rude. This sort of veiled rudeness by an enslaved person to his master was very popular with Roman audiences.
[5] *aiebat* (3rd person singular imperfect indicative active < *aio*: "say"; "say yes", "affirm").
[6] *uocari* = *te uocari*.
[7] *iubeo, -ere, iussi, iussum*: "order", "tell" (+ infinitive).
[8] *eloquere* (2nd person singular present imperative < *eloquor, eloqui, elocutus sum*: "speak out", "state", "say".
[9] *porrectior, porrectius* (comparative adjective): "wider"; translate *porrectiore fronte*: "with a less scowling forehead".
[10] *frons, frontis* (f.): "forehead", "face".
[11] *stultitia, -ae* (f.): "stupidity".
[12] *ei* (dative, referring to himself).
[13] *quoius* = *cuius*.
[14] *ei... quoius potestas plus potest*: "to one whose power is greater"
[15] *probus, -a, -um*: "good", "honest", "proper".
[16] *frugi* < *frugi bonae* (predicate dative used as adjectival phrase): "honest", "virtuous", "thrifty" (see note 171 on page 67 at line 255, II.iii.).
[17] *iam pridem*: "for a long time now".
[18] *arbitror, -ari, -atus sum*: "think".

quin,[19] si ita arbitrare, emittis me manu?[20] **Lysidamus:** quin 284-5
id uolo.

sed nihil est[21] me cupere factum,[22] nisi tu factis[23] adiuuas.[24]

Chalinus: quid uelis modo[25] id uelim[26] me scire.[27]
Lysidamus: aúsculta,[28] ego loquar.

Casinam ego uxorem promisi[29] uilico nostro dare.

Chalinus: at tua uxor filiusque promiserunt mihi.
Lysidamus: scio.

sed utrum[30] nunc tu caelibem[31] te ésse mauis[32] liberum 290

an maritum[33] seruom[34] aetatem[35] degere[36] et gnatos[37] tuos?

optio[38] haec tua est: utram[39] harum uis condicionem[40] accipe.

Chalinus: liber si sim, meo periclo[41] uiuam; nunc uiuo tuo.

de Casina certum[42] est concedere[43] homini nato nemini.[44]

---

[19] *quin*: "no, really", "I mean!"; "actually", "in fact", "but"; "why... not?"
[20] *emittere manu*: "manumit", "set free.
[21] *nihil est*: "it's no use", "there's no point" (+ accusative-infinitive).
[22] *factum*: "the thing (to be) done".
[23] *factis*: "by (means of) your actions".
[24] *adiuuo, -are, -iuui, -iutum*: "help".
[25] *modo* (adverb): "just", "just now"; "only".
[26] *uelim* (potential subjunctive) < *uolo, uelle, uolui, –*.
[27] *me scire* is the accusative-infinitive construction after *uelim*: "I'd like to know" (*id* is the direct object of *scire*, and also the antecedent of *quid*).
[28] *ausculto, -are, -aui, -atum*: "hear", "pay attention".
[29] *promitto, -ere, -misi, -missum*: "promise".
[30] *utrum* (adverb): "whether".
[31] *caelebs, caelibis*: "unmarried", "single".
[32] *mauis* (2nd person singular present indicative active) < *malo, malle, malui, –*: "prefer", "choose instead".
[33] *maritus, -a, -um*: "married".
[34] *seruom* = *seruum*.
[35] *aetas, aetatis* (f.): "age", "stage of life", "life".
[36] *dego, -ere, degi, –*: "spend", "pass" (time, life, etc.).
[37] *gnatos* = *natos* < *natus, -i* (m.): "son" (plural may refer to "sons and daughters" / "children").
[38] *optio, optinis* (f.): "choice", "option".
[39] *uter, utra, utrum*: "which (of two)".
[40] *condicio, -onis* (f.): "option", "alternative".
[41] *periclo* = *periculo* < *periculum, -i* (n.): "danger", "risk"; translate *meo periclo*: "at my own risk/expense".
[42] *certus, -a, -um*: "certain", "settled", "resolved".
[43] *concedo, -ere, concessi, concessum*: "give up", "submit" (+ dative of person submitted to).
[44] *certum est concedere homini nato nemini*: "I'm definitely not giving her up to any man born".

Lysidamus: intro⁴⁵ abi atque actutum⁴⁶ uxorem huc⁴⁷   295
euoca⁴⁸ ante aedis⁴⁹ cito,⁵⁰

et sitellam⁵¹ huc tecum ecferto⁵² cúm aqua et sortis.⁵³
Chalinus: sati'⁵⁴ placet.⁵⁵

Lysidamus: ego pol istam iam aliquouorsum⁵⁶ tragulam⁵⁷
decidero.⁵⁸

nam si sic nihil impetrare⁵⁹ potero, saltem⁶⁰ sortiar.⁶¹

ibi ego te et suffragatores⁶² tuos ulciscar.⁶³ **Chalinus:**
attamen⁶⁴

mihi obtinget⁶⁵ sors.⁶⁶ **Lysidamus:** ut quidem pol pereas⁶⁷   300
cruciatu⁶⁸ malo.⁶⁹

Chalinus: mihi illa nubet,⁷⁰ machinare⁷¹ quidlubet⁷²
quouis⁷³ modo.

---

45 *intro* (adverb): "inside", "into the house".
46 *actutum* (adverb): "immediately".
47 *huc* (adverb): "to this place".
48 *euoco, -are, -aui, -atum*: "call out", "summon".
49 *aedis/aedes, -is* (f.): "building", "house" (often used in the plural, as here).
50 *cito* (adverb): "quickly".
51 *sitella, -ae* (f.): "narrow-necked jar for drawing lots".
52 *ecferto = efferto* (2nd singular future imperative active) < *effero, efferre, extuli, elatum*: "bring out".
53 *sortīs = sortēs* (accusative plural) < *sors, sortis* (f.): "lot", "fate"; translate here: "lottery token".
54 *sati' = satis* (adverb): "enough", "sufficiently".
55 *placeo, -ere, placui, placitum*: "please", "be pleasing to" (+ dative); *sati' placet*: "sounds good to me".
56 *aliquouorsum* (adverb): "toward some place", "one way or another".
57 *tragula, -ae* (f.): "dart", "javelin" (here *tragula* implies a plot or attack).
58 *decido, -ere, decidi, decisum*: "cut down"; "put an end to", "settle"; translate here: "deflect".
59 *impetro, -are, -aui, -atum*: "accomplish", "get", "succeed", "be granted".
60 *saltem* (adverb): "at least".
61 *sortior, -iri, sortitus sum*: "draw lots".
62 *suffragator, -is* (m.): "supporter" (in an election), "partisan".
63 *ulciscor, -i, ultus sum*: "get revenge against", "punish" (+ accusative).
64 *attamen = at tamen*: "but yet", "however", "nevertheless".
65 *obtingo, -ere, obtigi, –*: "fall to the lot of", "occur" (+ dative).
66 *mihi obtinget sors*: "the lot will turn out in my favour".
67 *pereo, -ire, periui/-ii, peritum*: "die"; "be ruined"; "be lost".
68 *cruciatus, -ūs* (m.): "crucifixion", "torture", "agony" (for crucifixion references in Plautus see note 19 on page 48 at line 93, I.i).
69 *malo* (modifying *cruciatu*) may seem unnecessary, but the adjective was regularly paired with *crux* or *cruciatus*.
70 *nubo, -ere, -nupsi, nuptum*: "marry", "be married".
71 *machinare* (2nd person singular present indicative < *machinor, -ari, -atus sum*: "devise", "plot", "invent").
72 *quidlubet = quidlibet* < *quilibet, quaelibet, quidlibet*: "whoever / whatever you want".
73 *quiuis, quaeuis, quiduis*: "whoever/whatever you please".

Lysidamus: abin[74] hinc[75] ab oculis? **Chalinus:** inuitus[76] me uides, uiuam tamen. —

Lysidamus: sumne ego miser homo? satin[77] omnes res sunt aduorsae[78] mihi?

iam metuo,[79] ne Olympionem mea uxor exorauerit[80]

ne Casinam ducat:[81] si id factum est, ecce me nullum[82]   305
senem!

si non impetrauit, etiam specula[83] in sórtitust[84] mihi.

si sors autem decolassit,[85] gladium faciam culcitam[86]

eumque incumbam.[87] sed progreditur[88] optume[89] eccum[90] Olympio.

---

[74] *abin = abine.*
[75] *hinc* (adverb): "from this place".
[76] *inuitus, -a, -um*: "unwilling".
[77] *satin = satisne.*
[78] *aduorsus, -a, -um*: "hostile", "unfavourable".
[79] *metuo, -ere, metui, –*: "fear", "be afraid".
[80] *exoro, -are, -aui, -atum*: "persuade", "plead".
[81] *ducat = uxorem ducat* (see note 64 on page 49 at line 107, I.i).
[82] *nullus, -a, -um*: "not any", "none"; translate here: "of no account", "of no value".
[83] *specula, -a* (f.): "slight hope".
[84] *sortitust = sortitū est < sortitus, -ūs*: "the casting / drawing of lots", "the lottery", "fate".
[85] *decolassit = decolauerit < decolo, -are, -aui, -atum*: "trickle away"; "fail".
[86] *culcita, -ae* (f.): "mattress".
[87] *incumbo, -ere, -cubui, -cubitum*: "lie down upon".
[88] *progredior, -i, -gressus sum*: "come / go forth", "advance", "proceed".
[89] *optume = optime* (adverb): "most satisfactorily"; translate here: "excellent!", "oh good!".
[90] *eccum = ecce + eum* or *ecce + hum* (*= hunc*).

II.v OLYMPIO, LYSIDAMVS (309-352)

Scene summary: *Olympio comes out of the house telling Cleustrata, who's still indoors, that he won't do as she asks, and that her offer to give him his freedom in return for giving up Casina doesn't interest him, since he can buy his own freedom very cheaply. Lysidamus is much relieved, and reassures Olympio that he needn't worry about retribution from Cleustrata or anyone else while he (Lysidamus) is around, though Olympio comments that Lysidamus won't live forever. Lysidamus tells Olympio about his plan to let the gods decide who'll marry Casina by using the lottery.*

Olympio: Vna edepol opera[1] in furnum[2] calidum[3] condito[4]

atque ibi torreto[5] me pro[6] pane[7] rubido,[8] 310

erá,[9] qua istuc[10] ópera a me impetres,[11] quod postulas.[12]

Lysidamus: saluos[13] sum, salua spes est, ut uerba audio.

Olympio: quid[14] tu me tua, era, libertate[15] territas?[16]

qui[17] si tu nolis[18] filiusque etiam tuos,[19]

uobis inuitis[20] atque amborum[21] ingratiis[22] 315

una libella[23] liber possum fieri.

---

[1] *unā operā... quā operā*: "in the same manner... as", "at the same time... as"; translate here: "you might as well... as".
[2] *furnus, -i* (m.): "oven".
[3] *calidus, -a, -um*: "hot".
[4] *condito* (2nd person singular future imperative active) < *condo, -ere, -didi, -ditum*: "put", "insert".
[5] *torreto* (2nd person singular future imperative active) < *torreo, -ere, torrui, tostum*: "roast", "bake".
[6] *pro* (preposition + ablative): "before", "in front of"; "on behalf of", instead of".
[7] *panis, -is* (n.): "bread".
[8] *rubidus, -a, -um*: "red", "dark-red"; translate here: "golden-brown".
[9] *era, -ae* (f.): "mistress" (of the household, and of the enslaved members of the household).
[10] *istuc = istud* (Lindsay's text has *istam* instead of *istuc*, but Brix's suggested emendation to *istuc* works better).
[11] *impetro, -are, -aui, -atum*: "accomplish", "get", "succeed", "be granted".
[12] *postulo, -are, -aui, -atum*: "ask", "desire", "claim".
[13] *saluos = saluus < saluus, -a, -um*: "safe".
[14] *quid*: "why?".
[15] *libertas, -tatis* (f.): "freedom"; translate here: "talk of manumission".
[16] *territo, -are, -aui, -atum*: "frighten", "terrify".
[17] *qui*: "I, who..." (this relative clause continues on line 316 with *una libella liber possum fieri*).
[18] *nolo, nolle, nolui, –*: "be unwilling", "not want".
[19] *tuos = tuus*.
[20] *inuitus, -a, -um*: "unwilling".
[21] *ambo, -ae, -o*: "both".
[22] *ingratiis* (adverb): "against one's will"; translate *amborum ingratiis*: "against the will of you both", "with you both unwilling".
[23] *libella, -ae* (f.): "as" (a small silver coin equalling a tenth of a *denarius*).

Lysidamus: quid istúc est? quicum[24] litigas,[25] Olympio?

Olympio: cum eadem[26] qua tu semper.[27] **Lysidamus:** cum uxori[28] mea?

Olympio: quam tu mi[29] uxorem?[30] quasi[31] uenator[32] tu quidem es:

dies átque noctes cum cane[33] aetatem[34] exigis.[35]   320

Lysidamus: quid agit,[36] quid loquitur tecum? **Olympio:** órat, opsecrat[37]

ne Casinam uxorem ducam. **Lysidamus:** quid tu postea?[38]

Olympio: negaui[39] enim ipsi me concessurum[40] Ioui,[41]

si is mecum[42] oraret. **Lysidamus:** di te seruassint[43] mihi![44]

Olympio: nunc in fermento[45] totast,[46] ita turget[47] mihi.   325

Lysidamus: ego edepol illam mediam[48] diruptam[49] uelim.

Olympio: credo edepol esse,[50] siquidem[51] tu frugi bonae es.[52]

---

[24] *quicum = quocum*.
[25] *litigo, -are, -aui, -atum*: "quarrel".
[26] *idem, eadem, idem* (adjective): "the same".
[27] A repetition of *litigas* is implied, to complete the sentence.
[28] *uxori = uxore*.
[29] *mi = mihi*.
[30] An implied verb such as *dicis* completes the sentence: "what wife are you telling me about?"
[31] *quasi* (adverb): "as if", "just like".
[32] *uenator, -oris* (m.): "hunter".
[33] *canis, -is* (m./f.): "dog", "bitch".
[34] *aetas, aetatis* (f.): "age", "stage of life", "life".
[35] *exigo, -ere, -egi, -actum*: "lead", "spend", "pass" (one's life).
[36] *quid agit*: "what's she doing?", "what's she up to?".
[37] *opsecrat = obsecrat < obsecro, -are, -aui, -atum*: "beg", "implore".
[38] *postea* (adverb): "afterwords" (*dixisti* is implied to complete the sentence).
[39] *nego, -are, -aui, -atum*: "say... not", "deny".
[40] *concedo, -ere, concessi, concessum*: "give up", "submit" (+ dative of person submitted to).
[41] *Iuppiter, Iouis* (m.): "Jupiter".
[42] Translate *mecum* here as *me*.
[43] *seruassint = seruent* (present subjunctive) or *seruauerint* (perfect subjunctive) < *seruo, -are, -aui, -atum*: "save", "protect" (optative subjunctive, see Allen & Greenough 441).
[44] *mihi* (dative of reference).
[45] *fermentum, -i* (n.): "fermentation", "yeast"; "rage".
[46] *totast = tota est*: "she's completely".
[47] *turgeo, -ere, tursi, –*: "swell up"; "swell with anger at" (+ dative).
[48] *medius, -a, -um*: "in the middle".
[49] *diruptam = diruptam esse < dirumpo, -ere, dirupi, diruptum*: "burst", "break".
[50] *esse = illam diruptam esse*.
[51] *siquidem* (adverb): "if only", "if indeed".
[52] *frugi < frugi bonae* (predicate dative used as adjectival phrase): "honest", "virtuous",

uerum[53] edepol tua mihi odiosa[54] est amatio:[55]

inimica[56] est tua uxor mihi, inimicus filius,

inimici familiares.[57] **Lysidamus:** quid id refert tua?[58] 330

unus tibi hic[59] dum[60] propitius[61] sit Iuppiter,

tu istos minutos[62] caue[63] deos flócci feceris.[64]

Olympio: nugae[65] sunt istae magnae. quasi[66] tu nescias[67]

repente[68] ut[69] emoriantur[70] humani[71] Ioues.[72]

sed tandem si tu Iuppiter sis mortuos,[73] 335

quom[74] ad deos minores redierit[75] regnum tuom,[76]

quis mihi subueniet[77] tergo[78] aut capiti aut cruribus?[79]

"thrifty"; *frugi bonae es*: "you're doing your duty", "you're doing your job as her husband".

53 *uerum* (conjunction): "but".
54 *odiosus, -a, -um*: "tiresome", "unpleasant".
55 *amatio, -onis* (f.): "love", "love affair".
56 *inimicus, -a, -um*: "unfriendly", "hostile".
57 *familiaris, -is* (m./f.): "members of the household", "household slaves"; translate here: "fellow slaves".
58 *quid id rēfert tuā*: "what's it got to do with you?", "why's that your problem?".
59 *unus... hic... Iuppiter*: "this (one) Jupiter here" (Lysidamus means himself, see also line 230).
60 *dum*: "as long as" (+ subjunctive).
61 *propitius, -a, -um*: "propitious", "well-disposed".
62 *minutus, -a, -um*: "small", "insignificant", "less important".
63 *caueo, -ere, caui, cautus*: "beware", "avoid"; *caue* + subjunctive functions as a negative command (see Bennett 276b).
64 *flocci facere*: "to consider of any importance", "to take any account of" (+ accusative); *caue... flocci feceris*: "don't worry about", "you shouldn't care about".
65 *nuga, -ae* (f.): "nonsense".
66 *quasi* (conjunction): "as if", "as though", "just like" (+ subjunctive).; *quasi* here introduces a conditional clause of comparison (see Bennett 307).
67 *nescio, -ire, -iui, -itum*: "not know", "be unaware".
68 *repente* (adverb): "suddenly".
69 *ut*: "how".
70 *emorior, -i, emortuus sum*: "die".
71 *humanus, -a, -um*: "human".
72 *Ioues < Iuppiter, Iovis* (m).
73 *sis mortuos = sis mortuus < morior, -i, mortuus sum*: "die".
74 *quom = cum*.
75 *redeo, -ire, -ii, -itum*: "devolve", "revert" (+ *ad*); translate *ad deos minores redierit* here: "will be left to the lesser gods (as heirs)".
76 *tuom = tuum*.
77 *subuenio, -ire, -ueni, -uentum*: "rescue", "come to help" (+ dative).
78 *tergum, -i* (n.): "back".
79 *crus, cruris* (n.): "leg" (Olympio is referring to the physical abuse he, and these body parts of his, can expect to receive from Cleustrata and son if Lysidamus is no longer alive to protect him).

Lysidamus: opinione[80] melius res[81] tibi et tua,[82]

si hoc impetramus,[83] ut ego cum Casina cubem.[84]

Olympio: non hercle opinor[85] posse: ita uxor acriter[86] 340

tua instat[87] ne mihi detur.[88] **Lysidamus:** at ego sic agam:

coniciam[89] sortis[90] in sitellam[91] et sortiar[92]

tibi et Chalino. ita rem natam[93] intellego:

necessumst[94] uorsis[95] gladiis depugnarier.[96]

Olympio: quid si sors aliter[97] quam uoles euenerit?[98] 345

Lysidamus: benedice.[99] dis sum fretus,[100] deos sperabimus.[101]

Olympio: non ego istuc uerbum empsim[102] titibillicio;[103]

nam omnes mortales dis sunt freti, sed tamen

uidi ego dis fretos saepe multos decipi.[104]

---

[80] *opinio, -onis* (f.): "belief", "opinion".
[81] *res, rei* (f.): "thing", "circumstance", "situation", "matter", concern".
[82] *opinione melius res tibi et*: "your circumstances aren't as bad as you think".
[83] *impetro, -are, -aui, -atum* (see note 11 on page 75 at line 311, II.v).
[84] *cubo, -are, -aui, -atum*: "lie down", "go to bed".
[85] *opinor, -ari, -atus sum*: "think", "suppose", "imagine".
[86] *acriter* (adverb): "fiercely", "sharply".
[87] *insto, -are, institi, –*: "stand on"; "insist".
[88] Casina is the subject of *detur*.
[89] *conicio, -ere, conieci, coniectum*: "throw", "put".
[90] *sortīs = sortēs* (accusative plural) < *sors, sortis* (f.): "lot", "fate"; translate here: "lottery token".
[91] *sitella, -ae* (f.): "narrow-necked jar for drawing lots".
[92] *sortior, -iri, sortitus sum*: "draw lots".
[93] *res nata*: "the way things are".
[94] *necessumst = necessum est* (an older form of *necesse est*).
[95] *uorsis = uersis* < *uerto, -ere, uerti, uersum*: "turn", "turn about", "change".
[96] *depugnarier = depugnari* < *depugno, -are, -aui, -atum*: "fight", "do battle", "fight (it) out".
[97] *aliter* (adverb): "differently".
[98] *euenio, -ire, -ueni, -uentum*: "come about", "happen", "turn out".
[99] *benedico, -ere, -xi, -ctum*: "speak kindly"; translate here: "speak propitiously", "don't tempt fate".
[100] *fretus, -a, -um*: "relying on", "trusting in" (+ ablative).
[101] *spero, -are, -aui, -atum*: "hope"; "put one's hope in", "trust" (+ accusative).
[102] *empsim = emam* (present subjunctive) or *ēmerim* (perfect subjunctive) < *emo, -ere, ēmi, emptum*: "buy". *Empsim* is a potential subjunctive (see Allen & Greenough 446), hence the negative *non*.
[103] *titibillicium* is a word of obscure meaning, implying something worthless (*titibillicio* is ablative of price, see Bennett 225); translate *non ego istuc uerbum empsim titibillicio*: "I wouldn't pay a cent for that assurance of yours", "those are cheap words".
[104] *decipio, -ere, -cepi, -ceptum*: "cheat", "mislead", "deceive".

Lysidamus: st! tace parumper.[105] **Olympio:** quid uis? 350
Lysidamus: eccum[106] exit foras[107]

Chalinus intus[108] cum sitella et sortibus.

nunc nos conlatis[109] signis[110] depugnabimus.[111]

---

[105] *parumper* (adverb): "for a moment".
[106] *eccum = ecce + eum* or *ecce + hum* (= *hunc*).
[107] *foras* (adverb): "out of doors", "out of the house".
[108] *intus* (adverb): "inside"; translate here: "from inside".
[109] *confero, -ferre, contuli, conlatum*: "bring together", "gather".
[110] *signum, -i* (n.): "military standard", "military banner".
[111] *conlatis signis depugnabimus*: "we'll engage with our banners flying" (a military metaphor).

II.vi CLEVSTRATA, CHALINVS, LYSIDAMVS, OLYMPIO (353-423)

Scene summary: *Cleustrata and Chalinus (bringing the water jar and tokens) come out to where Lysidamus and Olympio are. Olympio and Chalinus exchange insults. Lysidamus accidentally mentions that he's hoping to get Casina for himself, and tries desperately to convince Cleustrata that he didn't mean it. Olympio and Chalinus each choose their token, and each prays to the gods that his token will come out first. Olympio and Chalinus then exchange more insults, and Olympio (urged on by Lysidamus) hits Chalinus. Cleustrata then tells Chalinus to hit Olympio back, which he does. Cleustrata takes out the first lottery token, which turns out to be Olympio's. Lysidamus tells Cleustrata to start preparing the wedding feast.*

Cleustrata: Face,[1] Chaline, certiorem[2] me[3] quid meu'[4] uir me uelit.[5]

Chalinus: ille edepol uidere[6] ardentem[7] te extra[8] portam[9] mortuam.[10]

Cleustrata: credo ecastor uelle.[11] **Chalinus:** at pol ego hau[12] credo, sed certo[13] scio.   355

Lysidamus: plus artificum[14] est mihi quam rebar:[15] hariolum[16] hunc eo domi.[17]

quid si propius[18] attollamus[19] signa[20] eamusque obuiam?[21]

---

[1] *Face = fac.*
[2] *certior, -ius:* "more certain", "clearer".
[3] *Face... certiorem me:* "let me know", "tell me".
[4] *meu' = meus.*
[5] *quid meu' uir me uelit:* "what my husband wants (to see) me for", "why my husband wants (to see) me".
[6] *uidere = uidere uult.*
[7] *ardeo, -ere, arsi, arsum:* "burn", "be burning".
[8] *extra* (preposition): "outside of" (+ accusative).
[9] *porta, -ae* (f.): "gate", "city gate" (burials had to take place outside of the city gates).
[10] *mortuus, -a, -um:* "dead".
[11] Lysidamus is the subject of *uelle.*
[12] *hau = haud:* "not at all".
[13] *certo* (adverb): "certainly", "with certainty".
[14] *artifex, -ficis* (m.): "skilled professional" (*artificum* is genitive of the whole after *plus*, see Bennett 201).
[15] *reor, reri, ratus sum:* "think", "suppose".
[16] *hariolus, -i* (m.): "soothsayer", "prophet" (a *hariolus* read the entrails of sacrificed animals).
[17] *domi* (locative case).
[18] *propius* (comparative adverb): "closer".
[19] *attollo, -ere, –, –:* "raise", "lift".
[20] *signum, -i* (n.): "military standard", "military banner".
[21] *obuiam* (adverb): "in the way"; translate here: "to meet" (them), "towards" (them).

sequere. quid uos agitis?²² **Chalinus:** adsunt quae imperauisti²³ omnia:

uxor, sortes, situla²⁴ atque egomet.²⁵ **Olympio:** te uno²⁶ adest plus quam ego uolo.

Chalinus: tibi quidem edepol ita uidetur; stimulus²⁷ ego nunc sum tibi,   360

fodico²⁸ corculum;²⁹ adsudascis³⁰ iam ex metu,³¹ mastigia.³²

Lysidamus: tace, Chaline. **Chalinus:** comprime³³ istunc.³⁴ **Olympio:** immo³⁵ istunc³⁶ qui didicit³⁷ dare.³⁸

Lysidamus: adpone³⁹ hic sitellam, sortis cedo⁴⁰ mihi. animum aduortite.⁴¹

atqui⁴² ego censui⁴³ aps⁴⁴ te posse hoc me⁴⁵ impetrare,⁴⁶ uxor mea,

Casina ut uxor mihi daretur; et nunc etiam censeo.   365

---

22   *quid uos agitis*: "what are you up to?", "how are you doing?".
23   *impero, -are, -aui, -atum*: "order".
24   *situla = sitella* (see note 91 on page 78 at line 342, II.v).
25   *egomet* (emphatic form of *ego*).
26   *te uno* (ablative of degree of difference, see Bennett 223); *te uno adest plus quam ego uolo*: "there's one more 'you' than I want".
27   *stimulus, -i* (m.): "goad", "spike" (used for torturing enslaved persons, see Plautus, *Asinaria* 548-552; here used metaphorically).
28   *fodico, -are, -aui, -atum*: "prod".
29   *corculum, -i* (n.): "little heart".
30   *adsudascis = assudascis/assudescis < assudasco/assudesco, -ere, –, –:* "sweat", "break out into a sweat".
31   *metus, -ūs* (m.): "fear".
32   *mastigia, -ae* (f.): "good-for-nothing", "rascal", "one who deserves a whipping".
33   *comprimo, -ere, -pressi, -pressum*: "press together", "restrain", "control"; this verb can also mean "sexually penetrate".
34   *istunc = istum*.
35   *immo* (adverb): "on the contrary".
36   *immo istunc*: "no, control **him**".
37   *disco, -ere, didici, –:* "learn", "learn how to".
38   *do, dare, dedi, datum*: "give"; "yield", "acquiesce"; *qui didicit dare*: "he's the one who learned how to give it up" (suggesting that Chalinus has been sexually penetrated by Lysidamus).
39   *adpone = appone < appono, -ere, -posui, -positum*: "put near".
40   *cedo* (archaic singular imperative related to *do, dare*): "give".
41   *animum aduortite*: "pay attention".
42   *atqui* (conjunction): "but anyhow"
43   *conseo, -ere, censui, censitum*: "think", "suppose".
44   *aps = ab*.
45   *me* is the accusative subject of *posse*.
46   *impetro, -are, -aui, -atum*: "accomplish", "get", "succeed", "be granted".

Cleustrata: tibi daretur illa? **Lysidamus:** mihi enim[47] — ah, non id uolui dicere:

dum 'mihi' uolui, 'huic'[48] dixi, atque adeo mihi dum[49] cupio — perperam[50]

iam dudum[51] hercle fabulor.[52] **Cleustrata:** pol tu quidem, atque etiam facis.[53]

Lysidamus: huic — immo hercle mihi — uah![54] tandem redii[55] uix[56] ueram in uiam.

Cleustrata: per pol[57] saepe peccas.[58] **Lysidamus:** ita fit,[59] ubi 370
quid[60] tanto opere[61] expetas.[62]

sed te uterque[63] tuo pro iure,[64] ego atque hic,[65] oramus. **Cleustrata:** quid est?

Lysidamus: dicam enim, mea mulsa:[66] de istac[67] Casina huic nostro uilico

gratiam facias.[68] **Cleustrata:** at pol ego neque facio neque censeo.

Lysidamus: tum igitur ego sortis utrimque[69] iam <diribeam>.[70] **Cleustrata:** quis uotat?[71]

---

[47] *enim*: "that is", "I mean".
[48] *huic* refers to Olympio.
[49] *adeo... dum*: "so long as".
[50] *perperam* (adverb): "wrongly", "incorrectly".
[51] *dudum* (adverb): "a little while ago", "formerly".
[52] *fabulor, -ari, -atus sum*: "talk", "make up a story".
[53] *atque etiam facis = atque etiam perperam facis*.
[54] *uah* (exclamation of joy or anger).
[55] *redeo, -ire, -iui/-ii, -itum*: "return", "go back".
[56] *uix* (adverb): "scarcely", "barely".
[57] *per pol*: "for Pollux's sake".
[58] *pecco, -are, -aui, -atus*: "do wrong", "blunder", "screw up".
[59] *fio, fieri, factus sum*: "be done", "be made", "happen", "take place".
[60] *quis, quid* (indefinite pronoun): "anyone / anything".
[61] *tanto opere*: "with such labour", "so much".
[62] *expeto, -ere, -iui, -itum*: "ask for", "look for"; "demand", "want", "desire", "be eager for".
[63] *uterque, utraque, utrumque*: "each" (of two), "both".
[64] *tuo pro iure*: "by virtue of your rights", "given your rights".
[65] *hic* refers to Olympio.
[66] *mulsa, -ae* (f.): "honeyed wine".
[67] *istāc = istā*.
[68] *gratiam facere*: "to do a favour" (for someone in the dative).
[69] *utrimque* (adverb): "on each side", "on both sides".
[70] *diribeo, -ere, – , diribitum*: "sort", "separate" (with reference to voting tokens).
[71] *uotat = uetat < ueto, -are, uotui, uotitum*: "forbid", "prevent".

Lysidamus: optumum[72] atque aequissumum[73] istuc[74] esse   375
iure[75] iudico.[76]

postremo,[77] <si> illuc[78] quod uolumus eueniet,[79]
gaudebimus;[80]

sin[81] secus,[82] patiemur[83] animis aequis. tene[84] sortem tibi.[85]

uide quid scriptumst.[86] **Olympio:** unum. **Chalinus:**
iniquomst,[87] quia isti prius quam[88] mihi est.[89]

Lysidamus: accipe hanc sis.[90] **Chalinus:** cedo.[91] mane,[92]
unum uenit in mentem[93] modo:[94]

uide ne quae[95] illic[96] insit[97] alia sortis[98] sub aqua.   380
Lysidamus: uerbero,[99]

men[100] te censes[101] esse? **Cleustrata:** nulla est. e quietum[102]
animum modo.

Chalinus: quod bonum atque fortunatum sit mihi —
Olympio: magnum malum[103]

---

[72] *optumum = optimum.*
[73] *aequissumum = aequissimum* (superlative < *aequus, -a, -um*: "fair").
[74] *istuc = istud.*
[75] *iure* (adverb): "justly", "rightly".
[76] *iudico, -are, -aui, -atum*: "judge".
[77] *postremo* (adverb): "finally".
[78] *illuc = illud.*
[79] *euenio, -ire, -ueni, -uentum*: "come about", "happen", "turn out".
[80] *gaudeo, -ere, gauisus sum* (semi-deponent): "rejoice", "be glad".
[81] *sin*: "if however", "but if".
[82] *secus* (adverb): "otherwise", "differently".
[83] *patior, -i, passus sum*: "bear", "tolerate", "put up with".
[84] *teneo, -ere, tenui, tentum*: "hold", "take hold of".
[85] *tibi* is dative of reference.
[86] *scriptumst = scriptum est.*
[87] *iniquomst = iniquum est*: "it's not fair".
[88] *prius quam*: "before".
[89] *isti... est* and *mihi est* are datives of possession (see Bennett 190).
[90] *sis = si uis.*
[91] *cedo* (see note 23 on page 155 at line 363, II.vi).
[92] *maneo, -ere, mansi, mansum*: "remain", "wait", "wait for".
[93] *mens, mentis* (f.): "mind".
[94] *modo* (adverb): "just", "just now".
[95] *quae* (indefininite adjective): "any".
[96] *illic = illi* (adverb): "there", "in there".
[97] *insum, -esse, -fui, -futurus*: "be in".
[98] *sortis = sors.*
[99] *uerbero, -onis* (m.): "rascal", "scum" (literally, someone who deserved a whipping).
[100] *men = mene* (*me* is the accusative subject of *esse*, while *te* is the predicate accusative).
[101] *censeo, -ere, censui, censitum* (see note 43 on page 81 at line 364, II.vi).
[102] *quietus, -a, -um*: "quiet", "calm".
[103] *malum, -i* (n.): "misfortune", "misery".

tibi quidem edepol credo[104] eueniet; noui[105] pietatem[106] tuam.

sed mane dum:[107] num[108] ista aut populna[109] sors aut abiegnast[110] tua?

Chalinus: quid tu id curas?[111] **Olympio:** quia enim metuo[112]   385
né in aqua summa[113] natet.[114]

Lysidamus: eugae![115] caue.[116] conicite[117] sortis[118] nunciam[119] ambo[120] huc.[121] eccere![122]

uxor, aequa.[123] **Olympio:** noli[124] uxori credere. **Lysidamus:** e animum bonum.

Olympio: credo hercle, hodie deuotabit[125] sortis si attigerit.[126] **Lysidamus:** tace.

Olympio: taceo. deos quaeso[127] — **Chalinus:** ut[128] quidem tu hodie canem[129] et furcam[130] feras.

---

[104] *credo* (interjection): "I suppose", "I dare say".
[105] *nosco, -ere, noui, notum*: "know", "come to know".
[106] *pietas, -tatis* (f.): "piety", "dutifulness".
[107] *dum* (enclitic, adding intensive force to the imperative *mane*); *sed mane dum*: "but wait a minute".
[108] *num* (interrogative): "it isn't possible that...?", "can it be that...?"; translate here: "I want to be sure"; (*num* is used when the speaker is anxious about a possible negative answer).
[109] *populnus, -a, -um*: "made out of poplar wood".
[110] *abiegnast = abiegna est; abiegnus, -a, -um*: "made out of fir wood".
[111] *curo, -are, -aui, -atum*: "take care of", "care about".
[112] *metuo, -ere, metui, –*: "fear", "be afraid".
[113] *summus, -a, -um*: "the top of"; *in aqua summa*: "on the top of the water".
[114] *nato, -are, -aui, -atum*: "swim", "float".
[115] *eugae* (exclamation): "well done", "good".
[116] *caueo, -ere, caui, cautus*: "beware", "avoid", "be careful".
[117] *conicio, -ere, -ieci, -iectum*: "throw together", "throw".
[118] *sortīs = sortēs* (accusative plural).
[119] *nunciam = nunc + iam* (emphatic form of *nunc*).
[120] *ambo, -bae, -bo*: "both".
[121] *huc* (adverb): "to this place"; translate here: "in here" (referring to the *sitella*).
[122] *eccere = ecce re*: "there!", "there you are".
[123] *aequus, -a, -um*: "fair", "level".
[124] *noli* (2nd person singular present imperative active < *nolo, nolle, nolui, –*: "not... want"; *noli* + an infinitive is a negative command.
[125] *deuoto, -are, -aui, -atum*: "bewitch", "curse", "put a spell on".
[126] *attingo, -ere, attigi, attactum*: "touch".
[127] *quaeso*: "I beg", "please" (< *quaeso, -ere, -iui/-ii*: "seek", "beg").
[128] Olympio began a prayer with *deos quaeso*, and now Chalinus finishes it for him with a substantive clause (*ut... feras*). In line 390, Olympio replaces Chalinus's substantive clause with his own: *ut eueniat...*, which Chalinus then replaces with *ut... pendeas*, and which Olympio then replaces again with *ut... emungare* (in line 391).
[129] *canis, -is* (m./f.): "dog"; translate here: "fetter", "chain", "device for physically restraining someone".
[130] *furca, -ae* (f.): "fork" (usually referring to a two-pronged fork used in the punishment of

Olympio: mihi[131] ut sortito[132] eueniat — **Chalinus:** ut quidem hercle pedibus[133] pendeas.[134] 390

Olympio: at tu ut oculos emungare[135] ex capite per nasum[136] tuos.

Chalinus: quid times? paratum[137] oportet[138] esse iam laqueum[139] tibi.

Olympio: periisti.[140] **Lysidamus:** animum aduortite[141] ambo. **Olympio:** taceo. **Lysidamus:** nunc tu, Cleustrata,

ne a me memores[142] malitiose[143] de hac re factum[144] aut suspices,[145]

tibi permitto:[146] tute[147] sorti.[148] **Olympio:** perdis[149] me. 395
Chalinus: lucrum[150] facit.[151]

Cleustrata: bene facis. **Chalinus:** deos quaeso — ut tua sors ex sitella ecfugerit.[152]

---

enslaved persons, see note 163 on page 53 at line 139, I.i).
[131] *mihi*: "in my favour".
[132] *sortito* (adverb): "by lot".
[133] *pes, pedis* (m.): "foot".
[134] *pendeo, -ere, pependi, –*: "hang", "be suspended"; *pedibus pendeas* might mean "that you be suspended by your feet", but MacCary and Willcock think it more likely to be "that you be suspended with your feet dangling". Roman slave owners are known to have inflicted punishment on slaves by suspending them by the wrists so that their feet were off the ground, the slave then being beaten in this position (MacCary and Willcock 1976: 144). Chalinus begins a new prayer with *deos quaeso* at line 396.
[135] *emungare* (2nd person singular present subjunctive passive) < *emungo, -ere, -nxi, -nctum*: "knock out", "blow out".
[136] *nasus, -i* (m.): "nose".
[137] *paro, -are, -aui, -atum*: "prepare".
[138] *oportet, oportere, oportuit, –* (impersonal verb): "it is right", "it is fitting"; translate here: "it ought".
[139] *laqueus, -i* (m.): "noose".
[140] *pereo, -ire, periui/-ii, peritum*: "die"; "be ruined"; "be lost"; translate here: "you're dead!".
[141] *animum aduortite* (see note 41 on page 81 at line 363, II.vi).
[142] *memoro, -are, -aui, -atum*: "remind of", "say", "tell", "claim".
[143] *malitiose* (adverb): "maliciously".
[144] *factum = factum esse*.
[145] *suspices = suspiceris < suspicor, -ari, -atus sum*: "suspect".
[146] *permitto, -ere, -misi, -missum*: "permit", "allow", "entrust" (+ dative of person entrusted).
[147] *tute = tu* (the *-te* adds emphasis to the pronoun).
[148] *sorti* (2nd person singular present imperative < *sortior, -iri, sortitus sum*: "draw lots").
[149] *perdo, -ere, perdidi, perditum*: "ruin", "destroy"; "lose".
[150] *lucrum, -i* (n.): "gain", "profit".
[151] *lucrum facit*: "he'll be better off then" (Chalinus chooses to take Olympio literally, and means that Lysidamus will be better off if Olympio were to be lost or destroyed).
[152] *ecfugerit = effugerit < effugio, -ere, -fugi, -fugitum*: "flee away", "run away".

Olympio: ain[153] tu? quia tute es fugitiuos,[154] omnis[155] te imitari[156] cupis?[157]

utinam tua quidem <ista>, sicut[158] Herculei[159] praedicant[160] quondam[161] prognatis,[162] in sortiendo[163] sors deliquerit.[164]

Chalinus: tú ut liquescas[165] ipse, actutum[166] uirgis[167] calefactabere.[168]   400

Lysidamus: hoc age[169] sis,[170] Olympio. **Olympio:** si hic litteratus[171] me sinat.[172]

Lysidamus: quod[173] bonum atque fortunatum mihi sit! **Olympio:** ita uero,[174] et mihi.

Chalinus: non. **Olympio:** immo[175] hercle. **Chalinus:** immo mihi hercle **Cleustrata:** hic uincet, tu uiues miser.

---

[153] *ain = aisne* (2nd person singular present indicative active < *aio*: "say"; "say yes", "affirm").
[154] *fugitiuos = fugitiuus* < *fugitiuus, -a, -um*: "runaway", "fugitive" (a term of abuse, implying that any runaway must be a criminal).
[155] *omnīs = omnēs*.
[156] *imitor, -ari, -atus sum*: "imitate", "act like".
[157] *cupio, -ere, -iui, -itum*: "wish", "desire".
[158] *sicut*: "just as", "just like".
[159] *Herculei* (alternative genitive singular) < *Hercules, -is*: "Hercules".
[160] *praedico, -ere, -dixi, -dictum*: "declare", "state".
[161] *quondam* (adverb): "once".
[162] *prognatis* (dative of reference) < *prognatus, -a, -um*: "descended from"; translate here: "descendants"; this is a reference to a myth involving the descendants of Hercules drawing lots to divide up the region of Messenia. One of the lottery tokens was made of baked clay, while the other was only sun-dried and so it dissolved in the water (see Pausanias 4.3.3-5 and Apollodorus 2.8.4).
[163] *sortiendo* (gerund < *sortior, -iri, sortitus sum*).
[164] *deliquerit = delicuerit* < *delinqueso, -ere, -licui, –*: "melt away", "dissolve".
[165] *liquesco, -ere, -licui, –*: "melt", "melt away".
[166] *actutum* (adverb): "immediately".
[167] *uirga, -ae* (f.): "switch", "stick", "rod".
[168] *calefactabere* (2nd person singular future indicative passive) < *calefacto, -are, -aui, -atum*: "heat", "make warm by a beating".
[169] *hoc age*: "pay attention to this".
[170] *sis = si uis*: "please".
[171] *litteratus, -a, -um*: "educated", "learned"; translate here: "wise guy", "smarty-pants".
[172] *sino, -ere, -siui, situm*: "allow", "let".
[173] *quod* (connecting relative pronoun, see Allen & Greenough 308f); translate here: "it", "the results" (of the lottery).
[174] *uero* (adverb): "truly", "certainly".
[175] *immo* (adverb): "on the contrary".

Lysidamus: percide[176] os tu illi odio.[177] age,[178] ecquid[179] fit?[180] caue obiexis[181] manum.[182]

Olympio: compressan[183] palma[184] an porrecta[185] ferio?[186]   405
Lysidamus: age ut uis. **Olympio:** em tibi![187]

Cleustrata: quid[188] tibi istunc[189] tactio[190] est?[191] **Olympio:** quia Iuppiter iussit[192] meus.

Cleustrata: feri[193] malam,[194] ut[195] ille, rusum.[196] **Olympio:** perii![197] pugnis[198] caedor,[199] Iuppiter.

Lysidamus: quid tibi tactio hunc fuit? **Chalinus:** quia iussit haec Iuno mea.

Lysidamus: patiundum est,[200] siquidem[201] me uiuo[202] mea uxor imperium exhibet.[203]

---

[176] *percido, -ere, -cidi, -cisum*: "punch", "hit".
[177] *odium, -ii* (n.): "hatred", "object of hatred" (*illi odio* is dative of reference, *odio* being an insulting reference to Chalinus).
[178] *age* (< *ago, -ere, egi, actum*): "come on", "go on".
[179] *ecquis, ecquid* (interrogative pronoun): "is there anyone who? / is there anything that".
[180] *ecquid fit*: "is anything going to happen?", "are you going to do anything?".
[181] *obiexis* = *ob(i)cias* (present subjunctive) or *obieceris* (perfect subjunctive) < *obicio, -ere, -ieci, -iectum*: "throw towards", "throw in the way"; *caue obiexis*: "don't raise your hand" (see Allen & Greenough 450 for negative prohibitions with *caue* + subjunctive).
[182] *caue obiexis manum*: "don't raise your hand" (Lysidamus addresses this to Chalinus, who evidently had put up a fist to defend himself).
[183] *compressan* = *compressane* < *comprimo, -ere, -pressi, -pressum*: "press together", "restrain", "control".
[184] *compressāne palmā*: "with clenched fist".
[185] *porrectus, -a, -um*: "stretched out"; translate here: "flat".
[186] *ferio, -ire, –, –*: "strike", "hit".
[187] *em tibi!*: "take that!", "that's for you!" (as Richlin points out, *em tibi* tends to accompany a physical blow given the the speaker – Richlin 2017: 90-93).
[188] *quid*: "why?".
[189] *istunc* = *istum*.
[190] *tactio, -onis* (f.): "physical contact".
[191] *quid tibi istunc tactio est*: "why are you hitting him?".
[192] *iubeo, -ere, iussi, iussum*: "order", "tell".
[193] *ferio, -ire* (see note 186 at line 405, II.vi).
[194] *mala, -ae* (f.): "cheek", "jaw".
[195] *ut*: "as".
[196] *rusum* = *rursum* = *rursus* (adverb): "again", "back", "in return".
[197] *pereo, -ire, periui/-ii, peritum*: "die"; "be ruined"; "be lost".
[198] *pugnus, -i* (m.): "fist".
[199] *caedo, -ere, cecidi, caesum*: "strike", "murder".
[200] *patiundum est* (passive periphrastic) < *patior, -i, passus sum*: "bear", "tolerate", "put up with".
[201] *siquidem* (adverb): "if only", "if indeed".
[202] *uiuus, -a, -um*: "alive"; *me uiuo*: "while I'm still alive".
[203] *exhibeo, -ere, -ui, -itum*: "show", "employ"; *imperium exhibet*: "exercise authority", "act like she's in charge".

Cleustrata: tam[204] huic loqui licere[205] oportet quam isti.   410
Olympio: qur[206] omen[207] mihi

uituperat?[208] **Lysidamus:** malo,[209] Chaline, tibi cauendum[210] censeo.[211]

Chalinus: temperi,[212] postquam oppugnatum est[213] os.[214]
Lysidamus: age,[215] uxor, nunciam[216]

sorti.[217] uos aduortite animum.[218] prae[219] metu[220] ubi sim nescio.

perii! cor[221] lienosum,[222] opinor, eo, iam dudum[223] salit.[224]

de labore[225] pectus[226] tundit.[227] **Cleustrata:** teneo sortem.   415
Lysidamus: ecfer[228] foras.[229]

Chalinus: iamne mortuo's?[230] **Olympio:** ostende.[231] mea <haec> est. **Chalinus:** mala crux[232] east[233] quidem.

---

[204] *tam... quam*: "as much... as".
[205] *licet, licere, licuit, licitum est*: "be allowed", "be permitted" (+ dative of person to whom it is permitted).
[206] *qur = cur*.
[207] *omen, ominis* (n.): "omen", "sign".
[208] *uitupero, -are, -aui, -atum*: "disparage"; "spoil".
[209] *malum, -i* (see note 103 on page 83 at line 382, II.vi); *malo* is ablative after *cauendum*.
[210] *malo... tibi cauendum*: "you'd better be careful of trouble", "you'd better watch your step".
[211] *censeo, -ere, censui, censitum* (see note 43 on page 81 at line 364, II.vi).
[212] *temperi* (adverb): "at the right time", "just in time" (meant ironically here).
[213] *oppugno, -are, -aui, -atum*: "attack", "assault".
[214] *os, oris* (n.): "mouth", "face".
[215] *age* (< *ago, -ere, egi, actum*): "come on", "go on".
[216] *nunciam = nunc + iam* (emphatic form of *nunc*).
[217] *sorti* (see note 148 on page 85 at line 395, II.vi).
[218] *aduortite animum* (see note 41 on page 81 at line 363, II.vi).
[219] *prae* (preposition + ablative): "before"; "because of".
[220] *metus, -ūs* (see note 31 on page 81 at line 361, II.vi).
[221] *cor, cordis* (n.): "heart", "mind".
[222] *lienosus, -a, -um*: "splenetic", "relating to the spleen"; "irritable" (< *lien, -enis*: "spleen").
[223] *dudum* (see note 51 on page 82 at line 368, VI.ii).
[224] *salio, -ire, -ui, saltum*: "jump", "bound"; translate *cor lienosum... salit*: "I think my poor heart is jumping out of my chest".
[225] *labor, -oris* (m.): "labour", "exertion"; "distress".
[226] *pectus, -oris* (n.): "chest"; "breast".
[227] *tundo, -ere, tutudi, tunsum/tussum/tusum*: "beat", "thump".
[228] *ecfer = effer* (2nd singular present imperative active) < *effero, efferre, extuli, elatum*: "bring out".
[229] *foras* (adverb): "out of doors"; translate here: "out of the jar".
[230] *mortuo's = mortuus es < mortuus, -a, -um*: "dead" (meaning: "have you lost?").
[231] *ostendo, -ere, -i, ostensum/ostentum*: "show".
[232] *crux, crucis* (f.): "cross" (see note 19 on page 48 at line 93, I.i); translate *mala crux*: "the worst luck".
[233] *east = ea est*.

Cleustrata: uictus es, Chaline. **Lysidamus:** quom[234] nos di iuuere,[235] Olympio,

gaudeo.[236] **Olympio:** pietate[237] factum est mea atque maiorum[238] meum.

Lysidamus: intro[239] abi, uxor, atque adorna[240] nuptias.[241]
Cleustrata: faciam ut iubes.

Lysidamus: scin[242] tu rus[243] hinc esse ad uillam[244] longe[245]   420
quo[246] ducat?[247] **Cleustrata:** scio.

Lysidamus: intro abi et, quamquam[248] hoc tibi aegre est,[249] tamen fac[250] accures.[251] **Cleustrata:** licet.[252] —

Lysidamus: eamus nos quoque[253] intro, hortemur[254] ut properent.[255] **Olympio:** numquid[256] moror?[257] —

Lysidamus: nam praesente[258] hoc[259] plura uerba <fieri>[260] non desidero.[261] —

---

[234] *quom = cum.*
[235] *iuuere* (3rd person plural perfect indicative active) < *iuuo, -are, iuui, iutum*: "help".
[236] *gaudeo, -ere, gauisus sum* (see note 80 on page 83 at line 376, II.vi).
[237] *pietas, -tatis* (see note 106 on page 84 at line 383, II.vi).
[238] *maiorum* < *maiores, -orum* (m. pl.): "ancestors". Enslaved persons were considered not to have a family of origin regardless of biological fact; this comment by Olympio about his ancestors would thus have struck the Roman audience as funny.
[239] *intro* (adverb): "inside", "into the house".
[240] *adorno, -are, -aui, -atum*: "get ready", "decorate".
[241] *nuptiae, -arum* (f. pl.): "marriage", "wedding".
[242] *scin = scisne.*
[243] *rus, ruris* (n.): "countryside".
[244] *uilla, -ae* (f.): "farm".
[245] *longe* (adverb): "a long way off".
[246] *quo* (adverb): "where (to)".
[247] *scin tu rus hinc esse ad uillam longe quo ducat* (indirect question within indirect discourse): "do you know that the countryside is far from here, to the farm where he'll take her?"
[248] *quamquam*: "although".
[249] *aegre esse alicui*: "to be annoying to someone".
[250] *fac* without *ut* can introduce a substantive clause, see Allen & Greenough 565; translate "make sure".
[251] *accuro, -are, -aui, -atum*: "take care of", "prepare with care".
[252] *licet* (see note 205 on the facing page at line 410, II.vi); translate here: "all right".
[253] *quoque* (adverb): "too", "also".
[254] *hortor, -ari, -tatus sum*: "urge", "encourage".
[255] *propero, -are, -aui, -atum*: "hurry", "be quick".
[256] *numquid* (interrogative adverb): "surely... not?"
[257] *moror, -ari, -atus sum*: "delay".
[258] *praesens, -entis* (adjective): "present", "at hand".
[259] *hoc* (refers to Chalinus); *praesente hoc* is ablative absolute.
[260] *fio, fieri, factus sum* (see note 59 on page 82 at line 370, II.vi).
[261] *desidero, -are, -aui, -atum*: "want"; *plura uerba fieri non desidero*: "I don't want there to be any more discussion".

II.vii CHALINVS (424-436)

Scene summary: *Chalinus, alone on the stage, expresses his dejection, and then, hearing Olympio and Lysidamus returning, hides so that he can overhear what they say.*

Chalinus: Si nunc me suspendam,[1] meam operam[2] luserim[3]

et praeter[4] operam restim[5] sumpti[6] fecerim[7] 425

et meis inimicis[8] uoluptatem[9] creauerim.[10]

quid opus est,[11] qui[12] sic mortuos?[13] equidem[14] tamen

sorti[15] sum uictus, Casina nubet[16] uilico.

atque id non tam aegrest[17] iam, uicisse uilicum,

quam id expetiuisse[18] opere tam magno[19] senem,[20] 430

ne ea míhi daretur atque ut illi[21] nuberet.

ut[22] illé trepidabat,[23] ut festinabat[24] miser!

ut sussultabat,[25] postquam uicit uilicus!

---

[1] *suspendo, -ere, -pendi, -pensus*: "hang", "hang up".
[2] *opera, -ae* (f.): "service", "activity", "effort".
[3] *ludo, -ere, lusi, lusum*: "play", "mock"; "make a mockery of" (+ accusative).
[4] *praeter* (adverb): "besides".
[5] *restim = restem < restis, -is* (f.): "rope".
[6] *sumpti = sumptūs < sumptus, -ūs* (m.): "expense", "expenditure".
[7] *restim sumpti fecerim*: "I'd have to pay for the rope".
[8] *inimicus, -i* (m.): "enemy".
[9] *uoluptas, -tatis* (f.): "pleasure", "delight".
[10] *creo, -are, -aui, -atum*: "produce", "create".
[11] *quid opus est*: "why's there any need?", "what's the point?".
[12] *qui*: "I who am", "since I'm".
[13] *mortuos = mortuus*.
[14] *equidem*: "indeed", "truly".
[15] *sorti = sorte < sors, sortis*.
[16] *nubo, -ere, -nupsi, nuptum*: "marry", "be married".
[17] *aegrest = aegre est*: "it's annoying / upsetting".
[18] *expeto, -ere, -iui, -itum*: "ask for", "look for"; "demand", "want", "desire", "be eager for".
[19] *opere... magno*: "particularly", "especially".
[20] *senem* is the accusative subject of *expetiuisse*, as *uilicum* is the subject of *uicisse* in line 429.
[21] *illi* refers to the *uilicus* Olympio.
[22] *ut*: "how" (as also for the following two instances of *ut*).
[23] *trepido, -are, -aui, -atum*: "tremble", "be anxious".
[24] *festino, -are, -aui, -atum*: "hurry".
[25] *sussultabat = subsultabat < subsulto, -are*: "leap up", "skip about".

attat!²⁶ concedam²⁷ huc,²⁸ audio aperiri²⁹ fores,³⁰
mei beneuolentes³¹ atque amici prodeunt.³²   435
hinc³³ ex insidiis³⁴ hisce³⁵ ego insidias dabo.³⁶

---

26   *attat* (exclamation of surprise).
27   *concedo, -ere, concessi, consessum*: "depart", "go away", "move".
28   *huc* (adverb): "to this place", "over here" (Chalinus means to one side of the stage where he will be able to eavesdrop without being seen by the other characters).
29   *aperio, -ire, -ui, apertum*: "open".
30   *foris, -is* (f.): "door", "gate".
31   *beneuolens, -ntis* (m./f.): "friend", "well-wisher".
32   *prodeo, -ire, -iui/-ii, -itum*: "come out".
33   *hinc* (adverb): "from this place".
34   *insidiae, -arum* (f. pl.): "ambush"; *ex insidiis*: "sneakily", "by a stratagem".
35   *hisce = his* (refers to Olympio and Lysidamus).
36   *insidias alicui dare*: "to lay a trap/ambush for someone".

II.viii OLYMPIO, LYSIDAMVS, CHALINVS (437-514)

Scene summary: *Chalinus overhears Olympio and Lysidamus planning to get Chalinus out to the farm so that Olympio can torture him. Lysidamus then starts talking about how much he wants to kiss and hold – Casina? – or Olympio? Chalinus interprets it as the latter, and thinks he now understands how Olympio got to be farm manager (in return for sexual favours), though he then seems to realize that Lysidamus is more obsessed with Casina. Lysidamus tells Olympio about his plan for the wedding night: he'll arrange for his neighbour Alcesimus and his wife Myrrhina to be out of their house so that, after the wedding, Olympio can bring Casina to the neighbours' empty house. Lysidamus will then have his "wedding night" with Casina while Cleustrata thinks Casina is at the farm with Olympio. Lysidamus sends Olympio off to the market to buy various types of fish with punning names for the wedding feast, while the hidden Chalinus says quietly that he'll tell everything he's heard to Cleustrata, and that he'll make a plan to get the better of Lysidamus and Olympio.*

Olympio: Sine[1] módo[2] rus[3] ueniat:[4] ego remittam[5] ad te uirum

cum furca[6] in urbem tamquam[7] carbonarium.[8]

Lysidamus: ita fieri[9] oportet.[10] **Olympio:** factum et curatum[11] dabo.[12]

Lysidamus: uolui Chalinum, si domi[13] esset, mittere   440

tecum opsonatum,[14] ut etiam in maerore[15] insuper[16]

---

[1] *sine* < *sino, -ere, siui, situm*: "allow", "let" (+ subjunctive here).
[2] *modo* (adverb): "just", "just now"; "only".
[3] *rus* (< *rus, ruris*) here is the accusative of limit of motion, see Bennett 182).
[4] Chalinus is the subject of *ueniat*.
[5] *remitto, -ere, -misi, -missum*: "send back".
[6] *furca, -ae* (f.): "fork" (usually referring to a two-pronged fork used in the punishment of slaves, though evidently a *furca* was also used by charcoal-burners to carry loads of charcoal).
[7] *tamquam* (adverb): "just like".
[8] *carbonarius, -i* (m.): "charcoal-burner", "charcoal-seller".
[9] *fio, fieri, factus sum*: "be done", "be made", "happen", "take place".
[10] *oportet, oportere, oportuit,* – (impersonal verb): "it is right", "it is fitting".
[11] *curo, -are, -aui, -atum*: "care for", take care of".
[12] *factum et curatum dabo*: "I'll make sure it's all taken care of" (*dare* + perfect participle can mean "to cause to be [done, taken care of, etc.*]", "to make sure [something] gets [done, taken care of, etc.*]; *depending on the verb of the perfect participle).
[13] *domi* (locative case).
[14] *opsonatum = obsonatum* (supine) < *obsono, -are, -aui, -atum*: "go grocery-shopping"; *Chalinum... mittere tecum opsonatum*: "to make Chalinus go grocery-shopping with you".
[15] *maeror, -oris* (m.): "grief", "sorrow".
[16] *insuper* (adverb): "on top", "additionally".

inimico[17] nostro miseriam hanc adiungerem.[18]

Chalinus: recessim[19] dabo me[20] ad parietem,[21] imitabor[22] nepam;[23]

captandust[24] horum clanculum[25] sermo[26] mihi.[27]

nam illorum me alter[28] cruciat,[29] alter macerat.[30]   445

at candidatus[31] cedit[32] hic mastigia,[33]

stimulorum[34] loculi.[35] protollo[36] mortem mihi;

certum[37] est, hunc Accheruntem[38] praemittam[39] prius.[40]

Olympio: ut[41] tibi ego inuentus sum[42] opsequens.[43] quod maxume[44]

---

[17] *inimicus, -i* (m.): "enemy".
[18] *adiungo, -ere, -iunxi, -iunctum*: "add to"; *ut... in maerore insuper... miseriam hanc adiungerem*: "so I could add an extra annoyance on top of his disappointment".
[19] *recessim* (adverb): "backwards".
[20] *dare se*: "to move oneself".
[21] *paries, parietis* (m.): "wall", "house wall"; *recessim dabo me ad parietam*: "I'll scoot myself back towards the wall".
[22] *imitor, -ari, -atus sum*: "imitate", "act like", "represent".
[23] *nepa, -ae* (m.?): "scorpion".
[24] *captandust = captandus est* (passive periphrastic) < *capto, -are, -aui, -atum*: "capture", "try to get"; translate here: "listen to".
[25] *clanculum* (adverb): "secretly".
[26] *sermo, -onis* (m.): "conversation".
[27] *mihi* (dative of agent after the passive periphrastic).
[28] *alter... alter*: "one... the other".
[29] *crucio, -are, -aui, -atum*: "crucify", "torture" (see note 19 on page 48 at line 93, I.i).
[30] *macero, -are, -aui, -atum*: "torment".
[31] *candidatus, -a, -um*: "dressed in white".
[32] *cedo, -ere, cessi, cessum*: "go", "move"; translate here: "come".
[33] *mastigia, -ae* (f.): "good-for-nothing", "rascal", "one who deserves a whipping".
[34] *stimulus, -i* (m.): "goad", "spike" (used for torturing slaves, see Plautus *Asinaria* 548-552; here used metaphorically).
[35] *loculi, -orum* (m. pl.): "container", "box"; *stimulorum loculi*: "box of spikes" (here a creative insult).
[36] *protollo, -ere*: "put off", "delay".
[37] *certus, -a, -um*: "certain", "settled", "resolved".
[38] *Accheruntem = Acheruntem < Acheruns, -untis* (m.): "Acheron" (river that leads to the underworld); *Accheruntem* is the accusative of limit of motion, see Bennett 182.4.
[39] *praemitto, -ere, -misi, -missum*: "send ahead", "send off".
[40] *prius* (adverb): "first".
[41] *ut*: "how".
[42] *inuenio, -ire, -ueni, -uentum*: "find", "find out".
[43] *opsequens, -entis*: "obedient", "accommodating", "submissive"; *ut tibi ego inuentus sum opsequens*: "look how accommodating I'm being to you".
[44] *maxume = maxime* (adverb): "especially".

cupiebas,[45] eiius[46] copiam[47] feci tibi.[48] 450

erit hodie tecum quod amas clam[49] uxorem. **Lysidamus:** tace.

ita me di bene ament ut ego uix[50] reprimo[51] labra[52]

ob[53] istanc[54] rem quin[55] te deosculer,[56] uoluptas[57] mea.

Chalinus: quid, deosculere?[58] quae res?[59] quae uoluptas tua?

credo hercle ecfodere[60] hic uolt uesicam[61] uilico.[62] 455

Olympio: ecquid[63] amas nunc me? **Lysidamus:** immo[64] edepol me quam te minus.[65]

licetne[66] amplecti[67] te? **Chalinus:** quid, 'amplecti'? **Olympio:** licet.

Lysidamus: ut,[68] quia te tango,[69] mel[70] mihi uideor lingere![71]

---

[45] *cupio, -ere, -iui, -itum*: "wish", "desire".
[46] *eiius = eius* (referring to what Lysidamus especially wanted).
[47] *copia, -ae* (f.): "supply"; "opportunity" (+ genitive).
[48] *quod cupiebas, eiius copiam feci tibi*: "I've provided you with the opportunity you especially wanted".
[49] *clam* (adverb): "secretly (from)", "unknown to" (+ accusative).
[50] *uix* (adverb): "scarcely", "barely".
[51] *reprimo, -ere, -pressi, -pressum*: "keep back", "
[52] *labrum, -i* (n.): "lip".
[53] *ob* (preposition): "because of" (+ accusative).
[54] *istanc = istam*.
[55] *quin* (conjunction + subjunctive): "so as to prevent", "so that... not".
[56] *deosculor, -ari, -atus sum*: "kiss".
[57] *uoluptas, -tatis* (f.): "pleasure", "delight".
[58] *deosculere* (2nd person sg. pres. subjunct. < *deosculor, -ari, -atus sum*).
[59] *res, rei* (f.): "thing", "circumstance", "situation", "matter", concern".
[60] *ecfodere = effodere < effodio, -ere, -odi, -ossum*: "dig out", "penetrate by digging" (sexual implication here).
[61] *uesica, -ae* (f.): "bladder"; slang: "vagina"; *ecfodere ... uesicam uilico* could mean "dig this *uilicus* some lady-parts" (see Richlin 2017: 106, note 49) or, as in the translation in this book, "explore the farm manager's interior".
[62] *uilico* is dative of reference.
[63] *ecquid* (interrogative pronoun): "at all...?".
[64] *immo* (adverb): "on the contrary".
[65] *me quam te minus = me quam te minus amo*: "I love myself less than I love you".
[66] *licere, licuit, licitum est* (impersonal): "is it allowed?", "is it permitted?".
[67] *amplector, -i, amplexus sum*: "embrace", "wrap one's arms about".
[68] *ut*: "how".
[69] *tango, -ere, tetigi, tactum*: "touch".
[70] *mel, mellis* (n.): "honey".
[71] *lingo, -ere, -nxi, -nctum*: "lick", "taste".

Olympio: ultro[72] te,[73] amator, apage[74] te a dorso[75] meo!

Chalinus: illuc[76] est, illuc, quod[77] hic hunc fecit uilicum: 460

et idem[78] me pridem,[79] quom[80] ei aduorsum ueneram,[81]

facere atriensem[82] uoluerat sub[83] ianua.[84]

Olympio: ut tibi morigerus[85] hodie, ut uoluptati fui![86]

Lysidamus: ut[87] tibi, dum uiuam, bene uelim plus quam mihi.

Chalinus: hodie hercle, opinor,[88] hi conturbabunt[89] pedes:[90]   465

solet[91] hic barbatos[92] sane[93] sectari[94] senex.

Lysidamus: ut ego hodie Casinam deosculabor,[95] ut mihi

bona multa faciam <clam>[96] meam uxorem! **Chalinus:** attatae![97]

nunc pol ego demum[98] in rectam redii[99] semitam.[100]

---

[72] *ultro* (adverb): "away", "off".
[73] *ultro te*: "you get away from me!".
[74] *apage* (< ἄπαγε): "go away".
[75] *dorsum, -i* (n.): "back".
[76] *illuc = illud*.
[77] *quod*: "because"; "the reason why".
[78] *idem = īdem*.
[79] *pridem* (adverb): "long ago".
[80] *quom = cum*.
[81] *ei aduorsum ueneram*: "I'd come to meet him" (a slave, sometimes referred to as an *aduorsitor / aduersitor*, would be expected to meet his master to escort him home from a party).
[82] *atriensis, -is* (m.): "manager of the atrium", "head house slave".
[83] *sub* (preposition): "under"; "near" (+ ablative).
[84] *ianua, -ae* (f.): "door".
[85] *morigerus, -a, -um*: "obedient", "accommodating".
[86] *tibi... uoluptati fui*: "I was a source of pleasure to you", "I pleased you" (*uoluptati* is dative of purpose or tendency, see Bennett 191.2a).
[87] *ut*: "so that" (+ subjunctive).
[88] *opinor, -ari, -atus sum*: "suppose", "imagine".
[89] *conturbo, -are, -aui, -atum*: "mix up"; *conturbare pedes* implies some sort of sexual activity.
[90] *pes, pedis* (m.): "foot".
[91] *soleo, -ere, –, solitus sum*: "be accustomed", "tend" (+ infinitive).
[92] *barbatus, -a, -um*: "bearded".
[93] *sane* (adverb): "certainly".
[94] *sector, -ari, -atus sum*: "run after", "pursue".
[95] *deosculor, -ari, -atus sum* (see note 56 on the preceding page at line 448, II.viii).
[96] *clam* (see note 49 on the facing page at line 451, II.viii).
[97] *attatae* (an expression of surprise or amazement).
[98] *demum* (adverb): "finally".
[99] *redeo, -ire, -iui/-ii, -itum*: "return", "go back".
[100] *semita, -ae* (f.): "path", "track".

hic ipsus[101] Casinam deperit.[102] eo uiros. 470

Lysidamus: iam hercle amplexari,[103] iam osculari[104] gestio.[105]

Olympio: sine[106] priu'[107] deduci.[108] quid, malum,[109] properas?[110] **Lysidamus:** amo.

Olympio: at non opinor fieri hoc posse hodie. **Lysidamus:** potest,

siquidem[111] cras censes[112] te posse emitti manu.[113]

Chalinus: enim uero huc aures magi'[114] sunt adhibendae[115] 475
mihi:[116]

iam ego uno in saltu[117] lepide[118] apros[119] capiam duos.

Lysidamus: apud hunc sodalem[120] meum atque uicinum[121] mihi

locus[122] est paratus:[123] ei ego amorem omnem meum

concredui;[124] is mihi se locum dixit dare.

Olympio: quid eiius[125] uxor? ubi erit? **Lysidamus:** lepide 480
repperi.[126]

---

[101] *ipsus = ipse.*
[102] *depereo, -ire, -iui/-ii, -itum:* "die", "be lost", "be desperately in love with (+ accusative)".
[103] *amplexor, -ari = amplector, -ari* (see note 67 on page 94 at line 457, II.viii).
[104] *osculor, -ari* means essentially the same as *deosculor, -ari*.
[105] *gestio, -ire, -iui/-ii, -itum:* "desire eagerly", "long to" (+ infinitive).
[106] *sino, -ere, siui, situm* (see note 1 on page 92 at line 437, II.viii).
[107] *priu' = prius* (see note 40 on page 93 at line 448, II.viii).
[108] *deduco, -ere, -duxi, -ductum* here means essentially the same as *duco, -ere,* with *uxorem* implied.
[109] *malum, -i* (n.): "misfortune", "misery"; here used as an expression of frustration/anger.
[110] *propero, -are, -aui, -atum:* "hurry", "be quick".
[111] *siquidem* (adverb): "if only", "if indeed".
[112] *censeo, -ere, censui, censitum:* "think", "suppose", "recommend".
[113] *emittere manu:* "to manumit", "to set free from slavery".
[114] *magi' = magis.*
[115] *adhibeo, -ere, -ui, -itum:* "hold towards", "use".
[116] *aures... sunt adhibendae mihi:* "I'd better use my ears".
[117] *saltus, -ūs* (m.): "forest pasture", "woodland", "thicket".
[118] *lepide* (adverb): "nicely", "agreeably", "excellently".
[119] *aper, apri* (m.): "wild boar".
[120] *sodalis, -is* (m.): "friend".
[121] *uicinus, -i* (m.): "(male) neighbour".
[122] *locus, -i* (m.): "place".
[123] *paro, -are, -aui, -atum:* "prepare".
[124] *concredo, -ere, -idi/-ui, -itum:* "entrust for safe keeping" (+ dative of person trusted).
[125] *eiius = eius.*
[126] *reperio, -ire, repperi, repertum:* "discover", "find out"; "devise", "figure out".

mea uxór uocabit[127] huc eam ad se in nuptias,[128]
ut hic[129] sit secum, se adiuuet,[130] secum cubet;[131]
ego iussi,[132] et dixit se facturam uxor mea.
illa hic cubabit, uir[133] ab[i]erit faxo[134] domo;[135]
tu rus uxorem duces: id rus hoc erit   485
tantisper[136] dum ego cum Casina faciam nuptias.[137]
hinc[138] tu ante lucem[139] rus cras duces postea.[140]
satin[141] docte?[142] **Olympio:** astute.[143] **Chalinus:** age[144] modo,[145] fabricamini,[146]
malo[147] hercle uostro[148] tam uorsuti[149] uiuitis.[150]

Lysidamus: scin[151] quid nunc facias? **Olympio:** loquere.   490
Lysidamus: tene marsuppium,[152]
abi atque opsona,[153] propera, sed lepide[154] uolo,

---

[127] *uoco, -are, -aui, -atum*: "call"; "invite".
[128] *in nuptias*: "for the wedding".
[129] *hīc* (adverb).
[130] *adiuuo, -are, -iuui, -iutum*: "help".
[131] *cubo, -are, -aui, -atum*: "lie down", "go to bed"; translate here: "stay the night".
[132] *iubeo, -ere, iussi, iussum*: "order", "tell".
[133] *uir*: "her husband" (referring to Lysidamus's *uicinus*).
[134] *faxo* (alternative form of the 1st person singular future indicative active of *facio, -ere*): "I'll make [it happen]", "I promise", "definitely".
[135] *domo* (ablative of place from which).
[136] *tantisper* (adverb): "for so long (as)" (+ *dum*).
[137] *tantisper dum ego cum Casina faciam nuptias*: "for as long as I need to have the wedding night with Casina".
[138] *hinc* (adverb): "from this place".
[139] *lux, lucis* (f.): "light", "dawn".
[140] *postea* (adverb): "afterwords".
[141] *satin = satisne*.
[142] *docte* (adverb): "cleverly"; *satin dicte*: "wasn't that quite clever?".
[143] *astute* (adverb): "craftily", "cunningly".
[144] *age* (< *ago, -ere, egi, actum*): "come on", "go on".
[145] *modo* (adverb): "just", "just now", "only".
[146] *fabricor, -are, -atus sum*: "build", "construct"; "devise"; translate here: "plot away!".
[147] *malo* (dative of reference) < *malum, -i* (n.): "misfortune", "misery".
[148] *uostro = uestro*.
[149] *uorsuti = uersuti* < *uersutus, -a, -um*: "clever", "crafty", "deceitful".
[150] *uiuo, -ere, uixi, uictum*: "live"; "be"; *malo... uostro tam uorsuti uiuitis*: "you are heading for misfortune, being so clever".
[151] *scin = scisne*.
[152] *marsuppium, -ii* (n.): "purse", "money-bag".
[153] *obsono, -are, -aui, -atum*: "go grocery-shopping".
[154] *lepide* (see note 118 on the facing page at line 476, II.viii).

molliculas[155] escas,[156] ut ipsa[157] mollicula est. **Olympio:** licet.

Lysidamus: emito[158] sepiolas,[159] lepadas,[160] lolligunculas,[161] hordeias,[162] — **Chalinus:** immo triticeias,[163] si sapis.[164]

Lysidamus: soleas.[165] **Chalinus:** qui[166] quaeso[167] potius quam sculponeas,[168]   495

quibu'[169] battuatur[170] tibi os,[171] senex nequissume?[172]

Olympio: uin[173] lingulacas?[174] **Lysidamus:** quid opust,[175] quando uxor domi[176] est?

ea lingulaca est nobis, nam numquam tacet.

Olympio: in re praesenti[177] ex copia[178] piscaria[179]

consulere[180] quid emam potero. **Lysidamus:** aéquom[181]   500
oras,[182] abi.

---

[155] *molliculus, -a, -um*: "delicate", "tender".
[156] *esca, -ae* (f.): "food", "dish".
[157] *ipsa* refers to Casina.
[158] *emito* (2nd person singular future imperative active) < *emo, -ere, emi, emptum*: "buy".
[159] *sepiola, -ae* (f.): "cuttlefish".
[160] *lepas, -adas* (f.): "limpet".
[161] *lolloguncula, -ae* (f.): "little squid".
[162] *hordeia, -ae* (f.): "barleyfish" (we have no idea what kind of fish was meant by *hordeia*, but the name sounds similar to *hordeum*, which means "barley").
[163] *triticeia, -ae* (f.): "wheatfish" (Chalinus has made up this name as a joke, since it sounds like *triticeus*, which means "made of wheat").
[164] *sapio, -ire, -iui/-ii, -itum*: "taste", "taste of"; "have good taste"; "show good sense".
[165] *solea, -ae* (f.): "sole".
[166] *qui*: "why".
[167] *quaeso*: "I beg", "please" (< *quaeso, -ere, -iui/-ii*: "seek", "beg").
[168] *sculponeae, -arum* (f. pl.): "clogs", "cheap wooden shoes".
[169] *quibu'* = *quibus*.
[170] *battuo, -ere*: "pound", "beat" (the subject of *battuatur* is *os*).
[171] *os, oris* (n.): "mouth", "face".
[172] *nequissume* = *nequissime* (< *nequam*): "most worthless", "completely useless".
[173] *uin* = *uisne*.
[174] *lingulaca, -ae* (f.): "tonguefish" (a kind of flatfish that looks like a mammalian tongue; *lingulaca* also meant "talkative woman", "(female) chatterbox").
[175] *opust* = *opus est*; *quid opus est*: "why's there any need?", "what's the point?".
[176] *domi* (locative case).
[177] *in re praesenti*: "at the scene of the action", "on the spot".
[178] *copia, -ae* (f.): "supply", "plenty".
[179] *piscarius, -a, -um*: "relating to fish"; *in re praesenti ex copia piscaria*: "when I'm at the fish market".
[180] *consulo, -ere, -sului, -sultum*: "consult", "decide".
[181] *aequom* = *aequum* < *aequus, -a, -um*: "fair", "level".
[182] *oro, -are, -aui, -atum*: "ask", "beg"; *aequom oras*: "good point".

argento parci[183] nolo,[184] opsonato[185] ampliter.[186]

nam mihi uicino hoc etiam conuento[187] est opus,[188]

ut quod mandaui[189] curet.[190] **Olympio:** iamne abeo?
Lysidamus: uolo. —

Chalinus: tribu'[191] non conduci[192] possum libertatibus[193]

quin[194] ego illis hodie comparem[195] magnum malum   505

quinque[196] hanc omnem rem meae erae[197] iam faciam palam.[198]

manufesto[199] teneo in noxia[200] inimicos meos.[201]

sed si nunc facere uolt era officium[202] suom,[203]

nostra omnis lis[204] est. pulchre praeuortar[205] uiros.

nostro omine[206] it dies; iam uicti uicimus.   510

ibo intro,[207] ut id quod alius condiuit[208] coquos,[209]

---

[183] *parco, -ere, peperci/parsi, parsum*: "be sparing" (+ dative).
[184] *argento parci nolo*: "don't be stingy with the money", "I want no expense spared".
[185] *opsonato = obsonato* (2nd person singular future imperative active < *obsono, -are*, see note 153 on page 97 at line 491, II.viii).
[186] *ampliter* (adverb): "sumptuously", "extravagantly".
[187] *conuenio, -ire, -ueni, -uentum*: "meet"; *uicino hoc... conuento* is ablative of means after *opus* (see Bennett 218.2c).
[188] *mihi uicino hoc etiam conuento est opus*: "I need to meet with this neighbour of mine".
[189] *mando, -are, -aui, -atum*: "order", "commission"; *quod mandaui*: "what I want done".
[190] *curo, -are, -aui, -atum* (see note 11 on page 92 at line 439, II.viii).
[191] *tribu' = tribus < tres, tria*.
[192] *conduco, -ere, -duxi, -ductum*: "hire".
[193] *tribu'... libertatibus*: "for three times the price of my liberty" (ablative of price, see Bennett 225).
[194] *quin* (conjunction + subjunctive; see note 55 on page 94 at line 453, II.viii).
[195] *comparo, -are, -aui, -atum*: "prepare", "plan".
[196] *quinque = quin + que*.
[197] *era, -ae* (f.): "mistress" (of the household, and of the enslaved members of the household).
[198] *palam* (adverb): "openly"; *facere palam*: "make public", "make known".
[199] *manufesto = manifesto* (adverb): "clearly".
[200] *noxia, -ae* (f.): "wrongdoing", "fault".
[201] *teneo in noxiā inimicos meos*: "I've caught my enemies in the act".
[202] *officium, -ii* (n.): "duty", "obligation".
[203] *suom = suum*.
[204] *lis, litis* (f.): "lawsuit"; "dispute".
[205] *praeuortar = praeuertar < praeuertor, -i, -uersus sum*: "forestall", "anticipate"; translate here "thwart", "get the better of".
[206] *omen, ominis* (n.): "omen"; *nostro omine*: "with a good omen for us", "with luck on our side" (ablative of attendant circumstances, see Bennett 221).
[207] *intro* (adverb): "inside", "into the house".
[208] *condio, -ire, -iui/-ii, -itum*: "season / flavour food".
[209] *coquos = coquus < coquus, -i* (m.): "cook" (this *coquos* is presumably meant to refer to Lysidamus).

ego nunc uicissim²¹⁰ ut²¹¹ alio pacto²¹² condiam,

quo²¹³ id quoi²¹⁴ paratum est²¹⁵ ut²¹⁶ paratum ne siet²¹⁷

sietque eí paratum quod paratum non erat.²¹⁸ —

---

²¹⁰ *uicissim* (adverb): "in turn".
²¹¹ This *ut* repeats the *ut* of line 511.
²¹² *pactum, -i* (n.): "agreement"; "manner", "method"; *alio pacto*: "in another way", "by another method".
²¹³ *quo*: "in order that" (*quo* introduces a relative clause of purpose, see Bennett 282.2).
²¹⁴ *quoi = cui* (refers to Lysidamus).
²¹⁵ *paro, -are, -aui, -atum* (see note 123 on page 96 at line 478, II.viii).
²¹⁶ *ut* repeats the meaning of *quo* at the beginning of the line, and is itself essentially repeated by *ne*.
²¹⁷ *siet = sit*.
²¹⁸ *quo id quoi paratum est ut paratum ne siet / sietque ei paratum quod paratum non erat*: literally: "so that what's been prepared for him won't have been prepared, and so what hadn't been prepared will be prepared for him"; less literally: "so he won't get what he's been planning to get, but he will get what he didn't plan for" (the cooking metaphor plays out later, beginning in act IV, scene i).

ACTVS III

III.i LYSIDAMVS, ALCESIMVS (515-530)

Scene summary: *Lysidamus arranges with his neighbour Alcesimus for the latter to leave his house empty that night. Alcesimus, although disapproving of Lysidamus's infatuation with Casina, agrees.*

Lysidamus: Nunc amici, ánne[1] inimici[2] sis imago,[3] Alcesime,   515

mihi sciam, nunc specimen[4] specitur,[5] nunc certamen[6] cernitur.[7]

qur[8] amem me castigare,[9] id ponito[10] ad compendium,[11]

'cano[12] capite', 'aetate[13] aliena'[14] eo[15] addito[16] ad compendium,

'quoi[17] sit uxor', id quoque illuc[18] ponito ad compendium.

Alcesimus: miseriorem ego ex amore quam te uidi neminem.   520

Lysidamus: fac[19] uacent[20] aedes.[21] **Alcesimus:** quin[22] edepol seruos ancillas domo[23]

---

[1] *anne*: "or".
[2] *inimicus, -i* (m.): "enemy".
[3] *imago, -ginis* (m.): "image", "likeness".
[4] *specimen, -inis* (n.): "proof", "sign".
[5] *specio, -ere, spexi, –*: "look at".
[6] *certamen, -minis* (n.): "contest", "struggle".
[7] *cerno, -ere, creui, cretum*: "perceive"; "decide", "decide by fighting".
[8] *qur = cur*
[9] *castigo, -are, -aui, -atum*: "find fault with", "blame", "reprove".
[10] *ponito* (2nd person singular future imperative active) < *pono, -ere, posui, positum*: "put".
[11] *compendium, -ii* (n.): "stash of savings", "profit"; *aliquid ponere ad compendium*: "to put something into one's savings"; translate here: "not to say something".
[12] *canus, -a, -um*: "white", "grey-haired".
[13] *aetas, aetatis* (f.): "age", "stage of life", "life".
[14] *alienus, -a, -um*: "unsuitable", "inappropriate" (to).
[15] *eo* refers to the first potential comment (*qur amem*) that Lysidamus is telling Alcesimus not to say.
[16] *addito* (2nd person singular future imperative active) < *addo, -ere, -didi, -ditum*: "add".
[17] *quoi = cui*.
[18] *illuc* (adverb): "in(to) there".
[19] *fac* without *ut* can introduce a substantive clause, see Allen & Greenough 565; translate "make sure".
[20] *uaco, -are, -aui, -atum*: "be empty", "unoccupied".
[21] *aedis/aedes, -is* (f.): "building", "house" (often used in the plural, as here).
[22] *quin*: "no, really", "I mean!"; "actually", "in fact", "but"; "why... not?"
[23] *domo* (ablative of place from which).

certum est[24] omnis mittere ad te. **Lysidamus:** oh, nimium[25] scite[26] scitus[27] es.

sed facitodum[28] merula[29] per uorsus[30] quod cantat[31] <tu> colas:[32]

'cum cibo[33] cum quiqui'[34] facito ut ueniant, quasi[35] eant Sutrium.[36]

Alcesimus: meminero.[37] **Lysidamus:** em,[38] nunc enim tu demum[39] nullo scito[40] scitus es.[41]   525

Lysidamus: cura,[42] ego ad forum[43] modo ibo: iam hic ero. **Alcesimus:** bene ambula.[44]

Lysidamus: fac[45] eant linguam[46] tuae aedes. **Alcesimus:** quid ita? **Lysidamus:** quom[47] ueniam, uocent.[48]

---

[24] *certum est = certum est mihi*: "I've decided".
[25] *nimium* (adverb): "too much", "excessively".
[26] *scitē* (adverb): "cleverly".
[27] *scitus, -a, -um*: "knowledgeable", "wise".
[28] *facitodum*: "make sure"; *facitodum = facito* (2nd person singular future imperative active < *facio*) + *dum* (enclitic, adding intensive force to the imperative verb).
[29] *merula, -ae* (f.): "blackbird".
[30] *uorsus = uersus* (< *uersus, -ūs*): "line of poetry"; "birdsong".
[31] *canto, -are, -aui, -atum*: "sing".
[32] *colo, -ere, -ui, cultum*: "take care of", "attend to"; *facitodum merula per uorsus quod cantat <tu> colas*: "make sure you attend to what the blackbird sings about in its song".
[33] *cibus, -i* (m.): "food".
[34] *quiqui* (neuter ablative singular < *quisquis, quidquid*): "with everything".
[35] *quasi* (conjunction): "as if", "as though", "just like" (+ subjunctive).
[36] *Sutrium, -ii* (n.): "Sutrium" (a town in Etruria); '*cum cibo cum quiqui' facito ut ueniant, quasi eant Sutrium*' apparently referred to a forced march by the Roman army against the Etruscan town of Sutrium, when the soldiers had to carry their food and everything else they might need. Lindsay suggested that *cum cibo cum quiqui* might have been memorialized in a song that featured a blackbird chirping the phrase (Lindsay 1892: 124; cited by MacCary and Willcock 1976: 157).
[37] *meminero* (1st person singular future perfect indicative active < *memini, meminisse*: "remember").
[38] *em*: "here/there you are!", "look!".
[39] *demum* (adverb): "finally", "at last".
[40] *scitum, -i* (n.): "decree", "resolution (of an assembly)".
[41] *nullo scito scitus es*: "you're smart even with no decree" (this, if the text is correct, may have worked as a joke in Latin because of the play on *scitum* and *scitus*).
[42] *curo, -are, -aui, -atum*: "take care of" (+ accusative).
[43] *forum, -i* (n.): "forum" (the forum was a big open area, the bustling economic and political centre of Rome).
[44] *ambulo, -are, -aui, -atum*: "walk".
[45] *fac* + subjunctive (see note 19 on the previous page at line 521, III.i).
[46] *lingua, -ae* (f.): "tongue".
[47] *quom = cum*.
[48] *uoco, -are* can mean "call", "invite", but was also an old variant of *uaco, -are*: "be vacant", "be unoccupied" (see note 20 on the preceding page at line 521, III.i). Lysidamus's joke is impossible to translate well into English: "make sure your house has a tongue... so it can

Alcesimus: attatae![49] caedundus[50] tú homo es: nimias[51] delicias[52] facis.[53]

Lysidamus: quid me amare refert,[54] nisi sim doctus <ac> dicaculus?[55]

sed tu caue[56] in quaesitione[57] mihi sis.[58] — **Alcesimus:**   530
usque[59] adero domi.[60] —

---

    invite me / be unoccupied when I come over". Alcesimus's response suggests the joke isn't much better in Latin.
[49] *attatae* (an expression of surprise or amazement).
[50] *caedo, -ere, cecidi, caesum*: "cut down", beat".
[51] *nimius, -a, -um*: "excessive", "too much".
[52] *deliciae, -arum* (f. pl.): "delight", "fun".
[53] *delicias facere*: "to joke", "to make jokes".
[54] *quid me amare refert*: "what's important about me being in love...?", "what the use of being in love...?".
[55] *dicaculus, -a, -um*: "witty".
[56] *caueo, -ere, caui, cautus*: "beware", "avoid", "be careful".
[57] *quaestio, -onis* (f.): "search", "inquiry".
[58] *caue in quaestione mihi sis*: "don't make me have to go looking for you".
[59] *usque* (adverb): "continuously", "constantly", "without interruption".
[60] *domi* (locative case).

III.ii CLEVSTRATA, ALCESIMVS

Scene summary: *Cleustrata, in order to foil Lysidamus's plans, tells Alcesimus she won't need his wife Myrrhina to help with the wedding preparations. Alcesimus, thinking Cleustrata has left, complains about the embarrassing situation Lysidamus has put him in. Cleustrata, overhearing, laughs about how she'll make fools of both Alcesimus and Lysidamus.*

Cleustrata: Hoc erat ecastor quod me uir tanto opere[1] orabat[2] meus,

ut properarem[3] arcessere[4] hanc <huc> ad me uicinam[5] meam,

liberae[6] aedes ut sibi essent Casinam quo[7] deducerent.[8]

nunc adeo[9] nequaquam[10] arcessam, <ne illis> ignauissumis[11]

liberi loci[12] potestas[13] sit, uetulis[14] ueruecibus.[15]   535

sed eccum[16] égreditur,[17] senati[18] columen,[19] praesidium[20] popli,[21]

meu'[22] uicinus, meo uiro qui liberum praehibet[23] locum.

---

[1] *tanto opere*: "with such labour", "so much".
[2] *oro, -are, -aui, -atum*: "ask", "beg".
[3] *propero, -are, -aui, -atum*: "hurry", "be quick".
[4] *arcesso, -ere, -iui, -itum*: "send for", "fetch".
[5] *uicina, -ae* (f.): "(female) neighbour".
[6] *liber, -era, -erum*: "free"
[7] *quo* (adverb): "where". "to which".
[8] *deduco, -ere, -duxi, -ductum*: "bring" (*uxorem deducere* is implied).
[9] *adeo* (adverb): "indeed", "even".
[10] *nequaquam* (adverb): "not at all".
[11] *ignauissimis < ignauus, -a, -um*: "lazy", "cowardly", "deadbeat".
[12] *locus, -i* (m.): "place".
[13] *potestas, -tatis* (f.): "power", "opportunity".
[14] *uetulus, -a, -um*: "elderly".
[15] *ueruex, -ecis* (m.): "wether", "castrated male sheep".
[16] *eccum = ecce + eum* or *ecce + hum* (= *hunc*).
[17] *egredior, egredi, egressus sum*: "come out", "go out".
[18] *senati = senatūs < senatus, -ūs* (m.): "senate".
[19] *columen, -inis* (n.): "column", "pillar"; *senati columen*: "pillar / prop of the senate".
[20] *praesidium, -ii* (n.): "defense-post", "guardian", "protector".
[21] *popli = populi < populus, -i* (m.): "people"; *praesidium popli*: "protector of the (Roman) people".
[22] *meu' = meus*.
[23] *praehibeo, -ere*: "offer".

non ecastor uilis[24] emptu'st[25] modius[26] qui[27] uenit[28] salis.[29]

Alcesimus: miror[30] huc iam non arcessi in proxumum[31] uxorem meam,

quae iam dudum,[32] si arcessatur, ornata[33] exspectat[34] domi. 540

sed eccam,[35] opino,[36] arcessit. salue,[37] Cleustrata. **Cleustrata:** et tu, Alcesime.

ubi tua uxor? **Alcesimus:** intus[38] illa te, si se[39] arcessas, manet;[40]

nam tuo'[41] uir me orauit ut eam isto[42] ad te adiutum[43] mitterem.

uin[44] uocem? **Cleustrata:** sine[45] eam: te nolo, si occupata[46] est. **Alcesimus:** otium[47] est.[48]

Cleustrata: nil moror,[49] molesta[50] ei esse nolo; post 545
conuenero.[51]

---

24   *uilis, -e*: "cheap", "of little value".
25   *emptu'st* = *emptu est* (< *emo, -ere, emi, emptum*: "buy"); *emptu* is a supine (see Bennett 340.2).
26   *modius, -ii* (m.): "bushel" (a *modius* was a unit of dry measurement, holding about 8.7 litres).
27   *qui* (an old ablative, here of price, see Bennett 225): "at whatever price".
28   *ueneo, -ire, -ii, -itum* (conjugated like *eo, ire*): "be sold".
29   *sal, salis* (m.): "salt"; *non ecastor uilis emptu'st modius qui uenit salis*: "by Castor, he's not cheap to buy at whatever price a bushel of salt is sold" (that is, "he isn't worth the price of a bag of salt").
30   *miror, -ari, -atus sum*: "wonder at", "be surprised".
31   *proxumum = proximum < proximus, -a, -um*: "nearest"; *huc... in proxumum*: "here next door".
32   *iam dudum* (adverbial): "a while ago", "formerly".
33   *orno, -are, -aui, -atum*: "prepare", "get ready", "dress up", "get dressed up".
34   *exspecto, -are, -aui, -atum*: "wait", "wait for", "expect".
35   *eccam = ecce + eam* or *ecce + ham* (= *hanc*).
36   *opino, -are = opinor, -ari*: "suppose", "imagine".
37   *salue* (salutation): "hello".
38   *intus* (adverb): "inside".
39   *se* is an indirect reflexive, and thus refers to the subject of the main clause (see Bennett 244.1.II).
40   *maneo, -ere, mansi, mansum*: "remain", "wait", "wait for".
41   *tuo' = tuos = tuus*.
42   *isto* (adverb): "to where you are", "over to you".
43   *adiutum* (supine) < *adiuuo, -are, -iuui, -iutum*: "help", "assist".
44   *uin = uisne*.
45   *sine < sino, -ere, siui, situm*: "allow"; "leave alone".
46   *occupatus, -a, -um*: "busy", "occupied".
47   *otium, -ii* (n.): "leisure".
48   *otium est = otium sibi est*: "she's not busy".
49   *moror, -ari, -atus sum*: "delay"; *nil moror*: "I don't mind", "not care (about/for)".
50   *molestus, -a, -um*: "annoying", "[a] bother".
51   *conuenio, -ire, -ueni, -uentum*: "meet", "visit", "go and see".

Alcesimus: non ornatis[52] isti[53] apud[54] uos nuptias?[55]
Cleustrata: orno et paro.[56]

Alcesimus: non ergo opus est[57] adiutrice?[58] **Cleustrata:** sati'[59] domist.[60] ubi nuptiae

fuerint, tum istam conuenibo.[61] nunc uale,[62] atque istanc[63] iube.[64] —

Alcesimus: quid ego nunc faciam? flagitium[65] maxumum[66] feci[67] miser

propter[68] operam[69] illius hirqui[70] ínprobí,[71] edentuli,[72]　　　550

qui hoc mihi contraxit;[73] operam uxoris polliceor[74] foras,[75]

quasi[76] catillatum.[77] flagitium hominis, qui dixit mihi

---

[52] *ornatis* (2nd person plural present indicative active).
[53] *isti* (adverb): "in that place", "where you are".
[54] *apud* (preposition): "near", "at", "at the house of" (+ accusative).
[55] *nuptiae, -arum* (f. pl.): "marriage", "wedding".
[56] *paro, -are, -aui, -atum*: "prepare".
[57] *opus est*: "there is need".
[58] *adiutrice* (ablative of means after *opus est*, see Bennett 218.2c) < *adiutrix, -tricis* (f.): "(female) helper".
[59] *sati'* = *satis* (adverb): "enough", "sufficiently".
[60] *domist* = *domi est*.
[61] *conuenibo* = *conveniam*.
[62] *uale*: "good bye" (< *ualeo, -ere, ualui, ualitum*: "be well").
[63] *istanc* = *istam*.
[64] *iubeo, -ere, iussi, iussum*: "order", "tell"; *iube* is probably an abbreivated form of the phrase *iube saluere*: "greet" or, more likely here, *iube ualere*: "say goodbye to", "wish (her) well".
[65] *flagitium, -ii/-i* (n.): "shameful act"; "disgrace".
[66] *maxumum* = *maximum*.
[67] *flagitum maxumum feci*: "I've gotten myself into the most disgraceful situation".
[68] *propter* (preposition): "because of".
[69] *opera, -ae* (f.): "service", "activity", "effort"; translate *propter operam*: "thanks to", "thanks to the meddling" (+ genitive).
[70] *hirqui* = *hirci* < *hircus, -i* (m.): "male goat".
[71] *inprobi* = *improbi* < *improbus, -a, -um*: "shameless", "wicked".
[72] *edentulus, -a, -um*: "toothless".
[73] *contraho, -ere, -traxi, -tractum*: "bring together"; "bring about", "cause".
[74] *polliceor, -eri, pollicitus sum*: "promise".
[75] *foras* (adverb): "out of doors"; translate here: "away from our home".
[76] *quasi* (adverb): "as if", "just like".
[77] *catillatum* (supine) < *catillo, -are, -aui, -atum*: "lick plates"; *quasi catillatum*: "as if (I were sending her over) to lick plates", "as if she needed the work" (the implication being that a husband who offered his wife's help to a neighbour would be doing so only because of dire poverty, and in the hopes that she would be able to eat some scraps while helping).

suam uxorem hanc arcessituram esse;[78] ea se eam négat[79] morarier.[80]

atque edepol mirum ni[81] subolet[82] iam hoc huic uicinae meae.

uerum[83] autem altrouorsum[84] quóm[85] eam mecum rationem[86] puto,[87]   555

siquid[88] eiius[89] esset, esset mecum postulatio.[90]

ibo intro, ut subducam[91] nauim[92] rusum[93] in puluinaria.[94] —

Cleustrata: iám hic est lepide[95] ludificatus.[96] miseri ut[97] festinant[98] senes![99]

nunc ego illúm nihili,[100] decrepitum[101] meum uirum ueniat uelim,[102]

---

[78] *arcessituram esse* (future active infinitive in indirect discourse < *arcesso, -ere, -iui, -itum*, see note 4 on page 104 at line 532, III.ii).
[79] *nego, -are, -aui, -atum*: "deny", "say... not".
[80] *morarier* = *morari* < *moror, -ari, -atus sum* (see note 49 on page 105 at line 545, III.ii); *ea... negat morarier*: "she says 'she doesn't mind'".
[81] *mirum ni* = *mirum est nisi*: "I'd be surprised if ... not".
[82] *subolet* < *subolet, subolere* (impersonal + accusative of thing suspected + dative of person detecting): "there is a suspicion"; *hoc subolet alicui*: "someone is suspicious about this", "someone smells a rat".
[83] *uerum* (conjunction): "but".
[84] *alterouorsum* (adverb): "on the other hand".
[85] *quom* = *cum*.
[86] *ratio, -onis* (f.): "reckoning", "calculation".
[87] *puto, -are, -aui, -atum*: "think"; *rationem puto*: "I think over the matter".
[88] *siquis, siquid* (indefinite pronoun): "if anyone / anything".
[89] *eiius* = *eius*.
[90] *postulatio, -onis* (f.): "demand for explanation", "complaint", "scolding".
[91] *subduco, -ere, -duxi, -ductum*: "draw up", "haul up".
[92] *nauim* = *nauem* < *nauis, -is* (f.): "ship".
[93] *rusum* = *rursum* = *rursus* (adverb): "again", "back", "in return".
[94] *puluinus, -i* (m.): "cushion"; "raised bank"; *ut subducam nauim rusum in puluinaria*: "to haul my ship back to its anchorage" (meaning he'll tell his wife that she won't be needed next door).
[95] *lepide* (adverb): "nicely", "agreeably", "excellently".
[96] *ludifico, -are, -aui, -atum*: "make a fool of".
[97] *ut*: "how".
[98] *festino, -are, -aui, -atum*: "hurry".
[99] *senex, senis* (adjective and noun): "old"; "old man".
[100] *nihili* (genitive of indefinite value; see Bennett 203.3); translate as "worthless", "nothing" (as an insult).
[101] *decrepitus, -a, -um*: "very old", "decrepit".
[102] *illum nihili, decrepitum meum uirum ueniat uelim*: "I'd like that worthless senile husband of mine to come" (*uirum* is accusative despite being the subject of *ueniat*, see MacCary and Willcock 1976: 161; *uolo* without *ut* can introduce a substantive clause, see Allen & Greenough 565).

ut eum ludificem uicissim,[103] postquam hunc delusi[104] 560
alterum.

nam ego aliquid[105] contrahere cupio[106] litigi[107] inter eos duos.

sed eccum[108] incedit.[109] at, quom[110] aspicias[111] tristem,[112] frugi[113] censeas.[114]

---

[103] *uicissim* (adverb): "in turn".
[104] *deludo, -ere, -si, -sum* = *ludifico, -are* (see note 96 on the previous page at line 558, III.ii).
[105] *aliquis, aliquid*: "some/any", "someone/something", "anyone/anything".
[106] *cupio, -ere, -iui, -itum*: "wish", "desire".
[107] *litigium, -ii/-i* (n.): "quarrel", "dispute"; *aliquid litigi*: "something of a quarrel", "some sort of quarrel".
[108] *eccum* (see note 16 on page 104 at line 536, III.ii).
[109] *incedo, -ere, -cessi, -cessum*: "walk", "proceed"; translate here: "he's arriving on the scene", "here he comes".
[110] *quom* = *cum* (*quom* introduces a present general conditional relative clause here, see Allen & Greenough 542).
[111] *aspicio, -ere, aspexi, aspectum*: "look at", "see".
[112] *tristis, -e*: "sad"; translate here: "serious", "stern".
[113] *frugi* < *frugi bonae* (predicate dative used as adjectival phrase): "honest", "virtuous", "thrifty".
[114] *censeo, -ere, censui, censitum*: "think", "suppose", "recommend"; *quom aspicias tristem, frugi censeas*: "whenever you see him looking serious you'd think he was an honest man".

III.iii LYSIDAMVS, CLEVSTRATA

Scene summary: *Lysidamus, returning home and complaining about having wasted time helping a friend in court, meets Cleustrata. She tells him that she did invite her neighbour Myrrhina over to help with the wedding preparations, but that Alcesimus had refused to allow his wife to go.*

Lysidamus: Stultitia[1] magna est, mea quidem sententia,[2]

hominém amatorem[3] ullum ad forum procedere,[4]

in eum diem[5] quoi[6] quod amet[7] in mundo[8] siet;[9]   565

sicut[10] ego feci stultus:[11] contriui[12] diem,

dum asto[13] aduocatus[14] quoidam[15] cognato[16] meo;

quem hercle ego litem[17] adeo[18] perdidisse[19] gaudeo,[20]

ne me nequiquam[21] sibi hodie aduocauerit.[22]

nam meo quidem animo[23] qui aduocatos aduocet   570

rogitare oportet[24] prius et contarier[25]

adsitne ei animus necne <ei> adsit[26] quem aduocet:

---

[1] *stultitia, -ae* (f.): "stupidity".
[2] *sententia, -ae* (f.): "opinion".
[3] *amator, -oris* (m.): "lover"; *hominem amatorem*: "a man that's in love".
[4] *procedo, -ere, -cessi, -cessum*: "advance", "go forth", "go".
[5] *in eum diem*: "on the very day", "on this day of all days".
[6] *quoi = cui* (refers to the *hominem* of the preceding line; dative after *in mundo*).
[7] *quo amet*: "what he loves", "the object of his love".
[8] *mundus, -a, -um*: "neat", "clean", "elegant"; *in mundo*: "in readiness", "ready".
[9] *siet = sit*; *in eum diem quoi quod amet in mundo siet*: "on the very day that the object of his love is ready for him".
[10] *sicut*: "just as", "just like".
[11] *stultus, -a, -um*: "stupid", "silly", "foolish"; *ego feci stultus*: "I myself acted foolishly".
[12] *contero, -ere, -triui, -tritum*: "waste".
[13] *asto, -are, -stiti, –*: "stand by", "support".
[14] *aduocatus, -i* (m.): "advocate", "witness" (that is, someone who has been called (*aduocare*) to act as character witness for a party in a lawsuit).
[15] *quoidam = cuidam < quidam, quaedam, quoddam*: "a certain".
[16] *cognatus, -i* (m.): "kinsman", "relative".
[17] *lis, litis* (f.): "lawsuit"; "dispute".
[18] *adeo* (adverb): "indeed", "even".
[19] *perdo, -ere, perdidi, perditum*: "ruin", "destroy"; "lose".
[20] *gaudeo, -ere, gauisus sum* (semi-deponent): "rejoice", "be glad".
[21] *nequiquam* (adverb): "in vain", "unsuccessfully".
[22] *aduoco, -are, -aui, -atum*: "call in to act as witness in court".
[23] *meo... animo*: "in my opinion".
[24] *oportet, oportere, oportuit, –* (impersonal verb): "it is right", "it is fitting".
[25] *contarier = contari < contor, -are, -atus sum*: "inquire".
[26] *adsitne ei animus necne <ei> adsit*: literally "whether there is willingness in him or not"; translate here: "whether he's willing or not".

si neget[27] adesse, exanimatum[28] amittat[29] domum.

sed uxórem ante aedis[30] eccam.[31] ei[32] misero mihi!

metuo[33] ne non sit surda[34] atque haec audiuerit.   575

Cleustrata: audiui ecastor cum malo[35] magno tuo.[36]

Lysidamus: accedam[37] propius.[38] quid agis,[39] mea festiuitas?[40]

Cleustrata: te ecastor praestolabar.[41] **Lysidamus:** iamne ornata[42] rest?[43]

iamne hanc traduxti[44] huc ad nos uicinam[45] tuam

quae te adiutaret?[46] **Cleustrata:** arcessiui,[47] ut[48] iusseras.[49]   580

uerum hic sodalis[50] tuos,[51] amicus optumus,[52]

nescioquid[53] se sufflauit[54] uxori suae:

negauit posse, quoniam[55] arcesso, mittere.

---

[27] *nego, -are, -aui, -atum*: "deny", "say... not".
[28] *exanimatum* (perfect passive participle < *exanimo, -are, -aui, -atum*): literally "deprived of *animus*", hence "exhausted", "dead"; translate here: "his unwilling friend".
[29] *amitto, -ere, -misi, -missum*: "send away".
[30] *aedis/aedes, -is* (f.): "building", "house" (often used in the plural, as here).
[31] *eccam* = *ecce* + *eam* or *ecce* + *ham* (= *hanc*).
[32] *ei* (exclamation): "oh!"
[33] *metuo, -ere, metui, –*: "fear", "be afraid".
[34] *surdus, -a, -um*: "deaf".
[35] *malum, -i* (n.): "misfortune", "misery".
[36] *cum malo magno tuo*: "to your great misery"; translate here: "and you'll live to regret it", "too bad for you!".
[37] *accedo, -ere, -cessi, -cessum*: "approach", "come near".
[38] *propius* (adverb): "nearer".
[39] *quid agis*: "how are you?".
[40] *festiuitas, -atis* (f.): "celebration", "joy".
[41] *praesolor, -ari, -atus sum*: "wait for" (+ accusative).
[42] *orno, -are, -aui, -atum*: "prepare", "get ready", "dress up", "get dressed up".
[43] *rest* = *res est*.
[44] *traduxti* = *traduxisti* < *traduco, -ere, -duxi, -ductum*: "bring across", "bring over".
[45] *uicina, -ae* (f.): "(female) neighbour".
[46] *adiutaret* < *adiuto, -are, -aui, -atum*: "help", "assist"; *quae te adiutaret* is a relative clause of purpose, see Bennett 282.2.
[47] *arcesso, -ere, -iui, -itum*: "send for", "fetch".
[48] *ut*: "as".
[49] *iubeo, -ere, iussi, iussum*: "order", "tell"
[50] *sodalis, -is* (m.): "friend".
[51] *tuos* = *tuus*.
[52] *optumus* = *optimus*.
[53] *nescioquid* (adverb): "a little bit".
[54] *sufflo, -are, -aui, -atum*: "blow", "blow up at"; "get enraged".
[55] *quoniam* (adverb): "since"; "after", "when".

Lysidamus: uitium[56] tibi istuc[57] maxumum[58] est, blanda[59] es parum.[60]

Cleustrata: non matronarum[61] officiumst,[62] sed meretricium,[63] 585

uiris alienis,[64] mi[65] uir, subblandirier.[66]

i tú atque arcesse illam: ego intus[67] quod[68] factost[69] opus[70]

uolo accurare,[71] mi uir. **Lysidamus:** propera[72] ergo. **Cleustrata:** licet.[73]

iam pol ego huic[74] aliquem[75] in pectus[76] iniciam[77] metum;[78]

miserrumum[79] hodie ego hunc ebo amasium.[80] — 590

---

[56] *uitium, -ii/-i* (n.): "fault".
[57] *istuc = istud.*
[58] *maxumum = maximum.*
[59] *blandus, -a, -um:* "charming".
[60] *parum* (adverb): "insufficiently", "not... enough".
[61] *matrona, -ae* (f.): "married woman".
[62] *officiumst = officium est < officium, -ii* (n.): "duty", "obligation", "function".
[63] *meretrix, -tricis* (m.): "prostitute", "sex-worker".
[64] *alienus, -a, -um:* "belonging to another"; *uiris alienis*: "to other people's husbands".
[65] *mi* (vocative masculine singular < *meus, -a, -um*).
[66] *subblandirier = subblandiri < subblandior, -iri, -:* "be charming to", "make up to".
[67] *intus* (adverb): "inside".
[68] *quod* is accusative by attraction to its unstated antecedent; normally it would be ablative, to agree with *facto*.
[69] *factost = facto est; facto* is is ablative of means after *opus* (see Bennett 218.2c).
[70] *opus est:* "there is need".
[71] *accuro, -are, -aui, -atum:* "take care of" (+ accusative).
[72] *propero, -are, -aui, -atum:* "hurry", "be quick".
[73] *licere, licuit, licitum est* (impersonal): "it is allowed", "it is permitted"; translate here; "all right".
[74] *huic* is dative of reference (see Bennett 188).
[75] *aliquis, aliquid:* "some/any", "someone/something", "anyone/anything".
[76] *pectus, -oris* (n.): "chest"; "breast".
[77] *inicio, -ere, -ieci, -iectum:* "throw into", "put into".
[78] *metus, -ūs* (m.): "fear".
[79] *miserrumum = miserrimum.*
[80] *amasius, -i* (m.): "lover".

III.iv ALCESIMVS, LYSIDAMVS

Scene summary: *Alcesimus expresses his anger at Lysidamus for having (as he thinks) falsely made him believe that Cleustrata would invite his wife over to help with the wedding preparations. Lysidamus expresses his anger at Alcesimus for having (as he thinks) refused to allow his wife to come over when Cleustrata invited her. Angrily, Alcesimus agrees to send his wife over after all. Lysidamus muses about love, until he hears shouting from inside his house.*

Alcesimus: Viso[1] huc, amator[2] si a foro rediit[3] domum,

qui me atque uxorem ludificatust,[4] larua.[5]

sed eccum[6] ante[7] aedis.[8] ad te hercle ibam commodum.[9]

Lysidamus: et hercle ego ad te. quid ais,[10] uir minimi preti?[11]

quid tibi mandaui?[12] quid tecum[13] oraui?[14] **Alcesimus:** quid est?   595

Lysidamus: ut[15] bene uociuas[16] aedis fecisti mihi,

ut traduxisti[17] huc ad nos uxorem tuam!

satin[18] propter[19] te pereo[20] ego atque occasio?[21]

---

[1] *uiso, -ere, uisi, -uisum*: "go to see", "go to look at".
[2] *amator, -oris* (m.): "lover", "loverboy", "a man in love", "womanizer".
[3] *redeo, -ire, -iui/-ii, -itum*: "return", "go back".
[4] *ludificatust = ludificatus est < ludifico, -are, -aui, -atum*: "make a fool of".
[5] *larua, -ae* (f.): "ghost"; "possessed by evil spirits", "demon" (term of abuse).
[6] *eccum = ecce + eum* or *ecce + hum* (= *hunc*).
[7] *ante* (preposition): "in front of".
[8] *aedis/aedes, -is* (f.): "building", "house" (often used in the plural, as here).
[9] *commodum* (adverb): "at the very moment"; "right now".
[10] *ais* (2nd person singular present indicative active < *aio*: "say"; "say yes", "affirm"); *quid ais*: "what have you got to say for yourself?".
[11] *preti = pretii < pretium, -i* (n.): "value", "price", "worth"; *minimi preti* (genitive of quality, see Bennett 203): "of very little value", "worthless".
[12] *mando, -are, -aui, -atum*: "order", "commission"; *aliquid alicui mandare*: "to tell someone to do something".
[13] Translate *tecum* here as *te*.
[14] *oro, -are, -āui, -atum*: "ask", "beg".
[15] *ut*: "how".
[16] *uociuus, -a, -um* (= *uaciuus, -a, -um*): "empty".
[17] *traduco, -ere, -duxi, -ductum*: "bring across", "bring over".
[18] *satin = satisne* (adverb): "enough", "sufficiently".
[19] *propter* (preposition): "because of".
[20] *pereo, -ire, periui/-ii, peritum*: "die"; "be ruined"; "be lost".
[21] *occasio, -onis* (f.): "occasion", "opportunity"; *pereo ego atque occasio*: "both I and my opportunity are lost".

Alcesimus: quin[22] tu suspendis[23] te? nemp'[24] tute[25] dixeras

tuam arcéssituram[26] esse uxorem uxorem meam.   600

Lysidamus: ergo arcessiuisse ait[27] sese, et dixisse te

eam nón missurum. **Alcesimus:** quin eapse[28] ultro[29] mihi

negauit eiius[30] operam[31] se morarier.[32]

Lysidamus: quin eapse me adlegauit[33] qui[34] istam
arcesserem.

Alcesimus: quin nihili[35] facio.[36] **Lysidamus:** quin me perdis.   605
Alcesimus: quin benest,[37]

quin etiam diu morabor,[38] quin cupio tibi —

Lysidamus: quin — **Alcesimus:** aliquid[39] aegre facere.[40]
Lysidamus: quin faciam lubens.[41]

numquam tibi hodie 'quin'[42] erit plus quam mihi.

Alcesimus: quin hercle di te perdant postremo[43] quidem!

Lysidamus: quid nunc? missurusne es ad me uxorem tuam?   610

---

[22] *quin*: "no, really", "I mean!"; "actually", "in fact", "but"; "why... not?"
[23] *suspendo, -ere, -pendi, -pensus:* "hang", "hang up".
[24] *nemp'* = *nempe*: "certainly".
[25] *tute* = *tu* (the *-te* adds emphasis to the pronoun).
[26] *arcesso, -ere, -iui, -itum*: "send for", "fetch".
[27] *ait* (3rd person singular present indicative active) < *aio* (defective verb): "say"; "say yes", "affirm".
[28] *eapse* = *ipsa*.
[29] *ultro* (adverb): "of his/her own accord", "on his/her own initiative".
[30] *eiius* = *eius*.
[31] *opera, -ae* (f.): "service", "activity", "effort".
[32] *morarier* = *morari* < *moror, -ari, -atus sum*: "delay"; *mihi negauit eiius operam se morarier*: "she told me 'she doesn't mind' about her help" (see lines 545 and 553), "she told me she didn't need her help".
[33] *adlegauit* = *allegauit* < *allego, -are, -aui, -atum*: "send as a representative", "employ as an agent".
[34] *qui ... arcesserem* (relative clause of purpose, see Bennett 282.2).
[35] *nihilum, -i* (n.): "nothing".
[36] *nihili facio*: "I don't care" (*nihili* is genitive of indefinite value; see Bennett 203.3).
[37] *benest* = *bene est*: "it's fine by me (that you're being destroyed)".
[38] *moror, -ari, -atus sum*: "delay"; translate *diu morabor* either: "I'll delay my wife longer", or "I'll delay things longer".
[39] *aliquis, aliquid*: "some/any", "someone/something", "anyone/anything".
[40] *aliquid aegre facere*: "to do something annoying / upsetting".
[41] *lubens* = *libens, -ntis*: "pleased", "willing" (often with adverbial sense); translate *faciam lubens* here: "I'll gladly do the same to you".
[42] *quin* is used as a noun here, as a joke about the number of times each old man has said it in the above argument.
[43] *postremo* (adverb): "finally", "at last"; Alcesimus has just uttered the last *quin*, so *postremo* refers obliquely to this fact (MacCary and Willcock 1976: 166).

Alcesimus: ducas, easque[44] in maxumam[45] malam crucem[46]

cum hác cum ístac,[47] cumque amica etiam tua.

abi et aliud cura,[48] ego iam per hortum[49] iussero[50]

meam istuc[51] transire uxorem ad uxorem tuam. —

Lysidamus: nunc tu mi[52] amicus es in germanum[53]   615
modum.[54]

qua ego hunc amorem mi esse aui[55] dicam datum[56]

aut quot[57] ego umquam erga[58] Venerem inique[59] fecerim,[60]

quoi[61] sic tot[62] amanti[63] mi obuiam[64] eueniant[65] morae? [66]

attat![67]

quid illúc[68] clamoris,[69] opsecro,[70] in nostrast[71] domo?   620

---

[44] *eas < eo, ire, iui/ii, itum.*
[45] *maxumum = maximum.*
[46] *crux, crucis* (f.): "cross"; *easque in maxumum malam crucem*: "you can go get crucified", "you can go crucify yourself on a giant cross".
[47] *istāc = istā.*
[48] *curo, -are, -aui, -atum*: "take care of" (+ accusative).
[49] *hortus, -i* (m.): "garden"
[50] *iubeo, -ere, iussi, iussum*: "order", "tell"
[51] *istuc* (adverb): "thither", "(to) there".
[52] *mi = mihi.*
[53] *germanus, -a, -um*: "full", "genuine".
[54] *in germanum modum*: "in a genuine way", "truly".
[55] *aui* (ablative singular) *< auis, -is* (f.): "bird"; translate here: "bird of ill omen".
[56] *datum = datum esse.*
[57] *quot* (indeclinable adjective): "how many?"; translate here as *quotiens*: "how many times?", or as modifying an unstated neuter plural object of *fecerim*: "how many things might I have done?"
[58] *erga*: "against".
[59] *inique* (adverb): "unfairly".
[60] *erga Venerem inique fecerim*: "might I have done/acted wrongly towards Venus", "might I have offended Venus".
[61] *quoi = cui.*
[62] *tot* (indeclinable adjective): "so many".
[63] *amans, -ntis* (m.): "lover", "being in love".
[64] *amanti mi obuiam*: "in my way when I'm in love".
[65] *euenio, -ire, -ueni, -uentum*: "come to pass", "befall".
[66] *mora, -ae* (f.): "delay", "hindrance", "obstacle".
[67] *attat* (exclamation of surprise).
[68] *illuc = illud.*
[69] *clamor, -oris* (m.): "loud shout"; *quid illuc clamoris*: "what's that shouting?".
[70] *opsecro = obsecro < obsecro, -are, -aui, -atum*: "beg", "implore"; *opsecro* (interjection): "please!".
[71] *nostrāst = nostrā est.*

III.v PARDALISCA, LYSIDAMVS

Scene summary: *Pardalisca comes dramatically out of the house, crying that terrible things are happening inside, and mentioning someone with a sword. Lysidamus asks her repeatedly what has been happening. Pardalisca, using the language of tragic drama, says that everyone will be killed, begs Lysidamus to hold her, and finally says that Casina has a sword and is chasing everyone with it. Pardalisca then claims that Casina has sworn to kill any man who tries to share her bed, that she will kill Lysidamus for making her marry Olympio, and that, in fact, she has two swords. Lysidamus, terrified, begs Pardalisca to persuade Cleustrata to persuade Casina to put the swords down.*

Pardalisca: nulla sum,[1] nulla sum, tota,[2] tota occidi,[3]

cor[4] metu[5] mortuomst,[6] membra[7] miserae[8] tremunt,[9]

nescio unde[10] auxili,[11] praesidi,[12] perfugi[13]

mi aut opum[14] copiam[15] comparem[16] aut expetam:[17]

tanta factu[18] modo[19] mira[20] miris modis[21]   625

intus[22] uidi, nouam atque integram[23] audaciam.[24]

---

[1] *nulla sum*: "I'm done for".
[2] *totus, -a, -um*: "whole", "entire"; translate tota here as adverbial: "wholly", "completely".
[3] *occido, -ere, -cidi, -casum*: "fall down", "die", "be destroyed".
[4] *cor, cordis* (n.): "heart", "mind".
[5] *metus, -ūs* (m.): "fear".
[6] *mortuomst = mortuum est < morior, -i, mortuus sum*: "die".
[7] *membrum, -i* (n.): "limb"; translate here: "legs".
[8] *miserae* is dative of reference (see Bennett 188).
[9] *tremo, -ere, -ui, –*: "tremble", "shake".
[10] *unde*: "from where".
[11] *auxilium, -ii/-i* (n.): "help", "assistance" (*auxili, perfugi, praesidi* and *opum* are genitives after *copiam*).
[12] *praesidium, -ii/-i* (n.): "protection".
[13] *perfugium, -ii/-i* (n.): "refuge", "place of safety".
[14] *ops, opis* (m): "help", "support".
[15] *copia, -ae* (f.): "supply".
[16] *comparo, -are, -aui, -atum*: "get together", "provide"; "muster".
[17] *expeto, -ere, -iui-/-ii, -itum*: "ask for", "look for"; "demand", "want", "desire", "be eager for".
[18] *factu* is a supine after *mira* (see Bennett 340.2).
[19] *modo* (adverb): "just", "just now"; "only".
[20] *mirus, -a, -um*: "surprising", "extraordinary"; *tanta factu mira*: "such "extraordinary/horrifying things done".
[21] *miris modis*: "in extraordinary/horrifying ways".
[22] *intus* (adverb): "inside".
[23] *integer, -gra, -grum*: "new", "not before attempted".
[24] *audacia, -ae* (f.): "daring", "audacity", "shamelessness".

caue[25] tibi, Cleustrata, apscede[26] ab ista, opsecro,[27]
nequid[28] in[29] te mali[30] faxit[31] ira[32] percita.[33]
eripite[34] isti[35] gladium,[36] quae suist[37] impos[38] animi.[39]

Lysidamus: nam quid est quod haec huc timida[40] átque   630
exanimata[41] exsiliuit?[42]

Pardalisca! **Pardalisca:** perii![43] únde méae usúrpant[44] aures[45]
sonitum?[46]

Lysidamus: respice[47] modo ad me. **Pardalisca:** o ere[48] mi[49]
— **Lysidamus:** quid tibi est? quid[50] timida es? **Pardalisca:**
perii.

Lysidamus: quid, periisti? **Pardalisca:** perii, ét tu periistí.
Lysidamus: a, perii? quid ita?

---

[25] *caueo, -ere, caui, cautum*: "be on one's guard", "beware", "look out for" (+ dative of person warned).
[26] *apscede = abscede < abscedo, -ere, -cessi, -cessum*: "go away", "get away".
[27] *opsecro = obsecro < obsecro, -are, -aui, -atum*: "beg", "implore"; *opsecro* (interjection): "please!".
[28] *nequid = ne quid.*
[29] *in*: "against".
[30] *mali* is genitive of the whole after *nequid* (see Bennett 201.2).
[31] *faxit = faciat* (present subjunctive) or *fecerit* (perfect subjunctive); *nequid in te mali faxit*: "don't let her do anything bad to you" (prohibition with *ne* + subjunctive, see Allen & Greenough 450).
[32] *ira, -ae* (f.): "rage", "anger".
[33] *percitus, -a, -um*: "stirred up", "disturbed", "overwrought".
[34] *eripio, -ere, -ripui, -reptum*: "take away", "snatch away".
[35] *isti* is dative of separation after a verb of "taking away" (see Bennett 188.2d).
[36] *gladius, -ii* (m.): "sword".
[37] *suist = sui est.*
[38] *impos, -otis*: "not having control".
[39] *sui impos animi*: "out of (her) mind".
[40] *timidus, -a, -um*: "frightened", "fearful".
[41] *exanimo, -are, -aui, -atum*: "terrify", "put out of one's senses with horror"; passive: "be breathless".
[42] *exsilio, -ire, -ui/-iui, –*: "leap up", "jump out".
[43] *pereo, -ire, periui/-ii, peritum*: "die"; "be ruined"; "be lost".
[44] *usurpo, -are, -aui, -atum*: "take possession of", "receive".
[45] *auris, -is* (f.): "ear".
[46] *unde meae usurpant aures sonitum*: "from where are my ears hearing this noise?", "whence comes this sound to my ears?" (this is meant to sound like the extravagant language of tragic drama).
[47] *respicio, -ere, -spexi, -spectum*: "look back", "look".
[48] *erus, -i* (m.): "master (of slaves)".
[49] *mi* (vocative masculine singular < *meus, -a, -um*).
[50] *quid*: "why?".

Pardalisca: uae tibi!⁵¹ **Lysidamus:** immo⁵² istuc⁵³ tibi sit.
Pardalisca: ne cadam,⁵⁴ amabo,⁵⁵ tene me.

Lysidamus: quidquid⁵⁶ est, eloquere⁵⁷ mi cito.⁵⁸ **Pardalisca:**   635-6
contine⁵⁹ pectus,⁶⁰

face⁶¹ uentum,⁶² amabo, pallio.⁶³ **Lysidamus:** timeo hoc   637-8
negoti⁶⁴ quid siet,⁶⁵

nisi haec meraco⁶⁶ se uspiam⁶⁷ percussit⁶⁸ flore⁶⁹ Liberi.⁷⁰   639/-40

Pardalisca: optine⁷¹ auris, amabo. **Lysidamus:** i in malam a
me⁷² crucem!⁷³

pectus, auris, caput teque di perduint!⁷⁴

nam nisi ex te scio, quidquid hoc est, cito, hoc⁷⁵

iam tibi istuc⁷⁶ cerebrum⁷⁷ dispercutiam,⁷⁸ excetra⁷⁹ tu,

---

51   *uae tibi:* "woe to you!".
52   *immo* (adverb): "on the contrary".
53   *istuc = istud* (referring to Pardalisca's word *uae*).
54   *cado, -ere, cecidi, casum:* "fall", "fall down".
55   *amabo:* "please", "I beg" (< *amo, -are, -aui, -atum*).
56   *quisquam, quaequam, quicquam / quidquid* (indefinite pronoun): "any(one) / any(thing)", "whoever / whatever".
57   *eloquere* (2nd person singular present imperative) < *eloquor, eloqui, elocutus sum:* "speak out", "state", "say".
58   *cito* (adverb): "quickly".
59   *contineo, -ere, -tinui, -tentum:* "hold".
60   *pectus,-oris* (n.): "chest"; "breast"; *contine pectus:* "hold me up".
61   *face:* the original form of the 2nd person singular present imperative active of *facio, -ere* (later *fac*).
62   *uentus, -i* (m.): "wind".
63   *pallium, -ii* (n.): "cloak"; *face uentum... pallio:* "fan (me) with (your) cloak".
64   *negotium, -ii/-i* (n.): "business", "concern"; "situation", "trouble"; *negoti* is a genitive of the whole after *quid* (see Bennett 201.2).
65   *siet = sit; timeo hic negoti quid siet:* "I'm afraid of what this could be about".
66   *meracus, -a, -um:* "undiluted", "straight" (usually referring to wine, which was usually mixed with water before drinking).
67   *uspiam* (adverb): "somewhere".
68   *percutio, -ere, -cussi, -cussum:* "strike", "afflict".
69   *flos, floris* (m.): "flower".
70   *Liber, -eri* (m.): "Liber" (god of vegetation, whom Romans came to identify with the Greek god of wine, Bacchus / Dionysus); *nisi haec meraco se uspiam percussit flore Liberi:* "unless she's got herself drunk somewhere on unmixed wine".
71   *optineo, -ere, -ui, -tentum:* "take hold of", "hold".
72   *a me:* "far away from me".
73   *in malam crucem* (see note 46 on page 114 at line 611, III.iv).
74   *perduint = perdant < perdo, -ere, perdidi, perditum:* "ruin", "destroy", "lose".
75   *hoc* must refer to his staff, with which he threatens to beat out her brains.
76   *istuc = istud.*
77   *cerebrum, -i* (n.): "brain".
78   *dispercutio, -ere:* "smash to pieces", "beat out".
79   *excetra, -ae* (f.): "snake", "dragon".

ludibrio[80] pessuma[81] adhuc[82] quae me uisti.[83] 645

Pardalisca: ere mi — **Lysidamus:** quid uis mea me ancilla?[84] 646-7

Pardalisca: nimium[85] saeuis.[86] **Lysidamus:** numero[87] dicis.

sed hoc quidquid est eloquere, in pauca[88] confer:[89]

quid intus tumulti[90] fuit? **Pardalisca:** scibis,[91] audi.

malum pessumumque[92] hic[93] modo intús — apud[94] nos 650

tua ancilla hoc pacto[95] exordiri[96] coëpit,[97]

quod haud[98] Atticam[99] condecet[100] disciplinam.[101]

Lysidamus: quid est id? **Pardalisca:** timor[102] praepedit[103] dicta linguae.[104]

Lysidamus: possum scire ego istuc[105] ex te quid negoti est?[106] **Pardalisca:** dicam.

tua ancilla, quam tu tuo uilico[107] uis 655

---

[80] *ludibrium, -ii* (n.): "mockery", laughing-stock". *ludibrio* is a dative of purpose with *uisti* (see Bennett 191).
[81] *pessuma = pessima.*
[82] *adhuc* (adverb): "thus far", "until now".
[83] *ludibrio... uisti:* "you've been making a fool of me".
[84] *ancilla, -ae* (f.): "enslaved woman/girl" (often used instead of *serva*).
[85] *nimium* (adverb): "too much", "excessively".
[86] *saeuio, -ire, -iui, -itum*: "be violently angry", "be in a rage".
[87] *numero* (adverb): "too quickly"; "too soon"; "exactly".
[88] *pauca, -orum* (n. pl.): "a few words".
[89] *confero, -ferre, contuli, collatum*: "bring together", "convey"; "direct"; "address" (words); *in pauca confer*: "tell me in a few words".
[90] *tumulti = tumultūs < tumultus, -ūs* (m.): "uproar", "disturbance"; *tumulti* is genitive of the whole (see Bennett 201.2).
[91] *scibis = scies.*
[92] *pessumum = pessimum.*
[93] *hīc* (adverb).
[94] *apud* (preposition): "near", "at", "at the house of" (+ accusative).
[95] *pactum, -i* (n.): "agreement"; "manner"; "method"; *hoc pacto*: "in this way".
[96] *exordior, -iri, -orsus sum*: "undertake", "start".
[97] *coepio, -ere, coepi, copetum*: "begin".
[98] *hau = haud*: "not at all".
[99] *Atticus, -a, -um*: "Attic", "Athenian" (relating to the customs of Athens or Attica).
[100] *condecet, -ere* (impersonal): "it is seemly", "it is keeping (with)" + accusative.
[101] *disciplina, -ae* (f.): "training", "upbringing", "discipline".
[102] *timor, -oris* (m.): "fear".
[103] *praepedio, -ire, -iui/-ii, -itum*: "shackle", "bind"; "obstruct", "impede".
[104] *lingua, -ae* (f.): "tongue", "speech". Pardalisca is again speaking in the extravagant language of tragic drama.
[105] *istuc = istud.*
[106] *quid negoti est* (see note 64 on the preceding page at line 638, III.v).
[107] *uilicus, -i* (m.): "slave-overseer", "(enslaved) farm manager".

dare uxorem, ea intus — **Lysidamus:** quid intus? quid est?

Pardalisca: imitatur[108] malarum malam disciplinam,

uiro quae suo interminatur:[109] uitam —

Lysidamus: quid ergo? **Pardalisca:** ah — **Lysidamus:** quid est? **Pardalisca:** interemeré[110] — ait[111] uelle uitam,

gladium[112] — **Lysidamus:** hem![113] **Pardalisca:** gladium —   660
Lysidamus: quid eum gladium?

Pardalisca: et. **Lysidamus:** ei[114] misero mihi! qur[115] eum et?

Pardalisca: insectatur[116] omnis[117] domi[118] per aedis[119]

nec quemquam[120] prope[121] ad se sinit[122] adire:

ita omnes sub arcis,[123] sub lectis[124] latentes[125]

metu[126] mussitant.[127] **Lysidamus:** occidi[128] atque interii![129]   665

quid illic[130] obiectumst[131] mali[132] tam[133] repente?[134]

---

[108] *imitor, -ari, -atus sum:* "imitate", "act like", "represent".
[109] *interminor, -ari, -atus sum:* "utter threats", "threaten" (+ dative).
[110] *interemere = interimere < interimo, -ere, -emi, -emptum:* "do away with", "destroy" (the object of *interemere* is *uitam* in line 658).
[111] *ait* (3rd person singular present indicative active) < *aio* (defective verb): "say"; "say yes", "affirm".
[112] *gladius, -ii* (see note 36 on page 116 at line 629, III.v).
[113] *hem* (expression of surprise and/or concern): "oh no!".
[114] *ei* (exclamation): "oh!"
[115] *qur = cur*.
[116] *insector, -ari, -atus sum:* "pursue", "chase".
[117] *omnīs = omnēs*.
[118] *domi* (locative case).
[119] *aedis/aedes, -is* (f.): "building", "house" (often used in the plural, as here).
[120] *quisquam, quaequam, quicquam / quidquid* (indefinite pronoun): "any(one) / any(thing)", "whoever / whatever".
[121] *proper* (adverb): "near", "nearby".
[122] *sino, -ere, siui, situm:* "allow".
[123] *arca, -ae* (f.): "chest", "cupboard".
[124] *lectus, -i* (m.): "bed".
[125] *lateo, -ere, -ui, –:* "hide".
[126] *metus, -ūs* (see note 5 on page 115 at line 622, III.v).
[127] *mussito, -are, -aui, -atum:* "be silent", "not let oneself be heard".
[128] *occido, -ere, -cidi, -casum* (see note 3 on page 115 at line 621, III.v).
[129] *intereo, -ire, -iui/-ii, -itum:* "become lost", "be ruined", "die".
[130] *illic = illi* (dative singular, referring to Casina).
[131] *obiectumst = obiectum est < obicio, -ere, -ieci, -iectum:* "throw towards", "throw in the way"; (passive) "happen", "befall".
[132] *mali* is genitive of the whole after *quid* (see Bennett 201.2).
[133] *tam* (adverb): "so", "to such a degree".
[134] *repente* (adverb): "suddenly".

Pardalisca: insanit.[135] **Lysidamus:** scelestissumum[136] me esse credo.

Pardalisca: immo[137] si scias dicta quae dixit hodie.

Lysidamus: istuc[138] expeto[139] scire. quid dixit? **Pardalisca:** audi.

per[140] omnis[141] deos et deas deierauit,[142] 670

occisurum[143] eum hac nocte quicum[144] cubaret.[145]

Lysidamus: men[146] occidet? **Pardalisca:** an quippiam[147] ad te attinet?[148] **Lysidamus:** uah![149]

Pardalisca: quid cum ea negoti[150] tibist?[151] **Lysidamus:** 673-4
peccaui:[152] illuc[153] dicere uilicum[154] uolebam.

Pardalisca: sciens de uia in semitam[155] degredere.[156] 675

Lysidamus: num[157] quid[158] mihi minatur?[159] **Pardalisca:** tibi[160] infesta[161] solist[162]

---

[135] *insanio, -ire, -iui, -itum*: "be insane", "act crazily".
[136] *scelestissumum = scelestissimum < scelestus, -a, -um*: "wicked"; translate here: "unlucky", "unfortunate".
[137] *immo* (see note 52 on page 117 at line 634, III.v).
[138] *istuc = istud*.
[139] *expeto, -ere, -iui/-ii, -itum* (see note 17 on page 115 at line 624, III.v).
[140] *per* (preposition): translate here: "by".
[141] *omnīs = omnēs*.
[142] *deiero, -are, -aui, -atum*: "swear".
[143] *occisurum* (indeclinable future active infinitive) = *occisuram esse < occido, -ere, -cidi, -cisum*: "strike down", "kill".
[144] *quicum = quocum* (an old ablative form).
[145] *cubo, -are, -aui, -atum*: "lie down", "go to bed".
[146] *men = mene*.
[147] *quippiam* (adverb): "at all", "in any respect", "somewhat".
[148] *attineo, -ere, -ui, -tentum*: "concern", "pertain", "relate".
[149] *uah* (exclamation of surprise, joy, anger, etc.).
[150] *negotium, -ii/-i* (n.): "business", "concern"; "situation", "trouble"; *negoti* is genitive of the whole after *quid* (see Bennett 201.2).
[151] *tibist = tibi est*.
[152] *pecco, -are, -aui, -atus*: "do wrong", "blunder", "screw up".
[153] *illuc = illud*: translate here: "that other thing/word".
[154] *uilicus, -i* (see note 107 on page 118 at line 655, III.v).
[155] *semita, -ae* (f.): "path", "track" (here implying dishonest behaviour).
[156] *degredior, -i, -gressus sum*: "go down", "descend".
[157] *num* (interrogative): "it isn't possible that...?", "can it be that...?".
[158] *quid* (internal or adverbial accusative): "at all".
[159] *minor, -ari, -atus sum*: "threaten" (+ dative of person threatened); *num quid mihi minatur?*: "she isn't threatening me at all, is she?".
[160] *tibi* is a dative after *infesta* (see Bennett 192.1).
[161] *infestus, -a, -um*: "hostile", "dangerous".
[162] *solist = soli est*; *soli* is dative singular, agreeing with *tibi*.

plus quam quoiquam.[163] **Lysidamus:** quámobrem?[164]
Pardalisca: quia se[165] des[166] uxorem Olympioni,

neque se[167] tuam nec suam neque uiri uitam sinere[168] in crastinum[169] protolli:[170] id[171] huc   678-80

missa sum tibi ut dicerem,

ab ea uti[172] caueas[173] tibi. **Lysidamus:** perii[174] hercle ego miser! **Pardalisca:** dig<nu's[175] tu>.[176]   682-3

Lysidamus: neque est neque fuit me senex quisquam[177] amator

adaeque[178] miser.[179] **Pardalisca:** ludo[180] ego hunc facete;[181]   685

nam quae facta dixi omnia huic falsa dixi:

era[182] atque haec dolum[183] ex proxumo[184] hunc protulerunt,[185]

ego huc missa sum ludere.[186] **Lysidamus:** heus[187] Pardalisca!

---

[163] *quoiquam = cuiquam < quisquam, quaequam, quicquam / quidquid* (indefinite pronoun): "any(one) / any(thing)", "whoever / whatever".
[164] *quamobrem = quam ob rem*: "why?", "for what reason?".
[165] *se* is an indirect reflexive, referring to Casina (see Bennett 244.1.II).
[166] *des < do, dare, dedi, datum* (*des* is subjunctive because it is implied indirect discourse, see Bennett 323 and 286.1).
[167] *se* is another indirect reflexive.
[168] *sino, -ere, siui, situm*: "allow"; translate here as indirect discourse with a verb of speaking implied (perhaps *minatur*).
[169] *in crastinum*: "till tomorrow".
[170] *protollo, -ere, –, –:* "extend", "defer", "prolong".
[171] *id* refers to the *uti* clause in the next line.
[172] *uti = ut* (+ subjunctive).
[173] *caueo, -ere, caui, cautum*: "be on one's guard", "beware", "look out for" (+ dative of person warned); *ab ea... caueas tibi*: "be on your guard against her".
[174] *pereo, -ire, -iui/-ii, -itum* (see note 43 on page 116 at line 631, III.v).
[175] *dignu's = dignus es*.
[176] *dignu's tu*: "you deserve it".
[177] *quisquam, quaequam, quicquam / quidquid* (see note 163 at line 677, III.v).
[178] *adaeque* (adverb): "equally", "as... as" (here with *me* as ablative of comparison).
[179] *neque est neque fuit me senex quisquam amator / adaeque miser*: there is ironic double meaning here, as the lines could also refer to Lysidamus's abject failure to play his role as *senex amator* successfully (see Christenson 2019: 61-62).
[180] *ludo, -ere, lusi, lusum*: "play", "mock"; "make a mockery of" (+ accusative).
[181] *facete* (adverb): "properly", "humorously".
[182] *era, -ae* (f.): "mistress" (of the house and of the slaves).
[183] *dolus, -i* (m.): "trickery", "cunning", "deceit".
[184] *proxumo = proximo < proximus, -a, -um*: "nearest"; *haec... ex proxumo*: "the woman next-door", "her next-door neighbour".
[185] *profero, -ferre, protuli, prolatum*: "bring forth", "invent".
[186] *ludere* is an infinitive of purpose, see Allen & Greenough 460c.
[187] *heus*: "hey!", "listen!" (used to try to get someone's attention).

Pardalisca: quid est? **Lysidamus:** est — **Pardalisca:** quid? **Lysidamus:** est quod uolo exquirere[188] ex te.

Pardalisca: moram[189] offers[190] mihi. **Lysidamus:** at tu mihi offers maerorem.[191]   690

sed etiamne et nunc Casina gladium?

Pardalisca: et, sed duos. **Lysidamus:** quid, duos? **Pardalisca:** altero[192] te

occisurum[193] ait,[194] altero uilicum hodie.

Lysidamus: occisissumus[195] sum omnium qui uiuont.[196]

loricam[197] induam[198] mi[199] optumum[200] esse opinor.[201]   695

quid uxor mea? non adît[202] atque ademit?[203]

Pardalisca: nemo[204] audet prope[205] accedere.[206] **Lysidamus:** exoret.[207] **Pardalisca:** orat:[208]

negat[209] ponere[210] alio modo[211] ullo profecto,[212]

nisi se sciat uilico non datum iri.[213]

---

[188] *exquiro, -ere, -siui, -situm*: "find out", "ask".
[189] *mora, -ae* (f.): "delay", "hindrance", "obstacle".
[190] *offero, -ferre, obtuli, oblatum*: "offer", "bring"; translate here: "cause".
[191] *maeror, -oris* (m.): "grief", "sorrow".
[192] *alter... alter*: "the one... the other" (*altero* is ablative of means).
[193] *occisurum = occisuram esse* (see note 143 on page 120 at line 671, III.v).
[194] *ait* (see note 111 on page 119 at line 659, III.v).
[195] *occisissumus = occisissimus* is a hyperbolic superlative form of the perfect passive participle < *occido, -ere, -cidi, -cisum*.
[196] *uiuont = uiuunt*.
[197] *lorica, -ae* (f.): "cuirass", "breastplate" (protective chest armour).
[198] *induo, -ere, indui, indutum*: "put on", "clothe oneself in".
[199] *mi = mihi*.
[200] *optumum = optimum*.
[201] *opinor, -ari, -atus sum*: "think", "suppose", "imagine".
[202] *adît = adiit* (*ad Casinam* is implied).
[203] *adimo, -ere, -emi, -emptum*: "take away" (*gladios* is implied).
[204] *nemo, neminis* (m./f.): "no one".
[205] *proper* (adverb): "near", "nearby".
[206] *accedo, -ere, -cessi, -cessum*: "approach", "come near".
[207] *exoro, -are, -aui, -atum*: "persuade", "plead".
[208] *oro, -are, -aui, -atum*: "ask", "beg".
[209] *nego, -are, -aui, -atum*: "deny", "say... not".
[210] *ponere = se posituram esse* (*gladios* is implied).
[211] *modus, -i* (m.): "way".
[212] *profecto* (adverb): "certainly".
[213] *datum iri* is future infinitive passive.

Lysidamus: atqui[214] ingratiis,[215] quia non uolt, nubet[216] 700
hodie.

nam qur[217] non ego id perpetrem[218] quod coëpi,[219]

ut nubat mihi — illud quidem uolebam,[220]

nostro uilico? **Pardalisca:** saepicule[221] peccas.[222]

Lysidamus: timor praepedit uerba.[223] uerum, opsecro[224] te,

dic med[225] uxorem orare[226] ut exoret[227] illam[228] 705

gladium ut ponat et redire me intro[229] ut liceat.[230] **Pardalisca:**
nuntiabo.[231]

Lysidamus: et tu orato.[232] **Pardalisca:** et ego orabo.
Lysidamus: at blande[233] orato, ut soles.[234] sed audin?[235]

si ecfexis[236] hoc, soleas[237] tibi dabo et anulum[238] in digito[239] 708-12
aureum[240] et bona pluruma.[241]

Pardalisca: operam dabo.[242]

---

[214] *atqui* (conjunction): "an nevertheless", "but certainly".
[215] *ingratiis* (adverb): "against (her) will".
[216] *nubo, -ere, -nupsi, nuptum*: "marry", "be married".
[217] *qur = cur*.
[218] *perpetro, -are, -aui, -atum*: "carry through", "bring about".
[219] *coepio, -ere, coepi, copetum*: "begin".
[220] *uolebam*: "I meant to say".
[221] *saepicule* (adverb): "often", "frequently", "repeatedly".
[222] *pecco, -are, -aui, -atus* (see note 152 on page 120 at line 674, III.v).
[223] *timor praepedit uerba* (Lysidamus copies Pardalisca's dramatic utterance at line 653).
[224] *opsecro* (see note 27 on page 116 at line 627, III.v).
[225] *med = me*.
[226] *dic med uxorem orare* (*med* is the accusative subject of the infinitive *orare*, while *uxorem* is the direct object of *dic*).
[227] *exoro, -are, -aui, -atum* (the subject of *exoret* is Cleustrata).
[228] *illam* refers to Casina.
[229] *intro* (adverb): "inside", "into the house".
[230] *licere, licuit, licitum est* (impersonal): "it is allowed", "it is permitted"; translate here; "all right"; *liceat* here takes an infinitive (*redire*) with subject accusative (*me*).
[231] *nuntio, -are, -aui, -atum*: "announce".
[232] *orato* (2nd person singular future imperative active) < *oro, -are, -aui, -atum*.
[233] *blande* (adverb): "sweetly", "flatteringly", "charmingly".
[234] *soleo, -ere, – , solitus sum*: "be accustomed", "tend".
[235] *audin = audine*.
[236] *ecfexis = effexis = effeceris < efficio, -ere, -eci, -ectum*: "bring about", "cause to occur".
[237] *solea, -ae* (f.): "slipper", "sandal".
[238] *anulus, -i* (m.): "ring".
[239] *digitus, -i* (m.): "finger".
[240] *aureus, -a, -um*: "gold", "made of gold".
[241] *plurimus, -a, -um* (superlative) < *multus, -a, -um*.
[242] *operam dare*: "take care", "give attention"; "help" (+ dative).

Lysidamus: face[243] ut impetres.[244]

Pardalisca: eo núnciam,[245]   715

nisi quippiam[246]

remorare[247] me.

Lysidamus: abi et cúra.[248]

redit eccum[249] tandem opsonatu[250] meus adiutor,[251] pompam[252] ducit.

---

[243] *face*: the original form of the 2nd person singular present imperative active of *facio, -ere* (later *fac*).
[244] *impetro, -are, -aui, -atum*: "accomplish", "get", "succeed", "be granted".
[245] *nunciam = nunc + iam* (emphatic form of *nunc*).
[246] *quippiam* (adverb): "at all", "in any respect", "somewhat".
[247] *remorare* (2nd person singular present indicative < *remoror, -ari, -atus sum*: "delay" + accusative of person delayed).
[248] *curo, -are, -aui, -atum*: "take care" "be careful".
[249] *eccum = ecce + eum* or *ecce + hum* (= *hunc*).
[250] *opsonatu = obsonatu < obsonatus, -ūs* (m.): "marketing", "grocery shopping" (*opsonatu* is ablative of place from which after *redit*).
[251] *adiutor, -oris* (m.): "helper", "assistant".
[252] *pompa, -ae* (f.): "solemn procession"; "retinue", "crew".

III.vi OLYMPIO, CHYTRIO, LYSIDAMVS

Scene summary: *Olympio makes some disparaging remarks about the catering staff (slaves hired to help prepare the wedding feast). He then speaks in an arrogant way with Lysidamus, making Lysidamus say that he (Lysidamus) is really Olympio's slave, and insisting that Lysidamus provide him with a nice meal in return for Olympio's cooperation in Lysidamus's plans for Casina. Lysidamus says he's scared to go into the house, since Casina has a sword, but eventually both he and Olympio go into the house.*

Olympio: Vide, fur,[1] ut sentis[2] sub signis[3] ducas! **Chytrio:**   720
qui[4] uero[5] hi sunt sentes?

Olympio: quia quod tetigere,[6] ilico[7] rapiunt, si eás[8] ereptum,[9] ilico scindunt:[10]

ita quoquo[11] adueniunt,[12] ubi ubi[13] sunt, duplici[14] damno[15] dominos multant.[16]

Chytrio: heia![17] **Olympio:** attat![18] cesso[19] magnufice[20] patriceque[21] amicirier[22] atque ita ero[23] meo ire aduorsum.[24]

---

[1] *fur, furis* (m./f.): "thief".
[2] *sentīs = sentēs < sentis, -is* (m.): "thorn".
[3] *sub signis* (a military metaphor).: "together", "in order"
[4] *qui* (an old ablative): "in what way?"
[5] *uero* (adverb): truly", "certainly"; translate here: "but".
[6] *tetigere* (3rd person plural perfect indicative active < *tango, -ere, tetigi, tactum*: "touch").
[7] *ilico* (adverb): "on the spot", "in that very place"; "at once", "there and then".
[8] *eas < eo, ire, iui/ii, itum*.
[9] *ereptum* (supine < *eripio, -ere, -ripui, -reptum*: "take away", "snatch away").
[10] *scindo, -ere, scidi, scissum*: "cut", "tear".
[11] *quoquo* (adverb): "(to) wherever".
[12] *aduenio, -ire, -ueni, -uentum*: "come to", "arrive at".
[13] *ubi ubi*: "wherever".
[14] *duplex, -plicis* (adjective): "double", "twofold".
[15] *damnum, -i* (n.): "damage", "loss".
[16] *multo, -are, -aui, -atum*: "punish"; "sentence to pay" (+ ablative of price paid).
[17] *heia* (exclamation, here implying pretended amusement).
[18] *attat* (exclamation of surprise).
[19] *cesso, -are, -aui, -atum*: "be remiss"; "delay", "cease from".
[20] *magnufice = magnifice* (adverb): "nobly", "magnificently".
[21] *patrice = patricie* (adverb): "in a patrician manner", "aristocratically".
[22] *amicirier = amiciri < amicio, -ire, -cui/-xi, -ctum*: "cover with an outer garment", "dress"; *cesso... amicirier*: "I'm being slow in dressing up", "it's time I dressed up".
[23] *erus, -i* (m.): "master (of slaves)".
[24] *ire aduorsum*: "go to meet" (+ dative of person met; see note 81 on page 95 at line 461, II.viii).

Lysidamus: bone uir,[25] salue. **Olympio:** fateor.[26] **Lysidamus:**   724-5
quid fit?[27] **Olympio:** tu amás: ego essurio[28] et sitio.[29]

Lysidamus: lepide[30] excuratus[31] incessisti.[32] **Olympio:** aha,[33]
hodie * * * * *

Lysidamus: mane uero, quamquam[34] fastidis.[35] **Olympio:**
fui fui![36] foetet[37] tuo'[38] mihi[39] sermo.[40]

Lysidamus: quae res?[41] **Olympio:** haec res. etiamne astas?[42]
enim uero πράγματά μοι παρέχεις.[43]

Lysidamus: dabo tibi

μέγα κακόν,[44]   729a

ut ego opinor,[45] nisi resistis.[46] **Olympio:** Ὦ Ζεῦ,[47]   730

potin[48] a me abeas,[49]

nisi me uis

uomere[50] hodie?   732a

---

[25] A *bonus uir* usually meant a member of the aristocracy, though in Plautus it is often used sarcastically when referring to low status characters (Cody 1976: 456).
[26] *fateor, fateri, fassus sum*: "admit", "confess" (Olympio is admitting that he is, indeed, a *bonus uir*).
[27] *fio, fieri, factus sum*: "be done", "be made", "happen", "take place".
[28] *essurio = esurio, -ire, –, -itum*: "be hungry".
[29] *sitio, -ire, -iui/-ii, –*: "be thirsty".
[30] *lepide* (adverb): "nicely", "agreeably", "excellently".
[31] *excuro, -are, -aui, -atum*: "take good care of", "attend to thoroughly".
[32] *incedo, -ere, -cessi, -cessum*: "walk", "proceed".
[33] *aha* (exclamation, here of reproof or protest).
[34] *quamquam*: "although".
[35] *fastidio, -ire, -iui/-ii, -itum*: "put on airs", "be haughty"; "feel disgust"; "be disdainful".
[36] *fui! fui!* (exclamations of disgust).
[37] *foeteo, -ere*: "stink", "have an unpleasant smell".
[38] *tuo' = tuos = tuus*.
[39] *mihi* is dative of person judging (a kind of dative of reference, see Bennett 188.2c.
[40] *sermo, -onis* (m.): "conversation" (the implication here is that Lysidamus's breath stinks when he talks).
[41] *res, rei* (f.): "thing", "circumstance", "situation", "matter", concern".
[42] *asto, -are, -stiti, —*: "stand still".
[43] πράγματά μοι παρέχεις (pronounced "*pragmata moi parecheis*"): "you're causing me trouble", "you're annoying me". Early second-century BCE Rome was a multicultural society, and Greek was commonly spoken by all social classes, including the enslaved.
[44] μέγα κακόν (pronounced "mega kakon"): "big trouble".
[45] *opinor, -ari, -atus sum*: "think", "suppose", "imagine".
[46] *resisto, -ere, -stiti, —*: "stand still".
[47] Ὦ Ζεῦ (pronounced "Oh Zeu"): "O Zeus".
[48] *potin = potisne < potis, pote* (adjective): "able", "capable"; "possible"; here supply *est*: "is it possible...?".
[49] *potin a me abeas*: "can't you keep away from me?".
[50] *uomo, -ere, -ui, -itum*: "vomit".

Lysidamus: mane. **Olympio:** quid est? quis hic est homo?

Lysidamus: eru'[51] sum. **Olympio:** quis erus? **Lysidamus:** quoius[52] tu seruo's.[53] **Olympio:** seruos ego? **Lysidamus:** ac meu'.[54] **Olympio:** non sum ego liber? 734-6

memento,[55] memento. **Lysidamus:** mane atque asta.[56] **Olympio:** omitte.[57]

Lysidamus: seruos sum tuós.[58] **Olympio:** optumest.[59] **Lysidamus:** opsecro[60] te,

Olympisce mi,[61] mi[62] pater,[63] mi patrone.[64] **Olympio:** em,[65]

sapis[66] sáne.[67] 740

Lysidamus: tuo'[68] sum equidem.[69] 740a

Olympio: quid mi[70] opust[71] seruo[72] tam nequam?[73]

Lysidamus: quid nunc? quam mox[74] recreas[75] me?

Olympio: cena[76] modo[77] si sit cocta.[78]

---

[51] *eru'* = *erus* < *erus, -i* (m.): "master (of slaves)".
[52] *quoius* = *cuius*.
[53] *seruo's* = *seruos es* = *seruus es*.
[54] *meu'* = *meus*.
[55] *memento* (2nd person singular future imperative active) < *memini, -isse*: "remember".
[56] *asto, -are, -stiti, —* (see note 42 on the facing page at line 728, III.vi).
[57] *omitto, -ere, -misi, -missum*: "let go"; "stop" (doing something).
[58] *tuos* = *tuus*.
[59] *optumest* = *optime est*: "that's better", "that's perfect".
[60] *opsecro* = *obsecro* < *obsecro, -are, -aui, -atum*: "beg", "implore"; *opsecro* (interjection): "please!".
[61] *Olympisce mi*: "my darling Olympio", "my little Olympio".
[62] *mi* (vocative masculine singular < *meus, -a, -um*).
[63] *pater, -tris* (m.): "father" (also used for someone respected like a father).
[64] *patronus, -i* (m.): "patron". "protector".
[65] *em*: "here/there you are!", "look!".
[66] *sapio, -ire, -iui/-ii, -itum*: "taste", "taste of"; "have good taste"; "show good sense".
[67] *sane* (adverb): "certainly".
[68] *tuo'* = *tuos* = *tuus*.
[69] *equidem*: "indeed", "truly".
[70] *mi* = *mihi*.
[71] *opust* = *opus est*: "there is need".
[72] *seruo* is ablative of means after *opus est* (see Bennett 218.2).
[73] *nequam* (indeclinable adjective): "worthless", "useless".
[74] *mox* (adverb): "soon".
[75] *recreo, -are, -aui, -atum*: "recreate", "make new", "restore"; "revive someone's spirits/mood".
[76] *cena, -ae* (f.): "dinner".
[77] *modo* (adverb): "just", "just now"; "only".
[78] *coquo, -ere, coxi, coctum*: "cook".

Lysidamus: hisce[79] ergo[80] abeant. **Olympio:** propere[81] cito,[82]   744-5
intro[83] ite et cito deproperate.[84]

ego iam intus[85] ero, facite cenam mihi ut ebria[86] sit.   746-7

sed lepide[87] nitideque[88] uolo, nil moror[89] barbarico[90] bliteo.[91]

stasne etiam? i sis,[92] ego hic[93] eo.[94] numquid[95] est ceterum[96]   749-50
quod morae[97] sit?[98]

Lysidamus: gladium Casinam intus ere ait,[99]

qui[100] me ac te interimat.[101]

Olympio: scio.[102] sic sine[103] ere;

nugas[104] agunt:[105] noui[106]

ego illas malas merces.[107]   754a

---

[79] *hisce* = *hi* (*hisce* is an alternative form of the nominative plural, used before vowels).
[80] *ergo* (adverb): "therefore".
[81] *propere* (adverb): "quickly", "speedily".
[82] *cito* (adverb): "quickly".
[83] *intro* (adverb): "inside", "into the house".
[84] *depropero, -are, –, –:* "make haste to complete" (*cenam* is an implied direct object).
[85] *intus* (adverb): "inside".
[86] *ebrius, -a, um:* "drunk"; "accompanied by drunkenness".
[87] *lepide* (adverb): "nicely", "agreeably", "excellently".
[88] *nitide* (adverb): "splendidly", "magnificently".
[89] *moror, -ari, -atus sum:* "delay"; *nil moror:* "I don't mind", "not care (about/for)".
[90] *barbaricus, -a, -um:* "barbarian", "foreign" (in Plautus, since the characters were supposed to be Greeks living in the Greek world, "barbarian" was used to refer to anyone not Greek, and usually meant "Roman" – apparently an endlessly funny joke to the Roman audiences).
[91] *bliteus, -a, -um:* "tasteless" (< *blitum, -i* (n.): "spinach").
[92] *sis* = *si uis*.
[93] *hīc* (adverb).
[94] *eo, -ere, -ui, -itum:* "have"; "dwell"; "live"; translate here: "stay".
[95] *numquid* (interrogative adverb): "surely... not?"
[96] *ceterum* (adverb): "else", "besides", "for the rest".
[97] *mora, -ae* (f.): "delay", "hindrance", "obstacle".
[98] *numquid est ceterum quod morae sit?:* "surely there's nothing else to delay you?"
[99] *ait* (3rd person singular present indicative active) < *aio* (defective verb): "say"; "say yes", "affirm".
[100] *qui* (an old ablative): "with which".
[101] *interemere* = *interimere* < *interimo, -ere, -emi, -emptum:* "do away with", "destroy".
[102] Since Olympio wasn't present when Pardalisca told Lysidamus about the sword, either he has heard from another source, or *scio* implies that Olympio knows now (because Lysidamus has just told him).
[103] *sino, -ere, siui, situm:* "allow".
[104] *nugae, -arum* (f. pl.): "nonsense".
[105] *nugas agunt:* "they're fooling (you)", "they're wasting their efforts".
[106] *nosco, -ere, noui, notum:* "know", "come to know".
[107] *merx, -cis* (f.): "commodity", "goods"; *mala merx:* "bad lot", "good-for-nothing".

quin[108] tu i modo mecum	755
domum. **Lysidamus:** at pol malum[109] metuo.[110]	755a
i tu modo, perspicito[111] prius[112]	
quid intus agatur.[113]	756a
Olympio: tam mihi mea uita	
tua quam tibi carast.[114]	757a
uerum[115] i modo. **Lysidamus:** si tu iubes,[116]	
em[117] ibitur[118] tecum.	758a

---

[108] *quin*: "no, really", "I mean!"; "actually", "in fact", "but"; "why... not?"
[109] *malum, -i* (n.): "misfortune", "misery".
[110] *metuo, -ere, metui, –*: "fear", "be afraid".
[111] *perspicito* (2nd person singular future imperative active) < *perspicio, -ere, -spexi, -spectum*: "look", "look into", "look at".
[112] *prius* (adverb): "first".
[113] *quid... agatur*: "what's going on".
[114] *carast = cara est < carus, -a, um*: "dear", "precious".
[115] *uerum* (conjunction): "but".
[116] *iubeo, -ere, iussi, iussum*: "order", "tell".
[117] *em*: "here/there you are!", "look!".
[118] *ibitur* (impersonal use of *eo, ire, iui/ii, itum*): translate here "I'll go".

ACTVS IV

IV.i PARDALISCA

Scene summary: *Pardalisca, alone on stage, laughs about how everyone in the house, including the hired caterers, are failing to get the meal ready, while Lysidamus is shouting at them to hurry up with the food. She says that Olympio is walking about in his wedding clothes, but that Cleustrata and Myrrhina are dressing up Chalinus as the bride Casina.*

Nec pol ego Nemeae[1] credo neque ego Olympiae[2]

neque usquam[3] ludos[4] tam festiuos[5] fieri[6]   760

quam hic[7] intus[8] fiunt ludi ludificabiles[9]

seni[10] nóstro et nostro Olympioni uilico.

omnes festinant[11] intus totis aedibus,[12]

senex ín culina[13] clamat,[14] hortatur[15] coquos:[16]

'quin[17] agitis hodie?[18] quin datis siquid[19] datis?   765

properate,[20] cenam[21] iám esse coctam[22] oportuit.'[23]

---

[1] *Nemeae* (locative) < *Nemea, -ae* (f.): "Nemea" (a Greek city about thirty km north of Argos; Nemea was the location of the prestigious Nemean games).
[2] *Olympiae* (locative) < *Olympia, -ae* (f.): "Olympia" (a region about twenty-five km east of the Greek city of Elis; Olympia was the location of the even more prestigious Olympic games).
[3] *usquam* (adverb): "anywhere".
[4] *ludus, -i* (m.): "game", "sport"; (plural): "festival", "public spectacles".
[5] *festiuus, -a, -um*: "festive", "enjoyable".
[6] *fio, fieri, factus sum*: "be done", "be made", "happen", "take place".
[7] *hīc* (adverb).
[8] *intus* (adverb): "inside".
[9] *ludificabilis, -e* (adjective found only in this play): "making a game (of)", "making a mockery (of)" (+ dative of person mocked).
[10] *senex, senis* (adjective and noun): "old"; "old man".
[11] *festino, -are, -aui, -atum*: "hurry".
[12] *aedibus* (ablative of place where, see Bennett 228.1d) < *aedis/aedes, -is* (f.): "building", "house" (often used in the plural, as here).
[13] *culina, -ae* (f.): "kitchen".
[14] *clamo, -are, -aui, -atum*: "shout", "complain loudly".
[15] *hortor, -ari, -tatus sum*: "urge", "encourage".
[16] *coquos = coquus < coquus, -i* (m.): "cook".
[17] *quin*: "no, really", "I mean!"; "actually", "in fact", "but"; "why... not?"
[18] *quin agitis hodie*: "why aren't you doing anything today?"
[19] *siquis, siquid* (indefinite pronoun): "if anyone / anything".
[20] *propero, -are, -aui, -atum*: "hurry", "be quick".
[21] *cena, -ae* (f.): "dinner".
[22] *coquo, -ere, coxi, coctum*: "cook".
[23] *oportet, oportere, oportuit*, – (impersonal verb): "it is right", "it is fitting".

uilicus is autem cum corona,[24] candide[25]
uestitus,[26] lautus[27] exornatusque[28] ambulat.[29]
illaec[30] autem[31] armigerum[32] ilico[33] exornant duae
quem[34] dent pro[35] Casina nuptum[36] nostro uilico.   770
sed nimium[37] lepide[38] dissimulant,[39] quasi[40] nil sciant
fore[41] huiius[42] quod futurumst;[43] digne[44] autem coqui
nimi'[45] lepide ei rei[46] dant operam,[47] ne cenet[48] senex,
aulas[49] peruortunt,[50] ignem[51] restinguont[52] aqua:
illarum oratu[53] faciunt; illae autem senem   775
cupiunt[54] extrudere[55] incenatum[56] ex aedibus,

---

[24] *corona, -ae* (f.): "wreath", "garland".
[25] *candide* (adverb): "in dazzling white".
[26] *uestio, -ire, -iui/-ii, -itum*: "dress", "clothe".
[27] *lauo, -are/-ere, laui, lauatum/lautum*: "wash", "bathe".
[28] *exorno, -are, -aui, -atum*: "deck out", "adorn".
[29] *ambulo, -are, -aui, -atum*: "walk".
[30] *illaec = illae*.
[31] *autem* (adverb): "on the other hand", "but", "moreover", "and in fact".
[32] *armiger, armigeri* (m.): "armour-bearer", "shield-bearer" (referring to Chalinus, who served in this capacity under the son of Lysidamus and Cleustrata, see line 55 in the prologue).
[33] *ilico* (adverb): "on the spot", "in that very place"; "at once", "there and then".
[34] *quem = ut eum* (relative clause of purpose, see Bennett 282.2).
[35] *pro* (preposition + ablative): "before", "in front of"; "on behalf of", instead of".
[36] *nuptum* (supine < *nubo, -ere, -nupsi, nuptum*: "marry", "be married"); *dent nuptum*: "they'll give in marriage".
[37] *nimium* (adverb): "too much", "excessively".
[38] *lepide* (adverb): "nicely", "agreeably", "excellently".
[39] *dissimulo, -are, -aui, -atum*: "disguise"; "conceal".
[40] *quasi* (conjunction): "as if", "as though", "just like" (+ subjunctive).
[41] *fore = futurum esse*: "(that) there will be".
[42] *huiius = huius* (genitive of the whole after *nil*; *huiius* is the antecedent of *quod*).
[43] *futurumst = futurum est* (active periphrastic, see Bennett 115); *quasi nil sciant fore huiius quod futurumst*: "just as though they didn't know anything about what's about to happen".
[44] *digne* (adverb): "worthily", "appropriately".
[45] *nimi' = nimis* (adverb): "too much", "excessively".
[46] *res, rei* (f.): "thing", "circumstance", "situation", "matter", concern".
[47] *operam dare*: "take care", "give attention"; "help" (+ dative).
[48] *ceno, -are, -aui, -atum*: "eat a meal", "dine".
[49] *aulas = ollas < olla, -ae* (f.): "pot".
[50] *peruortunt = peruertunt < peruerto, -ere, -ti, -sum*: "overturn", "throw down".
[51] *ignis, -is* (m.): "fire".
[52] *restinguont = restinguunt < restinguo, -ere, -nxi, -nctum*: "put out", "quench", "extinguish".
[53] *oratus, -ūs* (m.): "request" (*oratu* is ablative of cause, see Bennett 219).
[54] *cupio, -ere, -iui, -itum*: "wish", "desire".
[55] *extrudo, -ere, -si, -sum*: "drive away".
[56] *incenatus, -a, -um*: "not having eaten", "hungry".

ut ipsae solae uentris⁵⁷ distendant⁵⁸ suos.
noui⁵⁹ ego illas ambestrices:⁶⁰ corbitam⁶¹ cibi⁶²
comesse⁶³ possunt. sed aperitur⁶⁴ ostium.⁶⁵

---

57 *uentrīs = uentrēs < uenter, -tris* (m.): "stomach", "belly".
58 *distendo, -ere, -di, -tum*: "stretch out", "swell out", "fill".
59 *nosco, -ere, noui, notum*: "know", "come to know".
60 *ambestrix, -tricis* (f.): "gluttonous woman".
61 *corbita, -ae* (f.): "cargo ship"
62 *cibus, -i* (m.): "food".
63 *comedo, comesse/comedere, -edi, -es(s)um/-estum*: "eat up", "consume".
64 *aperio, -irir, -ui, apertum*: "open".
65 *ostium, -ii* (n.): "door".

IV.ii LYSIDAMVS, PARDALISCA

Scene summary: *Lysidamus, having given up on the hoped-for meal, tells Cleustrata that he's going to eat at the farm, to which he's decided to accompany Olympio and his new bride Casina. He accuses Pardalisca, who is still there, of spying on him.*

Lysidamus: Si sapitis,[1] uxor, uos tamen cenabitis,[2]   780
cena[3] ubi erit cocta;[4] égo ruri[5] cenauero.
nam nouom maritum[6] | et nouam[7] nuptam[8] uolo
rus[9] prosequi,[10] noui[11] hominum mores[12] maleficos,[13]
nequis[14] eam abripiat.[15] facite uostro animo uolup.[16]
sed properate[17] istum atque istam[18] actutum[19] emittere,[20]   785
tandem ut ueniamus luci;[21] ego cras hic[22] ero.
cras uero, uxor, ego tamen conuiuium.[23]

Pardalisca: fit[24] quod futurum[25] dixi: incenatum[26] senem

---

[1] *sapio, -ire, -iui/-ii, -itum*: "taste", "taste of"; "have good taste"; "show good sense".
[2] *ceno, -are, -aui, -atum*: "eat a meal", "dine".
[3] *cena, -ae* (f.): "dinner".
[4] *coquo, -ere, coxi, coctum*: "cook".
[5] *ruri = rure* (locative case) < *rus, ruris* (n.): "the country"; "the farm".
[6] *maritus, -i* (m.): "married man", "husband".
[7] *nouam* could be interpreted both as "new (bride)" or as "strange", given what the audience knows about the bride.
[8] *nupta, -ae* (f.): "bride".
[9] *rus* here is the accusative of limit of motion, see Bennett 182.
[10] *prosequor, -i, -secutus sum*: "follow", "accompany".
[11] *nosco, -ere, noui, notum*: "know", "come to know".
[12] *mos, moris* (m.): "custom", "it", "behaviour".
[13] *maleficus, -a, -um*: "wicked", "criminal".
[14] *nequis = ne quis*.
[15] *abripio, -ere, -ripui, -reptum*: "take forcibly away", "carry off".
[16] *uolup* (adverb): "agreeably", "delightfully"; *uolup facere* (+ dative): "cause pleasure (to)"; *facite uostro animo uolup*: "have a good time!".
[17] *propero, -are, -aui, -atum*: "hurry", "be quick".
[18] *istum atque istam* (refers to Olympio and Casina, respectively).
[19] *actutum* (adverb): "immediately".
[20] *emitto, -ere, -misi, -missum*: "send out", "send forth".
[21] *luci* (adverb): "by daylight".
[22] *hīc* (adverb).
[23] *conuiuium, -ii* (n.): "banquet".
[24] *fio, fieri, factus sum*: "be done", "be made", "happen", "take place".
[25] *futurum = futurum esse*.
[26] *incenatus, -a, -um*: "not having eaten", "hungry".

foras[27] extrudunt[28] mulieres.[29] **Lysidamus:** quid tu hic agis?

Pardalisca: ego eo quo[30] me ipsa[31] misit. **Lysidamus:** 790
ueron?[32] **Pardalisca:** serio.[33]

Lysidamus: quid[34] hic speculare?[35] **Pardalisca:** nil equidem speculor. **Lysidamus:** abi:

tu hic cunctas,[36] intus[37] alii festinant.[38] **Pardalisca:** eo. —

Lysidamus: abi hinc[39] sis[40] ergo,[41] pessumarum pessuma.[42]

iamne abiit illaec?[43] dicere hic quiduis[44] licet.

qui amat, tamen hercle, si essurit,[45] nullum essurit. 795

sed eccúm[46] progreditur[47] cum corona[48] et lampade[49]

meu'[50] socius,[51] compar,[52] commaritus[53] uilicus.

---

[27] *foras* (adverb): "out of doors"; translate here: "away from our home".
[28] *extrudo, -ere, -si, -sum*: "drive away".
[29] *mulier, mulieris* (f.): "woman".
[30] *quo* (adverb): "where", "to where".
[31] *ipsa* (refers to Cleustrata).
[32] *ueron = uerone; uero* (adverb): truly", "certainly".
[33] *serio* (adverb): "seriously", "honestly".
[34] *quid*: "why?".
[35] *speculor, -ari, -atus sum*: "watch", "look at"; "spy out".
[36] *cuncto, -are, – , – = cunctor, -ari, -atus sum*: "delay", "linger"; "hesitate".
[37] *intus* (adverb): "inside".
[38] *festino, -are, -aui, -atum*: "hurry".
[39] *hinc* (adverb): "from this place".
[40] *sis = si uis*.
[41] *ergo* (adverb): "therefore".
[42] *pessumarum pessuma = pessimarum pessima*.
[43] *illaec = illae*.
[44] *quiuis, quaeuis, quiduis*: "whoever/whatever (one) pleases".
[45] *essurio = esurio, -ire, – , -itum*: "be hungry".
[46] *eccum = ecce + eum* or *ecce + hum (= hunc)*.
[47] *progredior, -i, -gressus sum*: "come / go forth", "advance", "proceed".
[48] *corona, -ae* (f.): "wreath", "garland".
[49] *lampas, -adis* (f.): "torch".
[50] *meu' = meus*.
[51] *socius, -ii/-i* (m.): "companion", "partner", "accomplice", "ally".
[52] *compar, -paris* (m./f.): "partner", "comrade".
[53] *commaritus, -i* (m.) (word found only in this play < *cum+maritus*): "co-husband", "fellow husband".

IV.iii OLYMPIO, LYSIDAMVS

Scene summary: *Olympio sings the traditional Greek wedding song, and then he and Lysidamus complain about how long the food preparation is taking. To distract themselves from their hunger, the two sing the Greek wedding song together.*

Olympio: Age[1] tibicen,[2] dum illam educunt[3] huc nouam nuptam[4] foras,[5]

suaui[6] cantu[7] concelebra[8] omnem hanc plateam[9] hymenaeo[10] mi.[11]

Lysidamus et Olympio: hymen hymenaee o hymen![12]   800

Lysidamus: quid agis,[13] mea salus?[14] **Olympio:** esurio[15] hercle, atque adeo[16] hau[17] salubriter.[18]

Lysidamus: at ego amó. **Olympio:** at ego hercle nihili facio.[19] tibi amor pro[20] cibost,[21]

mihi iaiunitate[22] iam dudum[23] intestina[24] murmurant.[25]

---

[1] *age* (< *ago, -ere, egi, actum*): "come on", "go on".
[2] *tibicen, -inis* (m.): "performer on the tibia" (a tibia was a double reed instrument, perhaps like an oboe).
[3] *educo, -ere, eduxi, eductum*: "lead out"; "bring up", "rear".
[4] *nupta, -ae* (f.): "bride".
[5] *foras* (adverb): "out of doors".
[6] *suauis, -e* (adjective): "sweet", "agreeable".
[7] *cantus, -ūs* (m.): "song", "tune", "music".
[8] *concelebro, -are, -aui, -atum*: "celebrate in large numbers"; "fill (with singing)".
[9] *platea, -ae* (f.): "street".
[10] *hymenaeus, -i* (m.): "wedding song" (see note 12 below at line 800, IV.iii).
[11] *mi = mihi*. *mihi* is dative of reference (see Bennett 188).
[12] *hymen hymenaee o hymen* was the traditional Greek wedding song in honour of Hymen (Ὑμήν), a.k.a. Hymenaeus (Ὑμέναιος), the god of marriage.
[13] *quid agis*: "how are you?".
[14] *salus, -utis*: "health"; "safety"; translate here: "saviour".
[15] *essurio = esurio, -ire, –, -itum*: "be hungry".
[16] *adeo* (adverb): "indeed", "even".
[17] *hau = haud*: "not at all".
[18] *salubriter* (adverb): "healthily". There is a play on words with *salus* and *salubriter*, which have the same root.
[19] *nihili facere*: "to consider unimportant"; "not to care".
[20] *pro* (preposition + ablative): "before", "in front of"; "on behalf of", instead of".
[21] *cibost = cibo est < cibus, -i* (m.): "food".
[22] *iaiunitate = ieiunitate < ieiunitas, -tatis* (f.): "hunger", "emptiness of the stomach".
[23] *iam dudum* (adverbial): "a while ago", "formerly".
[24] *intestina, -orum* (n. pl.): "intestines", "guts".
[25] *murmuro, -are, -aui, -atum*: "rumble"; "murmur".

Lysidamus: nam quid[26] illaéc[27] nunc tam diu intus[28] remorantur[29] remeligines?[30]

quasi[31] ob industriam,[32] quanto[33] ego plus propero,[34] procedit[35] minus.   805

Olympio: quid si etiam <suffundam>[36] hymenaeum,[37] si qui[38] citius[39] prodeant?[40]

Lysidamus: censeo,[41] et ego te adiutabo[42] in nuptiis[43] communibus.[44]

Lysidamus et Olympio: hymen hymenaee o hymen!

Lysidamus: perii[45] hercle ego miser! dirrumpi[46] cantando[47] hymenaeum licet:[48]

illo morbo[49] quo dirrumpi cupio, non est copiae.[50]   810

---

[26] *quid*: "why?".
[27] *illaec = illae*.
[28] *intus* (adverb): "inside".
[29] *remoror, -ari, -atus sum*: "delay".
[30] *remeligo, -inis* (f.): "delayer", "dawdler".
[31] *quasi* (adverb): "as if", "just like".
[32] *industria, -ae* (f.): "activity", "industry", "purposefulness"; *ob industriam*: "on purpose".
[33] *quanto* (adverb): "by how much more", "the more".
[34] *propero, -are, -aui, -atum*: "hurry", "be quick".
[35] *procedo, -ere, -cessi, -cessum*: "advance", "go forth", "go"; translate here as impersonal: "[less] progress is made", "[the less] anything is done".
[36] *suffundo, -ere, -udi, -usum*: "pour on/in"; "cause to well up"; translate here: "sing".
[37] The manuscript tradition includes a corrupted first half of this line, which Lindsay's text retains: *quid si etiam †sit offendam hymenaeum*. Since it doesn't make much sense, I've replaced it with Leo's emendation: *quid si etiam suffundam hymenaeum* (Leo 1958: 259).
[38] *qui* (an old ablative); *si qui*: "if in any way", "if by any means".
[39] *citius* (comparative adverb < *cito*): "more quickly".
[40] *prodeo, -ire, -iui/-ii. -itum*: "come out".
[41] *censeo, -ere, censui, censitum*: "think", "suppose", "recommend"; translate here: "good idea".
[42] *adiuto, -are, -aui, -atum*: "help", "assist".
[43] *nuptiae, -arum* (f. pl.): "marriage", "wedding", "wedding festivities / rituals".
[44] *communis, -e* (adjective): "public"; "shared"; "joint".
[45] *pereo, -ire, periui/-ii, peritum*: "die"; "be ruined"; "be lost".
[46] *dirrumpo, -ere, -upi, -uptum*: "cause to burst"; passive: "burst"; to allow for the double entendre, translate *dirrumpi... licet* here as "I can wear myself out".
[47] *canto, -are, -aui, -atum*: "sing". The gerund *cantando* is ablative of means (see Bennett 338.4a).
[48] *licere, licuit, licitum est* (impersonal): "it is allowed", "it is permitted".
[49] *morbus, -i* (m.): "sickness"; "affliction"; "complaint" (referring here to Lysidamus's sexual frustration).
[50] *copia, -ae* (f.): "supply"; "opportunity"; *non est copiae*: "there isn't any opportunity"; translate *illo morbo quo dirrumpi cupio, non est copiae*: "I'm not getting the opportunity to wear myself out the way I want to".

Olympio: edepol ne[51] tu, sí equos[52] esses, esses indomabilis.[53]

Lysidamus: quo argumento?[54] **Olympio:** nimi'[55] tenax[56] es. **Lysidamus:** num[57] me expertu'[58] uspiam?[59]

Olympio: di melius faciant![60] sed crepuit[61] ostium,[62] exitur[63] foras.

Lysidamus: di hercle me cupiunt seruatum.[64]

---

[51] *ne* (interjection followed by a personal or demonstrative pronoun): "really", "indeed".
[52] *equos = equus*.
[53] *indomabilis, -e* (adjective): "untamable", "out of control".
[54] *quo argumento*: "how do you make that out?".
[55] *nimi' = nimis* (adverb): "too much", "excessively".
[56] *tenax, -acis* (adjective): "persistent", "headstrong".
[57] *num* (interrogative): "it isn't possible that...?", "can it be that...?".
[58] *expertu' = expertus es < experior, -iri, expertus sum*: "test", "put to the test", "find out (by experience)".
[59] *uspiam* (adverb): "somewhere".
[60] *di melius faciant!*: "may the gods grant a better outcome!".
[61] *crepo, -are, crepui, –*: "make a noise", "creak".
[62] *ostium, -ii* (n.): "door".
[63] *exitur*: (impersonal) "someone's coming out".
[64] *seruo, -are, -aui, -atum*: "save".

IV.iv CHALINVS, PARDALISCA, OLYMPIO, LYSIDAMVS, CLEVSTRATA

Scene summary: *Cleustrata and Pardalisca lead out Chalinus, who is dressed up as Casina in bridal clothes and heavily veiled. Pardalisca repeats mock-ritual words of advice to the bride, advising her to always dominate her husband. The two women go back into the house, and Lysidamus and Olympio quarrel over which of them gets to hold Casina (as they believe) first. The cross-dressed Chalinus uses his feet and elbow to fight back from Olympio's groping. The two men nevertheless lead her off without suspecting anything.*

Chalinus: iam oboluit[1] Casinus procul.	814a
Pardalisca: Sensim[2] super[3] attolle[4] limen[5] pedes,[6] noua nupta;[7]	815-6
sospes[8] iter[9] incipe[10] hoc, uti[11] uiro tuo	
semper sis superstes,[12]	
tuaque ut potior[13] pollentia[14] sit uincasque uirum uictrixque[15] sies,[16]	819-20
tua uox[17] superet tuomque[18] imperium:[19] uir te uestiat,[20] [tu] uirum despolies.[21]	821-2

---

[1] *oboleo, -ere, -ui, –*: "give off an odour".
[2] *sensim* (adverb): "gently", "carefully".
[3] *super* (preposition): "over".
[4] *attollo, -ere, – , –*: "raise", "lift".
[5] *limen, -inis* (n.): "threshold".
[6] *pes, pedis* (m.): "foot".
[7] *nupta, -ae* (f.): "bride".
[8] *sospes, -itis* (adjective): "fortunate"; "auspicious".
[9] *iter, itineris* (n.): "journey".
[10] *incipio, -ere, -cepi, -ceptum*: "begin", "start".
[11] *uti = ut.*
[12] *superstes, -itis* (adjective): "standing over" (as a victor over the body of an enemy); "surviving" (i.e. surviving the death of a relative; + dative of deceased person); *superstes* may mean dominance over a defeated husband here, or may refer to the bride outliving her husband.
[13] *potior, potius* (comparative adjective): "stronger", "better"; "better entitled to", "having greater control over" (+ genitive).
[14] *pollentia, -ae* (f.): "power".
[15] *uictrix, -icis* (f.): "(female) victor", "(female) conqueror".
[16] *sies = sis.*
[17] *uox, uocis* (f.): "voice".
[18] *tuom = tuum.*
[19] *imperium, -ii* (n.): "right to command", "dominion".
[20] *uestio, -ire, -iui/-ii, -itum*: "clothe", "provide with clothing".
[21] *despolio, -are, -aui, -atum*: "rob", "plunder".

noctuque[22] et diu[23] ut uiro subdola[24] sis,

opsecro,[25] memento.[26]

Olympio: malo[27] máxumo[28] suo[29] hercle ilicó,[30] ubi tantillum[31] peccassit.[32] 825

Lysidamus: tace. **Olympio:** non taceo. **Lysidamus:** quae res?[33] **Olympio:** mala malae male monstrat.[34]

Lysidamus: facies tun[35] hanc rem mi[36] ex parata[37] inparatam?[38] id

quaerunt,[39] id uolunt, haec ut infecta[40] faciant.

Pardalisca: age[41] Olympio, quando uis, uxo-

rem accipe hanc ab nobis. 830

Olympio: date ergo,[42] daturae si umquam estis[43] hodie uxorem.

Lysidamus: abite intro. **Pardalisca:** amabo, integrae[44] atque imperitae[45] huic

---

[22] *noctu* (adverb): "by night".
[23] *diu* (adverb): "by day".
[24] *subdolus, -a, -um*: "cunning", "sly", "sneaky".
[25] *opsecro* = *obsecro* < *obsecro, -are, -aui, -atum*: "beg", "implore"; *opsecro* (interjection): "please!".
[26] *memento* (2nd person singular future imperative active) < *memini, -isse*: "remember".
[27] *malum, -i* (n.): "misfortune", "misery".
[28] *maxumo* = *maximo*.
[29] *malo maxumo suo* is ablative of price (see Bennett 225), or more specifically ablative of the penalty (see Allen & Greenough 353). Translate here: "It'll cost her major misfortune", "she'll get the worst of it".
[30] *ilico* (adverb): "on the spot", "in that very place"; "at once", "there and then".
[31] *tantillum -i* (n.): "even a tiny bit", "ever so little".
[32] *peccassit* = *peccauerit* < *pecco, -are, -aui, -atus*: "do wrong", "blunder", "screw up".
[33] *res, rei* (f.): "thing", "circumstance", "situation", "matter", concern".
[34] *monstro, -are, -aui, -atum*: "show", "advise", "instruct" (+ dative of person advised/instructed).
[35] *tun* = *tune*.
[36] *mi* = *mihi*.
[37] *paratus, -a, -um*: "prepared".
[38] *inparatam* = *imparatam* < *imparatus, -a, -um*: "unprepared"; *facies tun hanc rem mi ex parata inparatam?*: "are you going to undo all my plans?"
[39] *quaero, -ere, quaesiui, quaesitum*: "ask", "inquire", "seek".
[40] *infectus, -a, -um*: "undone", "not accomplished".
[41] *age* (< *ago, -ere, egi, actum*): "come on", "go on".
[42] *ergo* (adverb): "therefore".
[43] *daturae... estis* (active periphrastic, see Bennett 115).
[44] *integer, -gra, -grum*: "untouched"; "virgin".
[45] *imperitus, -a, -um*: "inexperienced".

impercito.[46] **Olympio:** futurum est.

Pardalisca: ualete. **Olympio:** ite iám. **Lysidamus:** ite. **Cleustrata:** iam ualete. —

Lysidamus: iamne apscessit[47] uxor? **Olympio:** domist,[48] ne   835
time. **Lysidamus:** euax![49]

nunc pol demum[50] ego sum liber.

meum corculum,[51] melculum,[52] uerculum.[53] **Olympio:** heus[54] tu,

malo,[55] si sapis,[56] cauebis;[57]

meast[58] haec. **Lysidamus:** scio, sed meus fructust[59] prior.[60]

Olympio: tene hanc lampadém.[61] **Lysidamus:** immo[62] ego   840
hanc tenebo.

Venu' multipotens,[63] bona multa mihi

dedisti, huiius[64] quom[65] copiam[66] mi dedisti. **Olympio:** o

corpusculum[67] malacum![68]

mea uxorcula[69] — quae res?

---

[46] *impercito* (2nd person singular future imperative active) < *imperco, -ere, – , –:* "spare", "be gentle with" (+ dative).
[47] *apscessit = abscessit < abscedo, -ere, -cessi, -cessum:* "go away", "get away".
[48] *domist = domi est.*
[49] *euax!:* "hurray!", "excellent!".
[50] *demum* (adverb): "finally", "at last".
[51] *corculum, -i* (n.): "little heart".
[52] *melculum, -i* (n.): "little honey".
[53] *uerculum, -i* (n.): "little springtime", "fresh young thing".
[54] *heus:* "hey!", "listen!" (used to try to get someone's attention).
[55] *malo* is dative or ablative after *cauebis.*
[56] *sapio, -ire, -iui/-ii, -itum:* "taste", "taste of"; "have good taste"; "show good sense".
[57] *caueo, -ere, caui, cautum:* "be on one's guard against", "look out for" (+ dative/ablative).
[58] *meast = mea est.*
[59] *fructust = fructus est < fructus, -ūs* (m.): "enjoyment".
[60] *prior, prius* (comparative adjective): "first", "before".
[61] *lampas, -adis* (f.): "torch".
[62] *immo* (adverb): "on the contrary".
[63] *multipotens, -ntis* (adjective): "very powerful".
[64] *huiius = huius.*
[65] *quom = cum.*
[66] *copia, -ae* (f.): "supply"; "opportunity".
[67] *corpusculum, -i* (n.): "little body".
[68] *malacus, -a, -um:* "soft", "supple"; *corpusculum malacum* is accusative of exclamation, see Bennett 183).
[69] *uxorcula, -ae* (f.): "little wife".

Lysidamus: quid est? **Olympio:** institit[70] plantam[71]   845

quasi luca bos.[72] **Lysidamus:** tace sis,

nebula[73] haud est mollis[74] aeque atque[75] huius †est pectus†.[76]

Olympio: edepol papillam[77] bellulam[78] — ei[79] misero mihi!

Lysidamus: quid est? **Olympio:** péctus mi[80] icit[81] non cubito,[82] uerum ariete.[83]

Lysidamus: quid[84] tu ergo[85] hanc, quaeso,[86] tractas[87] tam   850
dura manu?

at mihi, qui belle[88] hanc tracto, non bellum[89] facit.

uah![90] **Olympio:** quid negotist?[91] **Lysidamus:** opsecro,[92] ut ualentulast![93]

paene exposiuit[94] cubito. **Olympio:** cubitum[95] ergo ire uolt.

Lysidamus: quin[96] imus ergo? **Olympio:** i, belle belliatula.[97]

---

[70] *insto, -are, institi, –*: "stand on"; "insist".
[71] *planta, -ae* (f.): "sole of the foot"; translate *institit plantam*: "she stomped on my foot".
[72] *luca bos, lucae bouis* (f.): "Lucanian cow" = "elephant".
[73] *nebula, -ae* (f.): "cloud".
[74] *mollis, -e*: "soft".
[75] *aeque atque*: "as... as", "as much as".
[76] *pectus,-oris* (n.): "chest"; "breast".
[77] *papilla, -ae* (f.): "breast".
[78] *bellulus, -a, -um*: "pretty", "lovely", "beautiful"; *papillam bellulam* is accusative of exclamation, see Bennett 183).
[79] *ei* (exclamation): "oh!"
[80] *mi = mihi*.
[81] *icio, -ere, ici, ictum*: "strike with a weapon".
[82] *cubitum, -i* (n.): "elbow".
[83] *aries, -ietis* (m.): "ram", "male sheep"; translate here: "battering ram".
[84] *quid*: "why?".
[85] *ergo* (adverb): "therefore".
[86] *quaeso*: "I beg", "please" (< *quaeso, -ere, -iui/-ii*: "seek", "beg").
[87] *tracto, -are, -aui, -atum*: "drag"; "handle".
[88] *belle* (adverb < *bellus, -a, -um*): "prettily","well", "politely .
[89] *bellum, -i* (n.): "war" (this is a pun on *belle*).
[90] *uah* (exclamation of surprise, joy, anger, etc.).
[91] *negotist = negotii est < negotium, -ii* (n.): "business"; *negotii* is a partitive genitive; translate *quid negotist*: "what's the matter?".
[92] *opsecro = obsecro < obsecro, -are, -aui, -atum*: "beg", "implore"; *opsecro* (interjection): "please!".
[93] *ualentulast = ualentula est < ualentulus, -a, -um* (diminutive < *ualens, -ntis*): "sturdy", "strong"; *ut ualentulast*: "how strong she is!", "what a feisty little thing she is!".
[94] *exposiuit = exposuit < expono, -ere, -posui, -positum*: "send (someone) sprawling", "lay (someone) out".
[95] *cubitum* (supine < *cubo, -are, -aui, -atum*: "lie down", "go to bed").
[96] *quin*: "no, really", "I mean!"; "actually", "in fact", "but"; "why... not?".
[97] *belliatulus, -a, -um*: "pretty little".

ACTVS V

V.i MYRRHINA, PARDALISCA, CLEVSTRATA

Scene summary: *Pardalisca, Myrrhina and Cleustrata, having enjoyed the wedding feast without the men, come outside and laugh about the trick they've played on Lysidamus and Olympio. Pardalisca is told to position herself so she can spy on the next door house without being seen.*

Myrrhina: Acceptae[1] bene et commode[2] eximus intus[3]   855

ludos[4] uisere[5] huc in uiam nuptialis.[6]

numquam ecastor ullo die risi[7] adaeque,[8]

neque hoc quod relicuom[9] est plus risuram opinor.[10]

Pardalisca: lubet[11] Chalinum quid agat scire,[12] nouom[13] nuptum[14] cum nouo marito.[15]

Myrrhina: nec fallaciam[16] astutiorem[17] ullu'[18] fecit   860

poeta[19] atque[20] ut[21] haec est fabre[22] facta ab nobis.

Cleustrata: optunso[23] ore[24] nunc peruelim[25] progrediri[26]

---

[1] *Acceptae*: "having been entertained".
[2] *commode* (adverb): "properly", "conveniently".
[3] *intus* (adverb): "inside"; translate here: "from inside".
[4] *ludus, -i* (m.): "game", "sport"; (plural): "festival", "public spectacles"; translate here: "fun", "entertainment".
[5] *uiso, -ere, uisi, uisum*: "go to see", "go to look at"; *uisere* is infinitive of purpose; see Allen & Greenough 460c.
[6] *nuptialis = nuptiales < nuptialis, -e*: "wedding-related", "nuptial".
[7] *rideo, -ere, risi, risum*: "laugh".
[8] *adaeque* (adverb): "equally", "as... as".
[9] *relicuom = reliquum < reliquus, -a, -um*: "remaining", "still to come".
[10] *est plus risuram opinor*: "I think/imagine I'll laugh at even more".
[11] *lubet = libet < libet, libuit, libitus est* (impersonal verb): "it is pleasing".
[12] *lubet Chalinum quid agat scire*: "I'd love to know what Chalinus is doing" (the accusative *Chalinum* is the subject of *agat*, see MacCary and Willcock 1976: 194).
[13] *nouom = nouum*.
[14] *nuptus, -i* (m.): "male bride", "boy-bride".
[15] *maritus, -i* (m.): "married man", "husband".
[16] *fallacia, -ae* (f.): "deception", "trick".
[17] *astutior, -ius* (comparative < *astutus, -a, -um*: "sly", "clever").
[18] *ullu' = ullus*.
[19] *poeta, -ae* (m.): "poet"; "playwright".
[20] *atque* (after words of comparison): "as", "than".
[21] *ut*: "how".
[22] *fabre* (adverb): "skillfully", "ingeniously".
[23] *optunso = obtunso < obtundo, -ere, -udi, -usum/-unsum*: "beat", "batter", "strike".
[24] *os, oris* (n.): "mouth", "face".
[25] *peruolo, -uelle, -uolui, –*: "wish greatly".
[26] *progrediri = progredi < progredior, -i, -gressus sum*: "come / go forth", "advance", "proceed".

senem, quo[27] senex nequior[28] nullu'[29] uiuit.

* * * * nisi illum quidem

nequiorem esse arbitrare[30] qui praebet[31] illi locum.[32]   865

* * * * <te> nunc praesidem[33]

uolo hic, Pardalisca, esse,[34] qui hinc exeat

eum ut * * ludibrio[35] eas.[36] **Pardalisca:** lubens[37] fecero

* * et solens.[38]

Cleustrata: * * spectato[39] hinc omnia: intus quid agant   870-1

<loquere. **Myrrhina:**> pone[40] med,[41] amabo.[42] **Cleustrata:** et ibi licet[43] audacius[44]

quae uelis libere proloqui.[45] **Myrrhina:** tace,

nostra foris[46] crepuit.[47]

---

[27] *quo* is ablative of comparison after *nequior* (see Bennett 217.1).
[28] *nequior, nequioris* (comparative adjective < indeclinable adjective *nequam*): "more worthless".
[29] *nullu'* = *nullus*.
[30] *arbitrare* (2nd person singular present indicative < *arbitror, -ari, -atus sum*: "think").
[31] *praebeo, -ere, -ui, -itum*: "offer", "supply", provide".
[32] *locus, -i* (m.): "place".
[33] *praesides, -idis* (m./f.): "guardian".
[34] <*te*> *nunc praesidem uolo hic... esse*: "now I want you to be in charge here".
[35] *ludibrium, -ii* (n.): "mockery", laughing-stock". *ludibrio* is a dative of purpose with *eas* (see Bennett 191).
[36] *eum... ludibrio eas*: "you can make fun of him".
[37] *lubens* = *libens, -ntis*: "pleased", "willing" (often with adverbial sense).
[38] *soleo, -ere, -ui, -itum*: "be accustomed", "be used"; translate *solens*: "as always".
[39] *spectato* (2nd person singular future imperative active) < *specto, -are, -aui, -atum*: "look at", "watch".
[40] *pone* = *postne*: "behind".
[41] *med* = *me*.
[42] *amabo*: "please", "I beg" (< *amo, -are, -aui, -atum*).
[43] *licere, licuit, licitum est* (impersonal): "it is allowed", "it is permitted".
[44] *audacius* (comparative adverb): "more boldly".
[45] *proloquor, -i, -locutus sum*: "speak out", "express".
[46] *foris, -is* (f.): "door", "gate".
[47] *crepo, -are, crepui, –*: "make a noise", "creak".

V.ii OLYMPIO, MYRRHINA, CLEVSTRATA, PARDALISCA

Scene summary: *Myrrhina, Cleustrata, and Pardalisca are spying on Alcesimus's house when Olympio comes out, very upset and talking aloud about the humiliation he experienced in the bridal bedroom. Pardalisca, urged on by Cleustrata, asks him to tell her all about it. Partly due to the fact that parts of the Latin text are missing, and partly due to Olympio's overwrought emotional state, his narrative is disjointed, but he talks about something huge that he thought was the sword, except that it wasn't cold. He says he tried to kiss her, but found himself kissing a bristly beard. Then he says that his bride kicked and punched him, so he ran out of the room, having left his cloak behind.*

Olympio: Neque quo[1] fugiam[2] neque ubi lateam[3] neque hoc dedecu'[4] quomodo[5] celem[6]   875

scio, tantum[7] erus[8] atque ego flagitio[9] superauimu'[10] nuptiis nostris,[11]

ita nunc pudeo[12] atque ita nunc paueo[13] atque ita inridiculo[14] sumus ambo.[15]

sed ego insipiens[16] noua nunc facio: pudet[17] quem priu'[18] non puditumst umquam.[19]

---

[1] *quo* (adverb): "where", "to which (place)".
[2] *fugio, -ere, fugi, fugitum*: "run away".
[3] *lateo, -ere, -ui, –*: "hide".
[4] *dedecu' = dedecus < dedecus, -oris* (n.): "shame", "dishonour".
[5] *quomodo* (adverb): "how", "in what manner", "in what way".
[6] *celo, -are, -aui, -atum*: "conceal", "keep secret".
[7] *tantum* (adverb): "so much", "to such a degree".
[8] *erus, -i* (m.): "master (of slaves)".
[9] *flagitium, -ii/-i* (n.): "shameful act"; "disgrace".
[10] *superauimu' = superauimus < supero, -are, -aui, -atum*: "excel", "outdo".
[11] *nuptiis nostris* is ablative of place where (see Bennett 228.1d)
[12] *pudeo, -ere, -ui, -itum*: "feel shame".
[13] *paueo, -ere, paui, –*: "be struck with terror", "tremble with fear".
[14] *inridiculo = irridiculo < irridiculum, -i* (n.): "laughing-stock"; *inridiculo* is dative of purpose or tendency, see Bennett 191.2a.
[15] *ambo, -bae, -bo*: "both".
[16] *insipiens, insipientis* (adjective): "foolish".
[17] *pudet, pudēre, pudit / puditum est* (usually impersonal): "make ashamed", "cause shame".
[18] *priu' = prius* (adverb): "before".
[19] *pudet quem priu' non puditumst umquam*: "I'm disgraced as I've never been disgraced before".

operam date,[20] dum mea facta itero:[21] est operae[22] pretium[23] auribus[24] accipere,[25]

ita ridicula[26] auditu,[27] iteratú[28] ea sunt quae ego íntus[29] turbaui.[30] 880

ubi intro[31] hanc nouam[32] nuptam deduxi,[33] recta uia[34] in conclaue[35] abduxi.[36]

sed tamen tenebrae[37] ibi erant tamquam[38] in puteo;[39] dum senex abest[40] 'decumbe'[41] inquam.[42]

conloco,[43] fulcio,[44] mollio,[45] blandior,[46]

ut prior[47] quam senex nup<tias[48] perpetrem>.[49]

tardus[50] esse ilico[51] coepi,[52] quoniam[53] * * * * 885

---

[20] *operam dare*: "take care", "give attention"; "help" (+ dative).
[21] *itero, -are, -aui, -atum*: "relate", "describe".
[22] *opera, -ae* (f.): "service", "activity", "effort".
[23] *pretium, -i* (n.): "value", "price", "worth"; *est operae pretium*: "it's worth your while".
[24] *auris, -is* (f.): "ear"; *auribus* is ablative of means.
[25] *auribus accipere*: "to hear".
[26] *ridiculus, -a, -um*: "laugle", "absurd".
[27] *auditu*: supine < *audio, -ire, -iui, -itum*.
[28] *iteratu*: supine < *itero, -are, -aui, -atum*: "repeat", "relate"; *ridicula auditu, iteratu*: "ridiculous to hear, ridiculous to describe".
[29] *intus* (adverb): "inside".
[30] *turbo, -are, -aui, -atum*: "stir up", "throw into disorder".
[31] *intro* (adverb): "inside", "into the house".
[32] See note 7 on page 133 at line 782, IV.ii.
[33] *deduco, -ere, -duxi, -ductum*: "bring"
[34] *rectā uiā* (adverbial): "directly".
[35] *conclaue, -is* (n.): "lockable room".
[36] *abduco, -ere, -duxi, ductum*: "lead away".
[37] *tenebrae, -arum* (f. pl.): "darkness".
[38] *tamquam* (adverb): "just like".
[39] *puteus, -i* (m.): "well"; "underground shaft/pit".
[40] *absum, abesse, afui, afuturus*: "be absent".
[41] *decumbo, -ere, decubui, –*: "lie down".
[42] *inquam* (1st person singular present indicative active): "I say".
[43] *conloco, -are, -aui, -atum*: "arrange", "position".
[44] *fulcio, -ire, fulsi, fultum*: "prop up".
[45] *mollio, -ire, iui, -itum*: "soften"; "make calm", "placate".
[46] *blandior, -iri, -itus sum*: "coax", "charm", "speak ingratiatingly to".
[47] *prior, prius* (comparative adjective): "first", "before".
[48] *nuptiae, -arum* (f. pl.): "marriage", "wedding".
[49] *perpetro, -are, -aui, -atum*: "accomplish", "perform" (an action/deed).
[50] *tardus, -a, -um*: "slow".
[51] *ilico* (adverb): "on the spot", "in that very place"; "at once", "there and then".
[52] *coepio, -ere, coepi, copetum*: "begin".
[53] *quoniam* (adverb): "since"; "after", "when".

respecto⁵⁴ identidem,⁵⁵ ne senex * * *

inlecebram⁵⁶ stupri⁵⁷ principio⁵⁸ eam sauium⁵⁹ posco⁶⁰ *,

reppulit⁶¹ mi⁶² manum,

neque enim dare sibi

sauium me siuit.⁶³   888a

enim iam magis⁶⁴ adpropero,⁶⁵ magi' iam lubet⁶⁶ in Casinam   889-90
inruere⁶⁷ *

cupio⁶⁸ illam operam⁶⁹ seni surruperé,⁷⁰ forem⁷¹ óbdo,⁷² ne
senex me opprimeret.⁷³

Cleustrata: agedum,⁷⁴ tu adi⁷⁵ hunc. **Pardalisca:** opsecro,⁷⁶
ubi tua noua nuptast?⁷⁷

Olympio: perii⁷⁸ hercle ego! manufesta⁷⁹ res [est].   893-5
Pardalisca: omnem in ordinem⁸⁰

---

54 *respecto, -are, -aui, -atum*: "keep on looking around/back".
55 *identidem*: "repeatedly".
56 *inlecebra, -ae* (f.): "enticement to" (+ genitive).
57 *stuprum, -i* (n.): "illicit sexual act", "fornication".
58 *principio* (adverb): "at first".
59 *sauium, -ii* (n.): "kiss" (usually an erotic kiss).
60 *posco, -ere, poposci, –*: "ask", "demand"; *eam sauium posco*: "I ask her for a kiss".
61 *repello, -ere, -puli, -pulsum*: "push away".
62 *mi = mihi. mihi* is dative of reference (see Bennett 188).
63 *sino, -ere, siui, situm*: "allow".
64 *magis* (adverb): "more," "rather", "instead".
65 *adpropero, -are, -aui, -atum*: "hurry", "go quickly".
66 *lubet = libet < libet, libuit, libitus est* (impersonal verb): "it is pleasing".
67 *inruo, -ere, -rui, -rutum*: "rush in", "make an attack upon", "charge at"; *lubet in Casinam inruere*: "I want to really throw myself on Casina" (the implication of *inruere* may be either a more persistent attempt at persuading her to cooperate, or a violent sexual assault).
68 *cupio, -ere, -iui, -itum*: "wish", "desire".
69 *opera, -ae* (f.): "service", "activity", "effort".
70 *surrupere = subripere < subripio, -ere, -ripui, -reptum*: "steal away", "get secretly"; *cupio illam operam seni surrupere*: "I want to steal a march on the old master".
71 *foris, -is* (f.): "door", "gate".
72 *obdo, -ere, -didi, -ditum*: "shut / fasten" (a door).
73 *opprimo, -ere, oppressi, oppressum*: "overpower", "take by surprise".
74 *agedum*: "come on!".
75 *adeo, -ire, -ii/-iui, -itum*: "go to".
76 *opsecro = obsecro < obsecro, -are, -aui, -atum*: "beg", "implore"; *opsecro* (interjection): "please!"; translate here: "excuse me".
77 *nuptast = nupta est; nupta, -ae* (f.): "bride".
78 *pereo, -ire, periui/-ii, peritum*: "die"; "be ruined"; "be lost".
79 *manufesta = manifesta < manifestus, -a, -um*: "clear", "evident"; "exposed", "brought to light".
80 *ordo, ordinis* (m.): "order".

fateri[81] ergo aequom[82] est. quid intus agitur?[83] quid agit Casina?

satin[84] morigera[85] est? **Olympio:** pudet[86] dicere. **Pardalisca:** memora[87] ordine, úti[88] occeperas.[89]　　897-8

Olympio: pudet hercle. **Pardalisca:** age. audacter[90]　　899

<post>quam decubuisti,[91] ind'[92] uolo. memora[93] quid est fáctum?[94]　　900

Olympio: flagitium[95] est. **Pardalisca:** cauebunt[96] qui audierint[97] faciant.[98]

Olympio: * * *[99] hoc magnumst.[100] **Pardalisca:** <rem>[101] perdis.[102] quin[103] tu pergis?[104] **Olympio:** ubi

* * * *us suptus[105] porro.[106]　　904-5

Pardalisca: quid? **Olympio:** babae![107]

Pardalisca: quid? **Olympio:** papae![108]　　906a

81　*fateor, fateri, fassus sum*: "admit", "confess".
82　*aequom = aequum < aequus, -a, -um*: "fair", "level".
83　*quid intus agitur*: "what's happening inside?".
84　*satin = satisne* (adverb): "enough", "sufficiently".
85　*morigerus, -a, -um*: "obedient", "accommodating".
86　*pudet, pudere, pudit / puditum est* (usually impersonal): "make ashamed", "cause shame".
87　*memoro, -are, -aui, -atum*: "remind of", "say", "tell", "claim".
88　*uti = ut*.
89　*occipio, -ere, -cepi, -ceptum*: "begin".
90　*audacter* (adv.): "bravely".
91　*decumbo, -ere, -cubui, –*: "lie down" (usually on a bed or couch).
92　*ind' = inde* (adv.): "from that place".
93　I have replaced Lindsay's *memora[re]* with *memora* (2nd person singular present imperative active < *memoro, -are, -aui, -atum*), to simplify translation.
94　For the use of the indicative in an indirect question, see Bennett 300.6.
95　*flagitium, -ii/-i* (n.): "shameful act"; "disgrace".
96　*caueo, -ere, caui, cautum*: "be on one's guard", "beware", "look out for"; *cauebunt... faciant*: "they'll be careful not to do it".
97　*audierint* (3rd person plural perfect subjunctive active); *qui audierint* is future-less-vivid conditional relative clause.
98　*cauebunt qui audierint faciant*: "anyone who hears will be careful not to do [what you did]".
99　The Latin text in the last three scenes of the play has been damaged; missing text is replaced with asterisks.
100　*magnumst = magnum est*.
101　*res, rei* (f.): "thing", "circumstance", "situation", "matter", concern".
102　*perdo, -ere, perdidi, perditum*: "ruin", "destroy"; "lose"; *rem perdis*: "you're losing focus".
103　*quin*: "why... not?"
104　*pergo, -ere, perrexi, perrectum*: "go on", "proceed".
105　*suptus = subtus* (adverb): "below", "underneath".
106　*porro* (adverb): "furthermore", "besides".
107　*babae* (exclamation of surprise or amazement).
108　*papae = babae*.

Pardalisca: * * * est? **Olympio:** oh, erat maxumum.[109]

<ferrum[110] né> eret metui: id quaerere[111] occepi.

dum gladium[112] quaero ne eat,[113] arripio[114] capulum.[115]

sed quom[116] cogito,[117] non uit gladium, nam esset frigidus.[118]   910

Pardalisca: eloquere.[119] **Olympio:** at pudet. **Pardalisca:** num[120] radix[121] fuit? **Olympio:** non fuit. **Pardalisca:** num cucumis?[122]

Olympio: profecto[123] hercle non fuit quicquam[124] holerum,[125]

nisi, quidquid erat, calamitas[126] profecto attigerat[127] numquam.

ita, quidquid erat, grande[128] erat.

Pardalisca: quid fit denique?[129] edisserta.[130] **Olympio:** íbi   915-6
appéllo,[131] 'Casina,' ínquam,[132]

---

[109] *maxumum = maximum.*
[110] *ferrum, -i* (n.): "iron", "iron implement"; "sword".
[111] *quaero, -ere, quaesiui, quaesitum:* "ask", "inquire", "seek".
[112] *gladius, -ii* (m.): "sword".
[113] *dum gladium quaero ne eat:* "while I'm checking if she has the sword".
[114] *arripio, -ere, -ripui, -reptum:* "seize", "snatch", "lay hold of".
[115] *capulus, -i* (m.): "handle", "hilt" (of a sword).
[116] *quom = cum.*
[117] *cogito, -are, -aui, -atum:* "think".
[118] *frigidus, -a, -um:* "cold".
[119] *eloquere* (2nd person singular present imperative) < *eloquor, eloqui, elocutus sum:* "speak out", "state", "say".
[120] *num* (interrogative): "it isn't possible that...?", "can it be that...?".
[121] *radix, radicis* (f.): "root"; translate here: "radish", "root vegetable".
[122] *cucumis, cucumeris* (f.): "cucumber".
[123] *profecto* (adverb): "certainly".
[124] *quisquam, quaequam, quicquam / quidquid* (indefinite pronoun): "any(one) / any(thing)", "whoever / whatever".
[125] *holus, holeris* (n.): "vegetable".
[126] *calamitas, -atis* (f.): "disaster"; "crop blight".
[127] *attingo, -ere, attigi, attactum:* "touch".
[128] *grandis, -e:* "full-grown", "large".
[129] *denique* (adverb): "then", "next", "finally".
[130] *edisserto, -are, -aui, -atum:* "explain", "relate".
[131] *appello, -are, -aui, -atum:* "call", "address", "solicit", "beseech".
[132] *inquam* (1st person singular present indicative active): "I say".

'amabo,[133] mea uxorcula,[134] qur[135] uirum tuom[136] sic me spernis?'[137]   917-8

nimis[138] tu quidem hercle inmerito[139]

meo mi[140] haec facis, quia mihi te expetiui.'[141]   920

illa hau[142] uerbum facit[143] et saepit[144] ueste[145] id qui[146] estis <mulieres>.[147]

ubi illum saltum[148] uideo opsaeptum,[149] rogo ut áltero[150] sinat[151] ire.

uolo, ut obuortam,[152] cubitis[153] im* * * * * * *[154]

ullum muttit[155] e* * * * * * * * * * *

surgo,[156] ut in eam in * * * * * * * * *   925

atque illam in * * * * * * * * * * *

Myrrhina: perlepide[157] narrat * * * * * * * * *

Olympio: sauium[158] * * * * * * * * * * *

---

[133] *amabo*: "please", "I beg" (< *amo, -are, -aui, -atum*).
[134] *uxorcula, -ae* (f.): "little wife".
[135] *qur = cur.*
[136] *tuom = tuum.*
[137] *sperno, -ere, spreui, spretum*: "despise", "reject".
[138] *nimis* (adverb): "too much", "excessively".
[139] *inmeritus, -a, -um*: "undeserved"; *inmerito meo*: "for no fault of mine".
[140] *mi = mihi.*
[141] *expeto, -ere, -petiui, -petitum*: "seek after", "covet", "desire".
[142] *hau = haud*: "not at all".
[143] *illa hau uerbum facit*: "that girl says not a single word".
[144] *saepio, -ire, saepsi, saeptum*: "fence in", "enclose"; "cover up".
[145] *uestis, -is* (f.): "clothing".
[146] *qui* (an old ablative).
[147] *id qui estis mulieres* (euphemistic phrase for female genitalia): "the bit that you women have down there".
[148] *saltus, -ūs* (m.): "forest pasture", "woodland", "thicket"; here implied: "vagina".
[149] *opsaeptum = obsaeptum < obsaepio, -ire, -si, -tum*: "block", "obstruct", "shield".
[150] *altero*: "by the other route" (probably implying anal intercourse).
[151] *sino, -ere, siui, situm*: "allow".
[152] *obuortam = obuertam < obuerto, -ere, -ti, -sum*: "turn towards".
[153] *cubitum, -i* (n.): "elbow".
[154] The Latin text is too damaged to get more than a general impression of Olympio's story here.
[155] *muttio, -ire, -iui, –*: "mutter", "speak in a low tone".
[156] *surgo, -ere, surrexi, surrectum*: "lift up"; "get up".
[157] *perlepide* (adverb): "very charmingly".
[158] *sauium, -ii* (n.) (see note 59 on page 146 at line 887, V.ii).

ita quasi[159] saetis[160] labra[161] mihi[162] compungit[163] barba[164] * * *

continuo[165] in genua[166] ut astiti,[167] pectu'[168] mihi pedibus[169] percutit.[170] 930

decido[171] de lecto[172] praecipes:[173] supsilit,[174] optundit[175] os[176] mihi.

inde[177] foras[178] tacitus[179] profugiens[180] exeo[181] hoc ornatu[182] quo uides,

ut senex hoc eodem poculo[183] quo ego bibi[184] biberet. **Pardalisca:** optume[185] est.

sed ubi est pálliolum[186] tuom?[187] **Olympio:** hic intu'[188] reliqui.

---

[159] *quasi* (adverb): "as if", "just like".
[160] *saeta, -ae* (f.): "hair", "bristle".
[161] *labrum, -i* (n.): "lip".
[162] *mihi* (here, as well as at line 930 and line 931) is dative of reference (see Bennett 188).
[163] *compungo, -ere, -nxi, -nctum*: "prick", "puncture", "sting".
[164] *barbā* (ablative) < *barba, -ae* (f.): "beard".
[165] *continuo* (adverb): "immediately".
[166] *genus, -us* (n.): "knee".
[167] *assisto, -ere, astiti, –*: "take up a position", "stand by".
[168] *pectu'* = *pectus* < *pectus, -oris* (n.): "chest".
[169] *pes, pedis* (m.): "foot".
[170] *percutio, -ere, -cussi, -cussum*: "strike", "beat".
[171] *decido, -ere, decidi, –*: "fall off".
[172] *lectus, -i* (m.): "bed".
[173] *praecipes= praeceps* < *praeceps, praecipitis* (adjective): "headlong", "falling head first".
[174] *supsilit = subsilit* < *subsilio, -ire, -lui, –*: "leap up".
[175] *optundit = obtundit* < *obtundo, -ere, -tudi, -tusus*: "strike", "beat".
[176] *os, oris* (n.): "mouth", "face".
[177] *inde* (see note 92 on page 147 at line 900, V.ii).
[178] *foras* (adverb): "out of doors".
[179] *tacitus, -a, -um*: "silent", "secret".
[180] *profugio, -ere, -fugi, –*: "escape", "run away from".
[181] *exeo, -ire, -iui/-ii, -itum*: "go out", "leave".
[182] *ornatus, -us* (m.): "outfit", "clothing".
[183] *poculum, -i* (n.): "cup", "drinking vessel".
[184] *bibo, -ere, bibi, bibitum*: "drink".
[185] *optume = optime* (adverb): "most satisfactorily"; *optume est*: "this is excellent!", "this is just perfect!".
[186] *palliolum, -i* (diminutive of *pallium, -ii* (n.): "cloak").
[187] *tuom = tuum*.
[188] *intu' = intus* (adverb): "inside".

Pardalisca: quid nunc? satin[189] lepide[190] adita est[191] uobis   935
manu'? **Olympio:** merito.[192]

sed concrepuerunt[193] fores.[194] num[195] illa me núnc sequitur?

---

[189] *satin* (see note 84 on page 147 at line 896, Vii).
[190] *lepide* (adverb): "nicely", "agreeably", "excellently".
[191] *adita est uobis manu'* (idiomatic phrase): "have you both been nicely tricked?".
[192] *merito* (adverb): "deservedly".
[193] *concrepo, -are, concrepui, concrepitum*: "creak".
[194] *foris, -is* (f.): "door", "gate".
[195] *num* (see note 120 on page 148 at line 911, V.ii).

V.iii LYSIDAMVS, CHALINVS

Scene summary: *Lysidamus now comes out of Alcesimus's house, without his cloak, having suffered similar treatment from the fake Casina. He says he's disgraced himself and that his wife will now beat him for his attempt to cheat on her. He asks the audience if anyone will take his beating for him, and then says he'll run away. Chalinus (still dressed up as Casina) comes out and calls to Lysidamus to stop, but Lysidamus keeps running.*

Lysidamus: Maxumo[1] ego ardeo[2] flagitio[3]

nec quid agam meis rebu'[4] scio,

nec meam ut[5] uxorem aspiciam[6]

contra oculis,[7] ita disperii;[8]   940

omnia palam[9] sunt probra,[10]

omnibus modis[11] occidi[12] miser.

* * * * * ita manufesto[13] faucibus[14] teneor[15]

* * * <nec> quibus modis purgem[16] scio me meae uxori

* * * * * <at>que expalliatus[17] sum miser,   945

* * * * * * <cla>ndestinae[18] nuptiae.[19]

* * * * * * * * censeo[20]

* * * * * mihi optumum[21] est.

intro[22] ad uxorem meam

---

[1] *maxumo = maximo.*
[2] *ardeo, -ere, arsi, arsum:* "burn", "be burning".
[3] *flagitium, -ii/-i* (n.): "shameful act"; "disgrace".
[4] *meis rebu':* "in my circumstances / condition".
[5] *ut:* "how".
[6] *aspicio, -ere, aspexi, aspectum:* "look at", "see".
[7] *contra oculis:* "in the eyes".
[8] *dispereo, -ire, -ii, –:* "be lost", "be ruined"; "die".
[9] *palam* (adverb): "openly"; (with *est/sunt*): "public", "out in the open".
[10] *probrum, -i* (n.): "disgraceful act", "dishonour".
[11] *modus, -i* (m.): "way".
[12] *occido, -ere, -cidi, -casum:* " fall down"; "die", "be ruined".
[13] *manufesto = manifesto* (adverb): "clearly", "openly".
[14] *fauces, faucium* (f. pl.): "throat", "neck".
[15] *teneor faucibus:* "I'm caught by the throat", "I feel a knife at my throat".
[16] *purgo, -are, -aui, -atum:* "cleanse"; translate here: "clear oneself", "justify oneself".
[17] *expalliatus, -a, -um* (word found only in this line): "cloakless", "having been robbed of one's cloak".
[18] *clandestinus, -a, -um:* "secret", "clandestine".
[19] *nuptiae, -arum* (f. pl.): "marriage", "wedding".
[20] *censeo, -ere, censui, censitum:* "think", "suppose", "recommend".
[21] *optumum = optimum.*
[22] *intro, -are, -aui, -atum:* "go into", "go inside".

sufferamque[23] ei meum tergum[24] ob[25] iniuriam.[26]   950

sed ecquis[27] est qui homo munus[28] uelit fungier[29]

pro me? quid nunc agam nescio, nisi ut   952-3

inprobos[30] famulos[31] imiter[32] ac domo fugiam.[33]

                                                                955-6
nam salus[34] nulla est scapulis,[35] si domum redeo.[36]

nugas[37] istic[38] dicere licet?[39] uapulo[40] hercle ego inuitus[41] tamen

etsi[42] malum[43] merui.[44]

hac[45] dabo[46] protinam[47] et fugiam. **Chalinus:** heus![48] asta[49]   959-60
ilico,[50] amator.[51]

Lysidamus: occidi![52] reuocor:[53] quasi[54] non audiam,[55]   961-2
abibo.[56]

---

[23] *suffero, -ferre, sustuli, sublatum*: "offer", "to place at a person's disposal".
[24] *tergum, -i* (n.): "back".
[25] *ob* (preposition): "because of" (+ accusative).
[26] *iniuria, -ae* (f.): "injury"; "wrongdoing", "bad behaviour".
[27] *ecquis, ecquid* (interrogative pronoun): "is there anyone who? / is there anything that".
[28] *munus, muneris* (n.): "service", "duty".
[29] *fungier = fungi < fungor, fungi, functus sum*: "perform", "discharge", "do".
[30] *inprobos = improbos < improbus, -a, -um*: "shameless", "wicked".
[31] *famulus, -i* (m.): "servant", "slave", "enslaved person".
[32] *imitor, -ari, -atus sum*: "copy"," imitate", "act like".
[33] *fugio, -ere, fugi, fugitum*: "run away".
[34] *salus, -utis* (f.): "health"; "safety".
[35] *scapulae, -arum* (f. pl.): "shoulders".
[36] *redeo, -ire, -iui/-ii, -itum*: "return", "go back".
[37] *nugae, -arum* (f. pl.): "nonsense".
[38] *istic* (adverb): "now", "here", "there".
[39] *licere, licuit, licitum est* (impersonal): "it is allowed", "it is permitted".
[40] *uapulo, -are, -aui, -atum*: "be beaten", "get a beating".
[41] *inuitus, -a, -um*: "unwilling".
[42] *etsi*: "although".
[43] *malum, -i* (n.): "misfortune", "misery".
[44] *mereo, -ere, merui, meritum*: "deserve", "earn".
[45] *hac* (adverb): "this way", "in this direction".
[46] *dabo = me dabo*: "I'll take myself off".
[47] *protinam* (adverb): "immediately".
[48] *heus*: "hey!", "listen!" (used to try to get someone's attention).
[49] *asto, -are, -stiti, –*: "stand still".
[50] *ilico* (adverb): "on the spot", "in that very place"; "at once", "there and then".
[51] *amator, -oris* (m.): "lover", "loverboy", "a man in love", "womanizer".
[52] *occido, -ere, -cidi, -casum* (see note 12 on the preceding page at line 942, V.iii).
[53] *reuoco, -are, -aui, -atum*: "call back", "recall".
[54] *quasi* (adverb): "as if", "just like".
[55] *quasi non audiam* is a conditional clause of comparison (see Bennett 307).
[56] *abeo, -re, -iui/-ii, -itum*: "go away".

V.iv CHALINVS, LYSIDAMVS, CLEVSTRATA, MYRRHINA, OLYMPIO

Scene summary: *Chalinus, still dressed as Casina but probably no longer veiled, and holding Lysidamus's staff, chases after Lysidamus. He invites him to come back to the bedroom for sex, and then threatens him with the staff. Lysidamus then runs right into Cleustrata and Myrrhina, who make it clear that they know about his planned adultery, and ask him what he's done with his cloak and staff. Olympio returns and tells the women about Lysidamus's plot to get a sneaky night with Casina. Lysidamus tries to deny it, but realizes that Cleustrata doesn't believe him, and begs her forgiveness. She forgives him, in order, she says, to keep the play from running on too long. She tells Chalinus to give Lysidamus's cloak and staff back to him. Chalinus ends the play by explaining that Casina will soon be discovered to be the freeborn daughter of the neighbours (presumably Alcesimus and Myrrhina), and will thus be able to marry Lysidamus's and Cleustrata's son (the absent Euthynicus).*

Chalinus: Vbi tu és, qui colere[1] mores[2] Massiliensis[3] postulas?[4]

nunc tu si uis subigitare[5] me, probast[6] occasio.[7]

redi[8] sis[9] in cubiculum;[10] periisti[11] hercle. age,[12] accede[13] huc   965
modo.[14]

---

[1] *colo, -ere, -ui, cultum*: "cultivate"; "practice", "devote oneself to".
[2] *mos, moris* (m.): "custom", "it", "behaviour".
[3] *Massiliensīs = Massiliensēs < Massiliensis, -e*: "of, or belonging to, Massilia"; *mores Massilienses* seem to have implied a willingness, by men, to allow sexual penetration, according to Athenaeus (*Deipnosophistae* 12.523c; cited by MacCary and Willcock 1976: 205). Romans did not, in general, consider sex between men to be wrong, as long as the one who penetrated the other was freeborn while the one being penetrated was enslaved.
[4] *postulo, -are, -aui, -atum*: "ask"; "desire".
[5] *subigito, -are, -aui, -atum*: "excite sexually", "arouse"; Christenson argues that, elsewhere in Plautus, *subigitare* means "to grope another man's woman", and that here it is used as a comment on the illicit nature of Lysidamus's claim to Casina's body (Christenson 2019: 74).
[6] *probast = proba est < probus, -a, -um*: "excellent".
[7] *occasio, -onis* (f.): "opportunity", "chance".
[8] *redi* (2nd person singular present imperative active < *redeo, -ire, -iui/-ii, -itum*: "return", "go back").
[9] *sis = si uis*.
[10] *cubiculum, -i* (n.): "bedroom".
[11] *pereo, -ire, periui/-ii, peritum*: "die"; "be ruined"; "be lost"; translate here: "you're dead!".
[12] *age* (< *ago, -ere, egi, actum*): "come on", "go on".
[13] *accedo, -ere, -cessi, -cessum*: "approach", "come near".
[14] *modo* (adverb): "just", "just now"; "only".

nunc ego tecum aequom[15] arbitrum[16] extra considium[17] captauero.[18]

Lysidamus: perii! fusti[19] defloccabit[20] iam illic[21] homo lumbos[22] meos.

hac[23] iter faciundumst,[24] nam illac[25] lumbifragiumst[26] obuiam.[27]

Cleustrata: iubeo te saluere,[28] amator.[29] **Lysidamus:** ecce autem uxor obuiamst:[30]

nunc ego intér sacrum[31] saxumque[32] sum nec quo[33] fugiam   970
scio.

hac lupi,[34] hac canes:[35] lupina[36] scaeua[37] fusti rem gerit;[38]

hercle opinor[39] permutabo[40] ego illuc[41] nunc uerbum[42] uetus:[43]

---

[15] *aequom = aequum < aequus, -a, -um*: "fair", "level".
[16] *arbiter, -tra, -trum*: "witness", "judge".
[17] *considium, -(i)i*: "court of justice".
[18] *capto, -are, -aui, -atum*: "try to get hold of".
[19] *fustis, -is* (m.): "staff".
[20] *deflocco, -are, -aui, -atum*: "rub the nap of (cloth)"; "strip of one's possessions", "fleece".
[21] *illic = illi* (adverb): "there", "in there".
[22] *lumbus, -i* (m.): "loin"; "genital area".
[23] *hac* (adverb): "this way", "in this direction".
[24] *faciundumst = faciundum est; hac iter faciundumst*: "I'll have to escape this way".
[25] *illac* (adverb): "that way", "in that direction".
[26] *lumbifragiumst = lumbifragium est; lumbifragium, -i* (n.): "ball-wreck", "ball-buster" (comic word coined by Plautus in imitation of *naufragium, -ii* (n.): "shipwreck").
[27] *obuiam* (adverb): "in the way".
[28] *iubeo te saluere*: "I greet you", "welcome!".
[29] *amator, -oris* (m.): "lover", "loverboy", "a man in love", "womanizer".
[30] *obuiamst = obuiam est*.
[31] *sacer, sacra, sacrum*: "sacred", "consecrated"; translate here: "sacrificial victim".
[32] *saxum, -i* (n.): "stone"; translate here: "flint knife"; *inter sacrum saxumque* (proverbial expression) "between a rock and a hard place", "in trouble".
[33] *quo* (adverb): "where", "to which (place)".
[34] *lupus, -i* (m.): "wolf".
[35] *canis, -is* (m./f.): "dog".
[36] *lupinus, -a, -um*: "wolf-like", "wolfish".
[37] *scaeua, -ae* (f.): "omen".
[38] *rem gerere*: "deal with the situation/matter".
[39] *opinor, -ari, -atus sum*: "think", "suppose", "imagine".
[40] *permuto, -are, -aui, -atum*: "exchange", "swap".
[41] *illuc = illud*.
[42] *uerbum, -i* (n.): "word"; translate here: "saying", "proverb".
[43] *uetus, ueteris* (adjective): "old", "aged".

hac ibo, caninam[44] scaeuam spero[45] meliorem[46] fore.[47]

Myrrhina: quid agis,[48] dismarite?[49] **Cleustrata:** mi uir, unde hoc ornatu[50] aduenis?[51]

quid fecisti scipione[52] aut quod uisti pallium?[53]   975

Myrrhina: in adulterio,[54] dum moechissat[55] Casinam, credo perdidit.[56]

Lysidamus: occidi![57] **Chalinus:** etiamne imus cubitum?[58] Casina sum. **Lysidamus:** i in malam crucem![59]

Chalinus: non amas me? **Cleustrata:** quin[60] responde, tuo quid factum est pallio?

Lysidamus: Bacchae[61] hercle, uxor — **Cleustrata:** Bacchae? **Lysidamus:** Bacchae hercle, uxor — **Myrrhina:** nugatur[62] sciens,

nam ecastor nunc Bacchae nullae ludunt.[63] **Lysidamus:**   980
oblitus[64] fui,[65]

sed tamen Bacchae — **Cleustrata:** quid, Bacchae?
<**Lysidamus:**> sin[66] id fieri[67] non potest —

---

44 *caninus, -a, -um*: "dog-like", "canine".
45 *spero, -are, -aui, -atum*: "hope".
46 *melior, melius* (comparative adjective < *bonus, -a, -um*).
47 *fore = futurum esse*.
48 *quid agis*: "how are you?".
49 *dismaritus, -i* (m.): "bigamist", "husband of two wives" (Greek-Latin hybrid word found only in this line).
50 *ornatus, -us* (m.): "outfit", "clothing".
51 *aduenio, -ire, -ueni, -uentum*: "come to", "arrive at".
52 *scipio, -onis* (m.): "staff", "stick" (ablative of specification; see Bennett 226). The form *scipione* makes more sense than *scipone[m]*, which is what appears in Lindsay's text.
53 *pallium, -ii* (n.): "cloak"; *pallium* is accusative because it has been attracted to the case of the relative pronoun *quod* (see Allen & Greenough 306a, note).
54 *adulterium, -(i)i* (n.): "adultery".
55 *moechisso, -are*: "commit adultery with" (+ accusative).
56 *perdo, -ere, perdidi, perditum*: "ruin", "destroy"; "lose" (*scipio* and *pallium* are implied direct objects of *perdidit*).
57 *occido, -ere, -cidi, -casum*: " fall down"; "die", "be ruined".
58 *cubitum* (supine < *cubo, -are, -aui, -atum*: "lie down", "go to bed").
59 *in malam crucem* (see note 46 on page 114 at line 611, III.iv).
60 *quin* + imperative adds force to the command; *quin responde*: "just answer".
61 *Baccha, -ae* (f.): "Bacchante", "female devotee of the god Bacchus".
62 *nugor, -ari, -atus sum*: "talk nonsense".
63 *ludo, -ere, lusi, lusum*: "play", "mock"; translate here: "amusing themselves".
64 *obliuiscor, -i, oblitus sum*: "forget".
65 *oblitus fui = oblitus sum*. Perfect passive forms that normally use *sum, eram*, or *ero* sometimes instead use *fui, fueram, fuero* (see Bennett 102, note 36).
66 *sin*: "if however", "but if".
67 *fio, fieri, factus sum*: "be done", "be made", "happen", "take place".

Cleustrata: times ecastor. **Lysidamus:** egone? mentire[68] hercle. **Cleustrata:** nam palles[69] male.[70]

ṇ . . . . quid me ụe . . . . ụṣ . . . . . am me rogạs?

* * * * * * mạlẹ ṛ * * * * * mihi.

* * * * * * * * * * gṛatulor.[71]   985

* * * * * * * qu * * * ṣenex.

họ * * * * * * * ọn * * ụ

* * * * * * * * ụnc̣ Cạsiṇust[72] | — |

qui hic̣ * * * lem frus . . . . . ṛam . . dịs   989/90

<**Olympio:**> qui etiam me miserum famosum[73] fecit flagitiis[74] suis.

Lysidamus: non taces? **Olympio:** non hercle uero[75] taceo. nam tu maxumo[76]

me opsecrauisti[77] opere[78] Casinam ut poscerem[79] uxorem mihi

tui amóris caussa.[80] **Lysidamus:** ego istuc[81] feci? **Olympio:**   994/5
immo[82] Hector Ilius[83] —

Lysidamus: te quidem oppresset.[84] feci ego istaec[85] dicta quae uos dicitis?

---

[68] *mentire* = *mentiris* < *mentior, mentiri, mentitus sum*: "lie".
[69] *palleo, -ere, -ui, –*: "look/be pale".
[70] *male* (adverb): "badly"; translate here: "awfully".
[71] *gratulor, -ari, -atus sum*: "rejoice"; "congratulate".
[72] *Casinust* = *Casinus est*.
[73] *famosus, -a, -um*: "much talked about"; "notorious".
[74] *flagitium, -ii/-i* (n.): "shameful act"; "disgrace".
[75] *uero* (adverb): truly", "certainly".
[76] *maxumo* = *maximo*.
[77] *opsecrauisti* = *obsecrauisti* < *obsecro, -are, -aui, -atum*: "beg", "implore".
[78] *maxumo... opere*: "with the greatest intensity", "most vehemently", "extremely".
[79] *posco, -ere, poposci, –*: "ask", "demand".
[80] *caussa* = *causa*; for a genitive + *causā* see Bennett 198.1).
[81] *istuc* = *istud*.
[82] *immo* (adverb): "on the contrary".
[83] *Ilius, -a, -um*: "of Ilium/Troy", "Trojan". "Hector of Ilium" may have had implications of sexual staying power, with perhaps a pun on *ilia* ("groin", "private parts"). Olympio could thus be mocking Lysidamus's lack of sexual potency, despite the latter's earlier boasts (Heil 2012: 485).
[84] *oppresset* = *oppressisset* (3rd person singular pluperfect subjunctive) < *opprimo, -ere, oppressi, oppressum*: "overpower", "take by surprise".
[85] *istaec* = *ista* (accusative neuter plural).

Cleustrata: rogitas[86] etiam? **Lysidamus:** si quidem hercle feci, feci nequiter.[87]

Cleustrata: redi[88] modo huc intro:[89] monebo,[90] si qui[91] meministi[92] minus.

Lysidamus: hercle, opinor, potius[93] uobis credam quod[94] uos dicitis.

sed, uxor, da uiro hanc ueniam[95] <mi>; Myrrhina, ora[96] Cleustratam;   1000

si umquam posthac[97] aut amasso[98] Casinam aut occepso[99] modo,

ne[100] ut eam amasso,[101] sí ego umquam adeo[102] posthac tale[103] admisero,[104]

nulla caussast[105] quin[106] pendentem[107] me, uxor, uirgis[108] uerberes.[109]

---

[86] *rogito, -are, -aui, -atum*: "keep asking".
[87] *nequiter* (adverb): "wickedly"; "badly", "unsuccessfully" "with poor results".
[88] *redi* (see note 8 on page 154 at line 965, V.iv).
[89] *intro* (adverb): "inside", "into the house".
[90] *monebo*: translate here: "I'll remind you".
[91] *qui* (an old ablative); *si qui*: "if in any way", "if by any means".
[92] *meministi* (2nd person singular perfect indicative active < *memini, meminisse*: "remember").
[93] *potius* (comparative adverb): "rather", "instead".
[94] *quod* is a cognate accusative (see Allen & Greenough 390c) or an accusative of result (see Bennett 176.2a).
[95] *uenia, -ae* (f.): "favour"; "pardon".
[96] *oro, -are, -aui, -atum*: "ask", "beg".
[97] *posthac* (adverb): "after this", "henceforth".
[98] *amasso* (future perfect < *amo, amare*); = *amauero*.
[99] *occepso = occepero < occipio, -ere, -cepi, -ceptum*: "begin".
[100] *ne = nedum*: "much less", "not to speak of".
[101] *ne ut eam amasso*: "not to speak of making love to her" (see MacCary and Willcock 1976: 209).
[102] *adeo* (adverb): "indeed", "even".
[103] *talis, -e*: "such", "of such a kind".
[104] *admitto, -ere, -misi, -missum*: "permit"; "become guilty of", "commit".
[105] *caussast = causa est; causa, -ae* (f.): "reason", "cause".
[106] *quin* (+ subjunctive): "except", "not without", "so that... not"; *nulla caussest quin*: "there is no reason why... not" (+ subjunctive).
[107] *pendeo, -ere, pependi, –*: "hang", "be suspended"
[108] *uirga, -ae* (f.): "switch", "stick", "rod".
[109] *uerbero, -are, -aui, -atum*: "whip", "beat"; *nulla caussast quin... uerberes*: "there's no reason not to beat...".

Myrrhina: censeo[110] ecástor ueniam hanc dandam,[111]
<Cleustrata>. **Cleustrata:** faciam ut iubes.[112]

propter[113] eam rem[114] hanc tibi nunc ueniam minu'[115]   1005
grauate[116] prospero,[117]

hanc ex longa[118] longiorem ne faciamus fabulam.[119]

Lysidamus: non irata's?[120] **Cleustrata:** non sum irata.
Lysidamus: tuaen[121] fide[122] credo? **Cleustrata:** meae.

Lysidamus: lepidiorem[123] uxorem nemo[124] quisquam[125]
quam ego eo hanc et.

Cleustrata: age[126] tu, redde[127] huic scipionem[128] et
pallium.[129] **Chalinus:** tene, si lubet.[130]

mihi quidem edepol insignite[131] factast[132] magna iniuria:[133]   1010

duobus[134] nupsi,[135] neuter[136] fecit quod nouae[137] nuptae[138]
solet.[139]

---

[110] *censeo, -ere, censui, censitum*: "think", "suppose", "recommend".
[111] *dandam* (gerundive modifying *ueniam*) < *do, dare, dedi, datum*.
[112] *iubeo, -ere, iussi, iussum*: "order", "tell".
[113] *propter* (preposition): "because of".
[114] *propter eam rem*: "for this reason".
[115] *minu'* = *minus*.
[116] *grauate* (adverb): "unwillingly", "grudgingly".
[117] *prospero, -are, -aui, -atum*: "make [someone] happy with" (+ accusative), "bring about".
[118] *ex longa*: "out of a[n already] long [play]".
[119] *fabula, -ae* (f.): "play".
[120] *irata's* = *irata est* < *irascor, -i, iratus sum*: "be angry".
[121] *tuaen* = *tuaene*.
[122] *fides, -ei* (f.): "trust", "good faith", "promise".
[123] *lepidior, -ius* (comparative adjective < *lepidus, -a, -um*: "charming", "witty").
[124] *nemo, neminis* (m./f.): "no one".
[125] *quisquam, quaequam, quicquam / quidquid* (indefinite pronoun): "any(one) / any(thing)", "whoever / whatever"; translate *nemo quisquam*: "no one at all".
[126] *age* (< *ago, -ere, egi, actum*): "come on", "go on".
[127] *reddo, -ere, reddidi, redditum*: "return", "repay" (+ dative of person).
[128] *scipio, -onis* (see note 52 on page 156 at line 975, V.iv).
[129] *pallium, -ii* (see note 53 on page 156 at line 975, V.iv).
[130] *lubet* = *libet* < *libet, libuit, libitus est* (impersonal verb): "it is pleasing".
[131] *insignite* (adverb): "extraordinarily", "notably".
[132] *factast* = *facta est*.
[133] *iniuria, -ae* (f.): "injury"; "wrongdoing", "bad behaviour".
[134] *duo, duae, duo* (numeral): "two".
[135] *nubo, -ere, nupsi, nuptum*: "marry", "be married" (+ dative).
[136] *neuter, -tra, -trum*: "neither".
[137] See note 7 on page 133 at line 782, IV.ii.
[138] *nupta, -ae* (f.): "bride".
[139] *soleo, -ere, -ui, -itum*: "be accustomed", "be used".

spectatores, quod futurumst[140] intus,[141] id memorabimus.[142]

haec Casina huiius[143] reperietur[144] filia esse ex proxumo[145]

eaque nubet Euthynico nostro erili[146] filio.[147]

nunc uos aequomst[148] manibus[149] meritis[150] meritam[151]   1015
mercedem[152] dare:

---

[140] *futurumst = futurum est*: "what's going to happen".
[141] *intus* (adverb): "inside".
[142] *memoro, -are, -aui, -atum*: "remind of", "say", "tell", "claim".
[143] *huiius = huius*.
[144] *reperio, -ire, repperi, repertum*: "discover", "find out"; "devise", "figure out".
[145] *proxumo = proximo < proximus, -a, -um*: "nearest"; *ex proxumo*: "from next door"; here: "of the next door neighbours".
[146] *erilis, -e*: "of the master/mistress".
[147] *nostro erili filio*: "to our young master".
[148] *aequomst = aequum est < aequus, -a, -um*: "fair", "level".
[149] *manus, -us* (f.): "hand".
[150] *mereor, -eri, -itus*: "deserve"; *meritis*: "to the deserving [actors]".
[151] *mereo, -ere, merui, meritum*: "deserve".
[152] *merces, -edis* (f.): "payment", "reward"; *manibus... meritam mercedem*: "well-deserved applause".

qui faxit,[153] clam[154] uxorem ducet[155] semper scortum[156] quod[157] uolet;

uerum[158] qui non manibus clare[159] quantum[160] poterit plauserit,[161]

ei pro[162] scorto supponetur[163] hircus[164] unctus[165] nautea.[166]

---

[153] *faxit = fecerit* (future perfect); *qui faxit... ducet* and *qui... plauserit...supponetur* (below) are future more vivid conditional sentences with relative clauses in the protases (see Allen & Greenough 519).

[154] *clam* (adverb): "secretly (from)", "unknown to" (+ accusative).

[155] *ducet*: "will bring home".

[156] *scortum, i* (n.): "sex worker", "mistress", "girlfriend" (literally: "skin", "hide").

[157] The antecedent of *quod* is *scortum*.

[158] *uerum* (conjunction): "but".

[159] *clare* (adverb < *clarus, -a, -um*: "clear", "loud").

[160] *quantum* (adverb): "as much as".

[161] *plaudo, -ere, plausi, plausum*: "clap", "applaud".

[162] *pro* (preposition + ablative): "before", "in front of"; "on behalf of", instead of".

[163] *suppono, -ere, -posui, -positum*: "substitute".

[164] *hircus, -i* (m.): "male goat".

[165] *unctus, -a, -um*: "anointed".

[166] *nautea, -ae* (f.): "tannery wastewater". Mature male goats anoint themselves with their own urine when in rut, hence their notorious stench; this particular goat would be worse smelling than usual, having been anointed with *nautea*. Gitner 2016 argues that *nautea* is cognate with *notia* ("white bryony"), the foul-smelling berries of which were used in tanning leather. Gitner further suggests that a salacious pun is intended here, and that the men in the audience are given the options of a *scortum* ("sex worker"), if they applaud loudly enough, or a literal *scortum* ("skin" or "hide"), that is, a goat in the revoltingly stinky process of being tanned (Gitner 2016: 123).

Casina (in Translation)

About the Translation

This translation aims to reflect the wit and irreverence of the Latin text, while retaining its connection to the world of mid-republican Rome. As any translator knows, there are constant compromises that must be made in the effort to be true to the original without creating a stiff, awkward translation. Because the Latin text of the play, with copious annotations, is included in the same volume, I had fewer compunctions when I felt that the Latin wording needed to be translated with a less literal English phrase, but I used a more literal translation wherever it would sound reasonably natural to do so. Readers of the translation who want to see how Plautus actually wrote a particular line can, with only intermediate knowledge of Latin, easily check for themselves in the Latin text of the play, included in this volume with copious grammatical notes to aid in understanding it.

Nevertheless this translation is not meant to look like a modern play. The world of mid-republican Rome was very different from the modern world, and I wanted to ensure that readers are immersed, as far as possible, in a world where slavery was unquestioned, and where a freeborn man of property was essentially supposed to be king (or, in this play, Jupiter – see lines 230, 331-335, and 406) of their households. Most of Plautus's jokes were and are funny partly because of this backdrop of extreme social hierarchy and injustice.

An example of such a historically-contextual joke appears at line 418 of the play (in act II, scene vi), when the enslaved farm manager (or *uilicus*) Olympio says, to explain why the gods have brought it about that he has drawn the winning lot, that "it's because I'm so dutiful, as were my ancestors before me" (*pietate factum est mea atque maiorum meum*). The joke is only mildly funny if we interpret it as Olympio being smugly complacent about the divine favour in which he basks, or about his own devotion to duty (*pietas*). The real joke, however, was that enslavement in the Roman world was supposed to delete the enslaved person's family relationships. An enslaved person, while obviously the biological child of their parents, was considered no longer to have parents or ancestors in any meaningful way, since they were now connected only to the slave-owner, even if they were subsequently manumitted. Olympio's comment about his ancestors, therefore, shows not just smug complacency about his divine favour, but also his grandiose notions about ancestors that contradict his actual enslaved status. We probably won't laugh more when we realize what the joke was really meant to be, but the Roman audience would have, and knowing this allows us to better understand the way Roman slavery worked.

Another, more complicated, example can be seen with a brief analysis of lines 216-278 (act II, scene iii). In this scene, the old married man Lysidamus prances on stage singing about his love for the sixteen-year-old Casina, and the humour translates well without too much dependence on explanatory footnotes. It was funny to the Romans, and is funny now, that he has drenched himself in cologne to make himself more attractive, as he thinks, to a girl who is at least four decades younger than he, and that he has failed to take into account the likelihood that his wife will smell the cologne and realize that he's planning on cheating on her.

Lysidamus's spending money on cologne in order to please Casina may, however, have struck an ancient Roman audience somewhat differently than it will strike a modern one. Would the Roman audiences have found it especially funny that Lysidamus was trying to please Casina, when, in a real Roman household, a slave-owner would not have needed to use persuasion on an enslaved person under his power? In this instance, we don't know if this was originally one aspect of the joke. An expensive gold bracelet, made to look like a snake coiling around the arm that wore it, was found on the arm of a woman who died just outside Pompeii in 79 CE. It was inscribed with the dedication *DOM[I]NVS ANCILLAE SVAE*, meaning "from the master to his slave-woman" (Edmondson 2011, 353), which suggests that Roman slave-owners might indeed have spent money on trying to please the object of their affections regardless of their servile status, though we cannot know how common or accepted it was.

Regardless of how the original jokes may have landed, the recurring references to slavery make it complicated for modern audiences to enjoy Plautus's humour unreservedly. Nevertheless, this translation is intended to provoke such complicated responses. It is meant to make readers laugh where possible, but also to make them understand a little of what life may have been like for the various different levels of society in the mid Roman republic. Information to provide context or explanations for obscure references in the play is provided in footnotes.

The *Casina* is even more full of polymetric *cantica* – passages in a variety of mixed metres that were sung with musical accompaniment – than any other play of Plautus,[1] but I have made no attempt to reflect these in my prose translation. A highly talented song-writer or poet may be able to write English songs that share the exuberant spirit of Plautus's songs, but they inevitably have to move further from the literal translation of the Latin than would have suited the purposes of this book. Richlin's translations of Plautus's plays *Curculio, Persa*, and *Poenulus* include English songs, set to various familiar tunes, that delightfully give us the spirit of Plautine polymetric *cantica* (Richlin 2005). Her translations are well worth reading, or rather, worth

---

[1] The polymetric *cantica* comprise 33.28% of this play, while the average percentage of polymetric *cantica* in the plays of Plautus is only 14.3% (Moore 2012: 397-398).

singing aloud. Franko's translation of the *Casina* succeeds in making the songs evident with a variety of stress-based English metres, and I encourage readers to read it as well (Franko 2001). Comparing multiple translations of the same work can be a great way for someone with only moderate Latin skills to get a fuller understanding of the play.

My translation of the *Casina* is, however, meant to retain, as far as possible, the Roman social context of the play. Turning Plautus's Latin into colloquial English inevitably required some loss of this social context, but more would have been lost with any attempt at turning Plautus's songs into English songs. My translation is also meant to work as a companion to the Latin text, and so I have tried to turn Plautus's Latin into fluent, familiar English, staying as true to the original as possible without sounding stilted. Readers who want to experience a fuller metrical understanding of the play will find some help and recommendations on page 28 of this volume.

I have also mostly stayed true to Lindsay's edition of the Latin text, which includes a few elements that are not original to Plautus. One such element is the division of the play into five acts. At least 100 years after the death of Plautus his plays were divided into acts in order to match the characteristics of Greek New Comedy, which featured, between each act, musical interludes that were non-essential to the development of the plot.[2] The act divisions can be useful, however, in locating specific scenes of the play, especially for jumping between the Latin and the English translation, so I retained them. Lindsay also lists the *senex* ("old man"), who is unnamed in the Latin manuscript traditions except in scene headings added later, by the name of Lysidamus.[3] Finally, I have retained Lindsay's choice to spell the *matrona*'s name Cleustrata, rather than using the spelling "Cleostrata" (the spelling used in the Latin manuscripts). The spelling "Cleustrata" better reflects the way the name was pronounced in Latin, with three syllables, not four.

---

[2] See Marshall 2006 on how the metre of *Casina* suggests four "arcs" that work better to identify the structure of the play as Plautus intended it (Marshall 2006: 210).

[3] A convenient summary of the scholarly debate around the *senex*'s name can be found in Franko 1999: 12, note 32.

Cast of Characters

[A rough guide to the English pronunciation of the characters' names appears in parentheses after each name; the stress falls on the syllable in ALL CAPS.]

Olympio (o-LIM-pee-o): Lysidamus's loyal farm manager (enslaved)

Chalinus (ka-LEE-nus): loyal servant to the son of Lysidamus and Cleustrata (enslaved)

Cleustrata (CLEW-stra-ta): wife of Lysidamus (free)

Pardalisca (par-da-LIS-ka): Cleustrata's elderly servant (enslaved)

Myrrhina (MIH-ri-na): wife of Alcesimus, and Cleustrata's friend and neighbour (free)

Lysidamus (li-si-DA-mus): the head of the household, and husband of Cleustrata (free)

Alcesimus (al-KESS-i-mus): Myrrhina's husband, neighbour to Cleustrata and Lysidamus (free)

Chytrio (KIH-tree-o): the hired cook (probably enslaved)

Note: For the acrostic *argumentum* (plot summary) that was added to the play perhaps around 150 CE, see page 220.

Prologue (lines 1-88)

The setting of the play is the Greek city of Athens. The characters in Plautus's plays are usually supposed to be Greek, and have Greek names, because his plays were reworkings of original Greek comedies. Because they were written for a Roman audience, however, the characters often represent comic versions of recognizably Roman types. They could safely do or say things that might have undermined strict Roman morality, though, because they were supposed to be Greeks. For a plot summary of the play, please see page 6, in the introduction. Scene summaries can be found before each scene in the Latin text.

Welcome,[1] all you excellent members of the audience! You guys seem very sincere – the goddess Sincerity[2] is totally on your side! Am I right? If so, give me a round of applause, so I'll know right from the start that you're here to have a good time [*pause for applause*]. Now, the smartest people are those who drink old wine, and enjoy watching the old plays. Since you guys like old-fashioned words and great works of the past, it's obvious that you'll prefer the old plays. The new comedies coming out now are worth less than the new coinage. When we found out from the rumour mill that you folks were insisting on the plays of Plautus, we decided to put on this classic comedy of his that some of you older folks thought was pretty good at the time. Now the younger folks in the audience aren't familiar with it, I know, but we'll make special efforts so they'll become fans of it too. When this was first acted, it beat out all the other plays.

Ah, those were the days, when playwrights really WERE playwrights! [*sighing*] But they've all gone now, to the place we're all headed for eventually. But [*brightening*] though gone, they can still make us laugh us just as if they were here.

I beg you all especially to pay kind attention to our actors. Cast out of your minds your worries and your bills, and make sure none of you is bothering about debt collectors. It's holiday time, and it's a holiday for the loan sharks as well. It's all relaxation and tranquility around the forum.[3] The loan sharks are reason-

---

[1] Part of this prologue appears to have been written by Plautus (in about 185 BC), and part by whoever put on a revival of the play about thirty years later.
[2] The goddess Sincerity is *Fides* in Latin, which can also mean "good faith", or "good credit".
[3] The forum was a big open area, the bustling economic and political centre of Rome and other towns and cities.

able, they don't demand payment during festivals! (of course, they don't repay what *they* owe to anyone even after the festival, am I right?).

Now, if your ears are ready, pay attention: I'm going to give you the name of this comedy. In Greek it's called "Clerumenoe", which we'd say in Latin was "The Lot-Drawers". Diphilus wrote the Greek version, which later the dog-named[4] poet, Plautus, rewrote in Latin.

Here's the plot:

An old married man lives here; he has a son, who lives with his father in that house there. The old master has a certain slave who's down with a sickness – I mean, by Hercules,[5] he's literally in bed! (so you won't see him). This slave, well it was sixteen years ago one evening just at dusk, he saw a newborn girl being abandoned.[6] Immediately he goes up to the woman and begs her to let him take the baby. He manages to persuade her, and he brings the little one home right away. He gives her to his mistress[7] and begs her to look after her and bring her up. His mistress agreed, and brought up the girl very carefully, just as though the girl were her own daughter.[8]

When the girl grew up and started looking attractive to the men, well, Lysidamus, master of the house (the one I was telling you about), falls madly in love with her – and likewise so does his son. Now each of them is busy planning his campaign, both father and son, keeping their plans secret from each other. Lysidamus has told his head slave – that is, his farm manager[9] – to

---

[4] The name Plautus is here said to be "dog-named" (literally "with a barking name"), probably because Plautus was a common name for a dog (*plautus* meant "flat", hence, according to the second century CE grammarian Festus, the name "Plautus" was often used as a name for dogs with broad flat ears that hung down – Paul. Fest. p. 231 M).
[5] On swearwords in the plays of Plautus, see note 124 on page 41.
[6] Exposure (abandoning unwanted babies) was considered a legitimate form of family planning in the Greek and Roman world. In reality, most of the infants must have died, but in Greek and Roman stories (comedy, novels, myth) they are always rescued.
[7] "His mistress" refers to the *matrona* Cleustrata.
[8] "Just as though the girl were her own daughter" is an important line, but needs some explanation for modern readers. To Plautus's original audiences, it would have meant that the girl was being brought up with the modesty and sexual inhibitions of a freeborn girl, and that she was sexually off-limits to anyone except her eventual husband. To the Roman audiences this was essential to the plot, since otherwise her subsequent recognition as a freeborn citizen would have been problematic.
[9] "Farm manager" refers to the *uilicus*, who usually was left in charge of the master's farm, overseeing the other slaves.

try to marry the girl, since he thinks if she becomes his slave's wife, that *he* – the master, that is – will get secret access to her without his wife knowing.

Meanwhile his son has told his own slave, who served him when he was in the army, to try to marry Casina (that's the girl's name), knowing that this would place her in his own household. Very handy for him!

The old man's wife knows that her husband is "interested" in the girl, so she's supporting her son's scheme. But the old master has figured out about his son also being in love with Casina, and he's worried his son might get in his way. So he's sent the boy off to foreign parts.

His mother, though, is looking after her son's "interests". Don't expect to see him in this play today, though. The playwright, Plautus, didn't feel like letting him return to the city, so he closed a bridge somewhere along his route home.

Now some of you here today are muttering to yourselves: "Come on, by Hercules, what's this nonsense? Slave weddings? Slaves getting married, or even arranging their own marriages? Nowhere does this happen, nowhere in the world!" But I'm telling you it is done! In Greece, in Carthage, and even closer to home, in Apulia. Slave weddings there are a bigger deal than the weddings of freeborn couples.[10] You don't believe me? I'll bet you a jar of honey wine it's true, as long as we have a Punic[11] judge, or a Greek – or even an Apulian for all I care. What, no takers? Well, I guess no one's thirsty!

Let me return to that foundling girl, the one those slave dudes are trying so hard to get as a wife. We're going to find out she's not just modestly brought up, but freeborn as well – an Athenian citizen, in fact![12] So she won't be having any inappropriate sex[13] in this comedy [*pause for groans of disappointment from the audience*] – yeah, I mean that. But soon, by Hercules – as soon as the

---

[10] This claim is exaggerated. Slaves could have marital relationships that were recognized more or less formally in different parts of the Mediterranean world, but slave "weddings" would rarely or never have been more elaborate than free persons' weddings.

[11] "Punic" here means "Carthaginian" (from the state of Carthage).

[12] Remember that this play is ostensibly set in Athens, although Plautus more or less played with this concept, making numerous references in the play to daily life in Rome.

[13] "Inappropriate sex" is a translation of the Latin *stuprum*, which could mean "rape" but could also just mean sex outside legitimate marriage (not something in which a freeborn citizen girl ought to be involved).

play is over, if anyone gives "her" some money I expect "she'll" do a bit of marrying,[14] and "she" won't be waiting around for the priests.[15] [*pause for coarse laughter from audience*]

That's all. Fare well, be successful, and conquer with true valour as you've done in the past.[16]

---

[14] Since actors in these sorts of Roman plays were all male, the "bit of marrying" was a sex work advertisement for the boy actor who usually played the parts of young women, and who might have played Casina in this play if she had had a walk-on part. Given the outcome of Lysidamus's and Olympio's attempt to have sex with "Casina" in the play, however, this offer to the audience was probably a joke that they would only fully appreciate after Lysidamus and Olympio describe their unfortunate wedding night (875-962).

[15] "Priests" here is a translation of *auspices*, people who were skilled in reading the signs from the gods, and who were therefore employed at weddings to ensure that everything was done properly (thus ensuring a prosperous marriage).

[16] This line was probably meant for the soldiers in the audience. Most freeborn Roman male citizens would have served in the army at some point, since Rome was almost constantly at war during the third and second centuries BCE.

Act I

I.i Scene with Olympio and Chalinus (lines 89-143)

A middle-aged man wearing the simple clothing of a slave comes on from stage right (that is, from the direction of the countryside), followed by a younger man, also a slave.

Olympio: [*turning around angrily*] Aren't I allowed to talk and think about my own affairs as I like without you eavesdropping? Why are you following me, shithead?

Chalinus: Because I'm like your shadow, wherever you go I'm sure to follow. By Pollux,[1] even if you go and get yourself crucified,[2] I'm bound to follow you. So have a guess at what's going to happen: you'll never be able to marry Casina like I know you want to, not without my knowing it, no matter how sneaky you are.

Olympio: Why, what business is it of yours?

Chalinus: What are you talking about, loser? Why are you, a stupid farm manager, creeping around in the city?

Olympio: 'Cuz I feel like it.

Chalinus: Why aren't you out in the country managing your realm?[3] Why don't you keep out of what's happening in the city, and instead focus on your proper work? You've come here to snatch my bride from me! Go away back to the farm, back to your official duties.

Olympio: Chalinus, I haven't forgotten my duties – I've appointed someone to look after everything on the farm, anyway. Meanwhile if I achieve what I came to the city for, I'll marry the girl that you're so desperately in love with, the lovely and charming Casina, your fellow slave. And when I take her as my wife to the country with me I'll sleep safe and sound in my rural domain.

Chalinus: You? Marry her? By Hercules I'd rather hang myself than let you become her husband!

---

[1] See note 124 on page 41 for information on swearing in the plays of Plautus.
[2] Slaves whose masters decided they deserved the death penalty would be crucified, which was a hideously painful and slow death. Perhaps because it was such a horrifying fate, slaves in Roman comedy frequently joke about other slaves getting crucified. It seems to have had the same casual meaning as "go to hell" does now.
[3] "Realm" is a translation of *praefectura*, which usually referred to a province over which a governor had authority, but here refers grandiosely to Lysidamus's farm.

Olympio: That girl is my prize:[4] so go put that noose around your neck.

Chalinus: You piece of shit! She? Your prize?

Olympio: You'll know it soon enough.

Chalinus: Just go and die!

Olympio: [*rubbing his hands together and grinning*] I'll make you miserable in so many ways at my wedding!

Chalinus: Oh yeah? [*pretending to be afraid*] What are you going to do to me?

Olympio: What am I going to do to you? First of all, you'll be the one holding a torch for my new bride; second of all, you'll always be a worthless piece of crap,[5] third of all, when you arrive at the farm, you'll be given one amphora,[6] and there's one narrow path, there's one water-source, one copper pot and eight big water casks. And if you don't keep them all filled up, I'll fill *you* up with whippings. I'll make your back properly bent from carrying water – I'll make a horse's ass strap[7] out of your hide. After that, unless you eat a whole pile of cattle fodder or eat dirt like a worm, if you ever ask to taste anything at all – well, by Pollux, there's no hunger equal to the hunger I'll make you feel when I get you down in the country. And after that? when you're exhausted and starved, I'll make sure you sleep the way you deserve to.

Chalinus: [*crossing his arms and smirking*] Yeah? What'll you do?

Olympio: I'll see you're securely imprisoned in a hole in the wall,[8] where you'll be able to listen to me kissing her, and her saying to me: [*in falsetto*] "my darling Olympio, my life, my little honey, my delight, let me kiss your dear little eyes, my delight! Let me love you, please, my festival day, my little sparrow, my dove, my hare!" [*speaking in his normal voice*] When she says these things to me then you (you worthless loser) will squirm

---

[4] "Prize" is a translation of *praeda*, which means prize, or booty, taken by soldiers from the defeated enemy.

[5] This line doesn't quite fit, so some scholars think it was mistakenly added to the play by a copyist.

[6] An amphora was a tall, narrow earthenware jar that was used for transporting liquids and grains.

[7] That is, a "crupper", which is a strap that runs from the saddle and loops under the horse's tail to prevent the saddle from slipping forward. This is probably a play on Chalinus's name, which means "bridle" (Franko 1999: 11, note 28).

[8] Richlin says, of this line, that Chalinus "must be envisioned as squeezed between the shutters [...] and the window bars that appeared in contemporary agricultural architecture and in security-minded houses in Plautus's own plays" (Richlin 2015: 56).

around in the middle of the wall like a mouse. Now, so you won't try to answer me back, I'm going into the house. Your conversation bores me. [*exit Olympio*]

Chalinus: I'm following *you* in. By Pollux, don't think you'll do anything without me watching. [*exit Chalinus*]

Act II

II.i Scene with Cleustrata and Pardalisca (lines 144-164)

A middle-aged woman dressed as a citizen wife appears at the door of her house, calling back to Pardalisca inside the house.

Cleustrata: Stamp the storeroom latch with the seal, and then bring me the ring.[1] I'm going over to my next door neighbour's. If my husband wants me for anything, send for me there.

Pardalisca: [*sticking her head out through the doorway*] But Lysidamus ordered a meal to be prepared for him.

Cleustrata: Shush! Be quiet and go away; I'm not preparing or cooking anything today, not when he's setting himself up against our son and me because of his own selfishness and his "love" affair – that disgusting man! I'll make that loverboy pay with hunger,[2] with thirst, with curses, and – more curses! By Pollux, I'll choke him properly with some pretty disagreeable things I'll tell him. I'll make him live the life he deserves, that Acheronfodder,[3] that scandal-chaser, that den of worthlessness! Now I'm going to vent about it to my neighbour. [*hearing a noise*] But her door just creaked, and look! My neighbour herself is going out. By Pollux, I haven't chosen my time well to visit her.

II.ii Scene with Myrrhina and Cleustrata (lines 165-216)

Another middle-aged woman, also dressed as a citizen wife, appears, coming out of the neighbouring house.

Myrrhina: Follow me closely, attendants. [*to other slaves within her house*] Listen up, you! Is anyone listening to what I'm saying? I'll be in here [*gesturing to Cleustrata's house*] if my husband or anyone wants me. When I'm home alone I get drowsy, and can't do my work as well. Didn't I tell you to bring my distaff[4] for me?

Cleustrata: Hello Myrrhina.

Myrrhina: By Castor![5] Hello! But is something wrong, dear?

---

[1] The *matrona* (female head of the household, or *mater familias*) was responsible for making sure the household slaves didn't steal supplies from the pantry. She therefore stamped the latch with her seal (in this case a seal ring), so any tampering would be obvious.
[2] Since a wife (*mater familias*) is in charge of the storeroom and of the food preparation, she could apparently punish her husband by refusing to feed him.
[3] The Acheron was a mythical river in the underworld.
[4] A distaff is a spindle used in winding wool or flax.
[5] See note 124 on page 41 for information on swearing in the plays of Plautus.

Cleustrata: [*bursting into tears*] There's always something wrong for women who are unhappily married. In the house, and out of the house, there's always enough to upset us. I was about to pay a call on you.

Myrrhina: Well, by Pollux, and I was coming to see you. But what's making you unhappy now? Whatever makes you sad makes me sad too.

Cleustrata: I know you mean that, by Castor, since I have no better friend and neighbour than you and there's no one who's got more of the sympathy I want.

Myrrhina: I'm your friend, and that's why I'm longing to know about it.

Cleustrata: I am being terribly disrespected at home.

Myrrhina: Oh no, what is it? Tell me about it again, please! I haven't quite understood your complaints, by Pollux.

Cleustrata: My husband has disrespected me in the worst way possible, and I'm not being allowed my rights.

Myrrhina: How shocking, if what you're saying is true. In general it's the husbands who aren't able to get their rights from us women.

Cleustrata: Against my will he wants to give my slave girl – who is *mine*! I brought her up at *my* expense! He wants to marry her to his farm manager! But really he wants to make her his mistress!

Myrrhina: Shsh! Please! [*shooing away the slave attendants hurriedly*]⁶

Cleustrata: We can talk now, as it's just the two of us.

Myrrhina: That's true. But in what way is she yours? A good wife shouldn't have any private property apart from her husband. If she does, she can't have come by it honestly, since either she's stolen it from her husband or she's received it from a lover. In my opinion everything you own is your husband's.

---

6   "Shsh" translates *tace*, which Lindsay replaced with *dice* in his edition. Linday also gave the next speech to Myrrhina, and the reply "That's true" to Cleustrata. I have reverted to the original *tace*, and followed MacCary and Willcock's speaker attribution. Feltovitch argues that Myrrhina's initially unsympathetic reaction to Cleustrata's complaints are consistent with a concern for the potentially negative consequences for wives if they stand up to their husbands too directly (Feltovitch 2015, in particular 253). It makes more sense, therefore, that Myrrhina's response should suggest that she is worried about the enslaved attendants reporting Cleustrata's open resentment to Lysidamus.

Cleustrata: Everything you're saying is an attack on me, your friend.

Myrrhina: Oh shush, don't be silly and listen to me: don't set yourself up against your husband. Let him have his love affair, let him do what he wants as long as you've got what you want at home.

Cleustrata: Are you crazy? You're saying things that aren't in your best interest.

Myrrhina: You're being foolish. You must always make sure your husband doesn't say those terrible words.

Cleustrata: What words?

Myrrhina: "I divorce you!"[7]

Cleustrata: Shush! Be quiet!

Myrrhina: What is it?

Cleustrata: Look!

Myrrhina: Who is it?

Cleustrata: Look, it's my husband coming; go back to your house, quickly! Go on, please!

Myrrhina: All right, I'm going.

Cleustrata: I'll tell you all about it soon, when we both have some free time: for now, good bye.

Myrrhina: Take care of yourself. [*exit Myrrhina*]

II.iii Scene with Lysidamus and Cleustrata (lines 217-278)

A man of about sixty years old comes on stage, dressed as a pater familias, *or male head of household, and walking with a sprightly step.*

Lysidamus: In my opinion, love matters more than anything, no matter how bright and shiny![8] And no one can say there's anything that's got more wit and charm than love. In fact I'm amazed that when cooks are seasoning the food they don't make more use of spicy love,[9] 'cuz it's better than all the others. Adding a dash of love will please everyone, I believe. Nothing can be

---

[7] *I foras mulier* literally means "Get out of the house, wife!" and was, apparently, the formula for divorce.

[8] This isn't supposed to make much sense. Lysidamus is euphoric, thinking about his love for Casina, and so his language is somewhat ornate.

[9] As MacCary and Willcock (1976) note, it is probably relevant here that the girl Casina's name sounds like the Latin word for the spice cinnamon (*casia*).

either salty[10] or sweet unless a pinch of love is mixed in. Bitter gall will become as sweet as honey, and a gloomy man will become charming and mild-mannered. I'm basing my reasoning on my own experience, not just from what other people say. Since falling in love with Casina, I look better, and I've become more elegant than Elegance herself. I'm constantly bothering all the perfume-sellers: wherever I find a charming cologne, I buy it and wear it just to please her. And I think she's pleased all right! But [*groaning*] my wife is torturing me – just by being alive! Wait – I see her standing there in a bad temper: I should butter her up, the old bag.

[*going up to Cleustrata and trying to embrace her*] My wife, my loveliness! How are you doing?

Cleustrata: Go away and stop pawing me!

Lysidamus: Now then my dear Juno,[11] it's not right that you should be so frowny to me, your Jupiter. [*Cleustrata begins to storm off and he grabs her wrist*] Where are you going now?

Cleustrata: Let go of me!

Lysidamus: Stay here!

Cleustrata: I won't.

Lysidamus: Then I'll follow you, by Pollux!

Cleustrata: Please! Are you in your right mind?

Lysidamus: Yes I am. I just love you, that's all.

Cleustrata: I don't want your love.

Lysidamus: You can't always get what you want.

Cleustrata: You're tiring me to death!

Lysidamus: [*quietly, not intending his wife to hear*] I only wish that was true!

Cleustrata: [*overhearing, and responding under her breath*] And I believe you mean it when you say that!

Lysidamus: [*aloud*] Look back at me, my sweet!

Cleustrata: [*sarcastically*] Of course, since you're *my* sweet, I suppose. What's that smell of cologne, please?

---

[10] The Latin word for "salty" can also mean "witty".
[11] Lysidamus is calling his wife "Juno" and himself "Jupiter" to emphasize the authority they have, respectively, over the members of their household.

Lysidamus: [*aside*] Uh-oh, I'm screwed! I'm completely trapped! I should have rubbed this stuff off of my head with my cloak. May the good god Mercury[12] smite you, perfume-sellers, for selling it to me.

Cleustrata: Gah! You – nothing! You grey-haired insect! I can barely keep myself from saying what you are! You deadbeat! Are you really strutting about the streets at your advanced age wearing cologne?

Lysidamus: [*with an air of outrage*] By Pollux! I have been helping a friend who was buying cologne.

Cleustrata: [*to the audience*] He came up with that lie pretty quickly! [*to her husband*] Does nothing shame you?

Lysidamus: Whatever you like.

Cleustrata: In what brothel have you been lying?

Lysidamus: [*gasping in outrage*] I? In a brothel?

Cleustrata: I know more than you think I know.

Lysidamus: [*worried*] What? What do you know?

Cleustrata: I know that, of all old men, no one is more of a loser than you, you old has-been. Where are you coming from, loser? Where have you been? Where've you been whoring? Where've you been carousing? You are drunk, by Castor: look at how wrinkled your cloak is!

Lysidamus: [*outraged*] May the gods shower us both with bad luck if I've put a single drop of wine into my mouth today.

Cleustrata: Fine, do whatever you like, drink, eat, waste your money.

Lysidamus: Hey, that's enough, woman: control yourself and don't be so shrill. Save some of your eloquence so you can quarrel with me about it again tomorrow. But what do you say? Have you calmed down enough to do what your husband wants instead of setting yourself against him?

Cleustrata: What are you talking about?

Lysidamus: How can you ask? I'm talking about the slave girl Casina being married off to Olympio my farm manager, who's an honest slave. She'll have plenty of firewood, hot water, food, and clothing with him. She'll be able to raise sons with him properly,

---

[12] Mercury was the god of, among other things, buying and selling, messages, travellers, and trickery.

as opposed to what she'd have with that worthless, dishonest shield-bearing[13] slave you'd like to give her to, who doesn't have a penny saved up.[14]

Cleustrata: I'm amazed, by Castor, that you've forgotten your duty in your old age.

Lysidamus: What do you mean?

Cleustrata: If you were acting rightly and properly, you'd allow me to look after the slave girls, since that's MY job.

Lysidamus: Why, for the gods' sake, do you want to give her to a shield-bearer?!

Cleustrata: Because we should do what benefits our only son.[15]

Lysidamus: He may be my only son, but I'm just as much his only father: it's more fair for him to give in to me than for me to give up what I want to him.

Cleustrata: By Castor, you're looking for trouble.

Lysidamus: [*under his breath*] Uh-oh, I think she smells a rat... [*aloud*] Wh-who, m-me?

Cleustrata: Yes, you! What makes you stammer like that? Why are you so keen on getting your way in this?

Lysidamus: I just want her married to an honest slave, rather than to a dishonest one.

Cleustrata: What if I manage to persuade your farm manager to let Chalinus marry the girl?

Lysidamus: And what if I manage to persuade that shield-bearer to let my farm manager marry her? I think I could persuade him, too.

---

[13] Remember (see line 55 of the prologue) that Chalinus had been armour-bearer (soldier's assistant) to the couple's son.

[14] Enslaved people in Roman society were often allowed to have *peculia* (singular: *peculium*), which was money or property they would have acquired as gifts from (usually) their masters or their master's friends. Technically the master owned whatever the slave owned, but allowing their enslaved dependants to have *peculia* was a way of encouraging their ongoing obedience and cooperation.

[15] As Richlin points out, the most cynical element to the plot of the *Casina* is that Cleustrata's actions are directed towards ensuring that her son, rather than her husband, can use Casina (the girl she's brought up like a daughter) for sex (Richlin 2015: 50). Casina's best interests are not Cleustrata's priority, although, until Casina's freeborn status is discovered, the Roman audience likely considered that Cleustrata's planned outcome was the best an enslaved girl in Casina's position could expect.

Cleustrata: OK, I agree. Do you want me to call Chalinus out here for you? You try to win him over, while I try to win over your farm manager.

Lysidamus: Good idea.

Cleustrata: He's coming over now. Let's see which of us is more persuasive. [*exit Cleustrata*]

Lysidamus: [*to the audience*] Now I can say it out loud: I wish Hercules and the gods would smite her down. I'm tortured by my passion and she's interfering on purpose. My wife guesses what I'm planning: that's why she's helping the armour-bearer.

II.iv Scene with Lysidamus and Chalinus (lines 279-308)

Lysidamus: [*seeing Chalinus come out of the house*] I wish all the gods and goddesses would smite him down!

Chalinus: Your wife was saying that! [*quickly correcting himself*] – uh, she was saying that you were calling for me.

Lysidamus: Yes, I did.

Chalinus: Go ahead then.

Lysidamus: First of all, I want you to speak to me without that scowl on your face: only an idiot looks sullen in front of someone more powerful. [*changing his tone*] I've always considered you an honest and upright man.

Chalinus: Oh...kay..? But if that's what you think, why don't you set me free?

Lysidamus: I'd like to, really I would, but there's no point in me wanting it, unless you help a bit.

Chalinus: I just want to know what you want.

Lysidamus: Listen up, and I'll tell you: I promised to give Casina as a wife to my farm manager.

Chalinus: But your wife and son promised her to me.

Lysidamus: I know, but would you rather be a free single man, or a married man, with you and your children living out your lives as slaves? This is your choice, it's one or the other.

Chalinus: If I were free, I'd be living at my own expense. As it is, I live at your expense.[16] And there's no man on earth I'd give

---

[16] This sort of comment by enslaved characters in Plautus probably hit different members of the Roman audience differently. The members of the audience who had some expe-

up Casina to.

Lysidamus: Get out of here! Go into the house and call my wife out here now. And also bring the big jar out with you, full of water, and the lottery tokens.

Chalinus: All right, I will.

Lysidamus: By Pollux, I'll put a stop to her scheming[17] one way or another. If I can't get what I want one way, then at least I'll have a chance by drawing lots. Then I'll get my revenge on you and those who're taking your part.

Chalinus: But I'LL draw the winning token.

Lysidamus: By Pollux, you can go get yourself crucified!

Chalinus: She'll be marrying me, no matter what tricks you try to pull.

Lysidamus: Will you get out of my sight?!

Chalinus: I know you don't want to look at me, but I can live with that. [*exit Chalinus*]

Lysidamus: I must be the unluckiest man alive – everything is stacked against me! Now what if my wife persuades Olympio to agree not to marry Casina: if she does that, I'll be one pathetic old man! If she hasn't succeeded, there's a slight hope for me in the drawing of lots; but if the lottery goes against me, I'll use my sword as a bed and throw myself down on it. But look! Good, Olympio is coming out.

II.v Scene with Olympio and Lysidamus (lines 309-352)

Olympio: [*coming out of the house while speaking to Cleustrata, who remains in the house*] By Pollux, you might as well put me into a hot oven and bake me, instead of a loaf of golden-brown bread, ma'am, as get me to do what you're asking.

Lysidamus: Whew! There's still hope, from what I'm hearing!

Olympio: Why are you scaring me, ma'am, with this talk about manumission? Even if you and your son weren't interested in

---

rience of slavery may have understood that, in the play, Chalinus knows perfectly well that he can't trust Lysidamus's offer of freedom, and so he rejects it. The slave-owners in the audience, on the other hand, may have interpreted it as evidence for the servile and dependent nature of enslaved persons. We certainly can't take Chalinus's comment, however, as evidence for how enslaved people really felt.

17 Literally: "I'll put an end to this attack" or "I'll beat down that missile".

freeing me, if both of you were completely against it, I can buy my freedom for practically nothing.[18]

Lysidamus: What's going on there? Who are you quarrelling with, Olympio?

Olympio: The same person you're always quarrelling with.

Lysidamus: With my wife?

Olympio: What wife are you talking about? You're just like a hunter, spending your life, days and nights, with your hound bitch.

Lysidamus: What's she up to? Why's she talking with you?

Olympio: She's begging – she's pleading with me – not to marry Casina.

Lysidamus: What did you say?

Olympio: I said I wouldn't give place to Jupiter himself,[19] if he begged me.

Lysidamus: May the gods protect you!

Olympio: Now she's fit to burst, she's so angry with me.

Lysidamus: By Pollux, I wish she'd split herself in two.

Olympio: Haw haw, by Pollux, I bet she's already been split in two, if you're a proper husband! [*making a crude gesture*] By Pollux, though, your love affair is a pain for me: your wife hates me, your son hates me, the other slaves hate me.

Lysidamus: Why's that your problem? As long as Jupiter [*pointing to himself*] is on your side, you shouldn't care what those lesser gods are up to.

Olympio: That's a load of crap: as if you don't know how suddenly human Jupiters can up and die. If you, Jupiter [*pointing a finger at Lysidamus*], go and die, and your realm is inherited by those lesser gods, who'll save me, or my back, or my head, or my legs then?[20]

---

[18] Literally: "I can become free for a *libella* (1/10th of a *denarius*)." Olympio means that Lysidamus will allow him to buy his freedom very cheaply (provided that he remain loyal to him).

[19] Remember that Lysidamus referred to himself as Jupiter at line 230, and is about to do so again at line 331. It will become clear that Olympio means that he will try not to give Casina up even to his master, despite having agreed to it.

[20] "Me, or my back, or my head, or my legs" refers to Olympio, and particularly these body parts, being susceptible to physical abuse by Cleustrata and son if Lysidamus were to die and not be around to protect him.

Lysidamus: It'll go better than you think, if we get what I want, and I can get Casina into bed.

Olympio: By Hercules, I don't think that's going to happen. Your wife is so fiercely opposed to letting me marry Casina.

Lysidamus: Here's what I'll do: I'll throw lottery tokens into a jar and I'll assign lots to you and Chalinus. I think, the way things are, we'll have to switch to new weapons in this fight.

Olympio: What if the lottery results aren't what you want?

Lysidamus: Don't tempt fate! I'm relying on the gods. We'll have to trust the gods.

Olympio: Those are cheap words! All mortals rely on the gods, but I've seen lots of people that were relying on the gods ending up disappointed.

Lysidamus: Shush! Pipe down for a moment.

Olympio: Why?

Lysidamus: Look, Chalinus is coming out of the house with a jar and the lottery tokens: now we'll engage, with our banners flying.[21]

II.vi Scene with Cleustrata, Chalinus, Lysidamus, and Olympio (lines 353-423)

Cleustrata: [*coming out of the house with Chalinus*] Chalinus, what does my husband want with me?

Chalinus: By Pollux, what he wants is to see you dead and being cremated outside the city gates.

Cleustrata: [*sadly*] By Castor, I believe he does.

Chalinus: Well I don't just "believe he does", by Pollux – I know it for a certainty!

Lysidamus: [*to Olympio, having overheard Chalinus*] I have more skilled workers on my estate than I thought: I've got a soothsayer on staff![22] [*nervously*] How about we signal the troops to advance – that is, shall we go up to them? Follow me. [*to Chalinus*] What are you doing?

Chalinus: Everything you ordered is here: wife, lottery tokens, jar, and even myself.

---

[21] This is another military metaphor.
[22] "I've got a soothsayer on staff" means that Lysidamus thinks Chalinus must be clairvoyant to have learned about his secret wish that his wife would die.

Olympio: Even you yourself? You've brought one more thing than I wanted.

Chalinus: I bet that's true, by Pollux! I really am a thorn in your side, pricking your sweet little heart... You're sweating from fear now, you whipping post.

Lysidamus: Shut up, Chalinus.

Chalinus: That guy needs to be held down and given what he deserves.

Olympio: Oh really? *He's* the one that's used to being held down... [*smirking*][23]

Lysidamus: Put the jar down here, and give me the lottery tokens. Pay attention. [*to Cleustrata*] But anyhow, I thought I'd be able to get what I want from you – to get Casina for my wife; and I still think so.

Cleustrata: For *your* wife?

Lysidamus: Yes, my – that is, no, I didn't mean to say that! [*babbling nervously*] I meant to say "my" but I said "his", and although I may want her ... by Hercules, I said it wrong just now, didn't I?

Cleustrata: You said it wrong, by Pollux, and you've acted wrong.

Lysidamus: [*pointing to Olympio*] HIS wife – I mean MY – by Hercules, whoo! (*wiping his sweaty forehead, and giving a wide artificial grin*) There, I've finally managed to get back on solid ground.

Cleustrata: You make a lot of mistakes, by Pollux.

Lysidamus: Well, that's often the way, when you want something so much. Now, Olympio and I, both of us, we ask you, given your rights in this matter...

Cleustrata: What?

Lysidamus: Well I'll tell you, my sweetie: about that Casina – you might do a favour for this farm manager of ours [*gesturing to Olympio*].

Cleustrata: By Pollux, I'm not doing it, and I don't approve of it.

---

[23] In Latin, Chalinus said *comprime* (translated here as "to be held down and given what he deserves"), which can mean "restrain" or "control", but can also mean "penetrate sexually". Olympio's response is to suggest that Chalinus has regularly been sexually penetrated by Lysidamus. For Roman attitudes around sex between men, see note 4 on page 216 in the English translation at line 963, V.iv.

Lysidamus: In that case, then, I'll start sorting the lottery tokens for each side.

Cleustrata: Who's stopping you?

Lysidamus: I rightly consider this to be the best and fairest way. We'll be pretty happy if it turns out the way we want in the end; but if it doesn't, we'll accept it calmly. [*to Olympio*] Choose your token. Look what's written on it.

Olympio: [*reading it*] It says "number 1".

Chalinus: It isn't fair – he got one before I did.

Lysidamus: Take the other token, please.

Chalinus: Give it here. Wait a minute – I've just had an idea: make sure there isn't another token already in the jar, under the water.[24]

Lysidamus: [*enraged*] You lowlife, do you think I'd stoop to your kind of tricks?

Cleustrata: [*to Chalinus*] There's no other token: just keep your cool.

Chalinus: [*praying dutifully*] Let whatever good fortune that may be in store for me...

Olympio: [*interrupting*] I suppose it's whatever *bad* fortune will come to you, by Pollux! I know your so-called piety. Just wait a minute though, I want to be sure: is your token made out of poplar wood, or fir?[25]

Chalinus: Why should you care about that?

Olympio: Because one of them might float higher – that's my fear.

Lysidamus: Good, now take care and both of you cast your tokens in here [*holding the jar of water*]. There [*offering the jar to Cleustrata so she can draw the lots*], it's level.[26]

Olympio: Hey, don't trust your wife!

Lysidamus: Don't worry.

---

[24] Chalinus suspects Lysidamus or Olympio might have added an extra token to the jar with their winning number on it, which would increase their chances of winning.

[25] Another way of cheating would be to use a token made out of a lighter wood, which would float to the top of the jar.

[26] The lot-taking probably involved shaking the urn to randomize the placement of the tokens, and then waiting till the water was level again before drawing the lots (MacCary and Willcock 1976: 144).

Olympio: By Hercules, I think she'll bewitch whatever token she touches.

Lysidamus: Be quiet.

Olympio: OK, I won't talk. [*praying in an undertone*] Please gods!...

Chalinus: [*interrupting*] May you be chained and held down for a beating today.[27]

Olympio: [*continuing his interrupted prayer*] ... May the lottery work in my favour...

Chalinus: [*interrupting*] ... May you be strung up with your feet dangling, by Hercules.[28]

Olympio: And may you blow your eyes out of your head through the nose!

Chalinus: What are you afraid of? It should be ready by now – your noose, I mean.

Olympio: You're so dead!

Lysidamus: Pay attention, both of you.

Olympio: OK.

Lysidamus: Now, Cleustrata, just so you won't claim I did anything underhand, or suspect that I did, I'll let you do it: go on, draw the lot.

Olympio: [*groaning anxiously*] You're destroying me.

Chalinus: He'll be better off without you, then.[29]

Cleustrata: [*reponding to Lysidamus's proposal that she draw the lots*] That's fair.

Chalinus: Please gods... let your token be a run-away, and run right out of the jar.

Olympio: What are you saying? Just because you're a delinquent runaway slave,[30] you want everyone to act like you?

---

[27] Chalinus literally wishes Olympio to be bound with a fetter or chain (*canem*) and held down to the ground by a two-pronged fork (*furcam*) over his neck, in preparation for a beating.

[28] Slave-owners sometimes punished their slaves by hanging them up by their wrists and then having them beaten in this position.

[29] Chalinus pretends to take Olympio literally, and suggests that Lysidamus will be better off if Olympio were to be destroyed.

[30] In the skewed morality of slave-owning Rome, enslaved people that ran away were considered morally bad for doing so (while those who enslaved others were morally justified). In the plays of Plautus, calling someone a "runaway slave" (*fugitivus*) was a generalized insult.

Chalinus: I hope your token does what they say happened with Hercules' great great grandsons: dissolve during the shaking of the lots.[31]

Olympio: You'll soon be warmed up by such a good beating that you'll dissolve!

Lysidamus: Pay attention, Olympio!

Olympio: If this wise guy lets me.

Lysidamus: I hope the results are good and lucky for me!

Olympio: Yes, and for me!

Chalinus: Uh... no, actually!

Olympio: Yes for me, by Hercules!

Chalinus: For me, actually, by Hercules!

Cleustrata: [*smugly*] He's going to win, and your life's going to be pitiable.

Lysidamus: Punch him in the face for that spite. Go on, are you going to do anything? [*to Chalinus*] Don't you raise your hand!

Olympio: Do you want me to punch him or slap him?

Lysidamus: Whatever you like.

Olympio: [*striking Chalinus*] There!

Cleustrata: Why are you hitting him?

Olympio: Because my Jupiter here [*gesturing to Lysidamus*] ordered me to.

Cleustrata: [*to Chalinus*] Hit him hard.

Olympio: Ow! Jupiter, I'm being pounded!

Lysidamus: [*to Chalinus*] Why are you hitting him?

Chalinus: Because my Juno here [*gesturing to Cleustrata*] ordered me to.

Lysidamus: [*to Olympio*] You'll have to put up with it, if my wife is going to act like the boss while I'm still alive.

Cleustrata: Chalinus has got just as much right as Olympio to speak if he wants to.

---

[31] This is a reference to a myth involving the descendants of Hercules drawing lots to divide up the region of Messenia. One of the lottery tokens was made of baked clay, while the others were only sun-dried and so they dissolved in the water (see Pausanias 4.3.3-5 and Apollodorus 2.8.4).

Olympio: Why does he get to spoil my praying?[32]

Lysidamus: [*threateningly*] You'd better watch your step, Chalinus!

Chalinus: It's a bit late for that – after I've been punched in the face.

Lysidamus: [*to Cleustrata*] Go on, draw the lot now. You two [*to Chalinus and Olympio*] pay attention. [*to himself*] I don't even know where I am, I'm so anxious. I'm in a funk! I think I've got heart palpitations. My heart is pounding.

Cleustrata: [*fishing with her hand in the jar*] I've got hold of the token.

Lysidamus: [*anxiously*] Take it out.

Chalinus: [*hopefully, to Olympio*] Have you lost?

Olympio: Let's see it... [*jumping up joyously*] It's mine!

Chalinus: [*crushed*] Oh crucify me.

Cleustrata: You've lost, Chalinus.

Lysidamus: [*skipping with glee*] When the gods are good to us, Olympio, I'm so happy!

Olympio: [*piously*] It's because I'm so dutiful, as were my ancestors before me.[33]

Lysidamus: Go inside, dear, and prepare the wedding.

Cleustrata: [*resignedly*] I'll do what you command.

Lysidamus: You do know that it's way out in the countryside, to the farm where Olympio's going to have to bring Casina?

Cleustrata: Yes, I know.

Lysidamus: Go inside, and even though you don't like how it's turned out, make sure you do a good job.

Cleustrata: All right. [*exit Cleustrata*]

Lysidamus: Let's go inside too, to hurry things along.

Olympio: [*eagerly*] Am I slowing you down? [*exit Olympio*]

---

[32] A more literal translation would be "why is he spoiling my omen?" Olympio is referring to his interrupted prayer for success, begun at line 389. The Romans believed that interrupting a ritual rendered it ineffective.

[33] This is a joke, since enslaved persons in the Roman world were considered no longer to have parents, let alone ancestors.

Lysidamus: I don't want to say any more about it with this guy still here [*gesturing to Chalinus*]. [*exit Lysidamus*]

II.vii Scene with Chalinus (lines 424-436)

Chalinus: [*dejectedly*] OK, so if I go and hang myself I'd be making a game of all my efforts so far. And besides, I'd have to pay for the rope. And I'd just be making my enemies happy. What's the point, anyway, since I'm totally screwed? I've lost the lottery, and Casina will be marrying the farm manager. The worst part isn't even that the farm manager won – it's that the old man wanted so badly for her to marry Olympio instead of being given to me. How anxious he was, and in such a hurry, poor fool! And how he skipped about when the farm manager won.

Oops! I hear the door opening. I'd better get out of their way. My oh-so-friendly well-wishers are coming out. I'll sneak around here and spy on them.

II.viii Scene with Olympio, Lysidamus, and Chalinus (lines 437-514)

Olympio: [*coming out of the house with Lysidamus*] Just let me get him to the farm: I'll send you back a man with a forked stick just like a charcoal seller.[34]

Lysidamus: That's what he deserves!

Olympio: I'll see it's all taken care of.

Lysidamus: I'd have liked to send Chalinus out with you to get groceries, if he were around, so I could pile an extra annoyance onto our enemy, on top of his disappointment at losing.

Chalinus: [*quietly*] I'll scoot myself back towards the wall, like a scorpion; I've got to overhear their conversation! One of them's crucifying me and the other's tormenting me. But [*singing quietly*] here comes the blight [*referring to Olympio, dressed as a bridegroom*], all dressed in white! [*in his speaking voice again*] The perfect thing to stick spikes into. OK, wait – I'll put off suicide for a bit; I'll certainly send this guy to the underworld first.

Olympio: Look how accommodating I'm being to you! I've got you just the opportunity you wanted. Today you're going to get

---

[34] Olympio's plan is to torture Chalinus with the aid of a *furca*, or forked stick, to hold him down by the neck (see footnote 27 on page 187). But charcoal sellers perhaps carried their charcoal on forked sticks, which is why Olympio makes the comparison.

what you desire without your wife knowing.

Lysidamus: That's enough from you. The gods love me so well! I can hardly keep my lips from kissing you because of it, my sweet![35]

Chalinus: [*aside*] What? Kissing? What's going on? What "sweet" is he talking about? By Hercules, I think he wants to explore the farm manager's interior.

Olympio: Do you care about me at all now?

Lysidamus: More than I care about myself, by Pollux! Can I take you in my arms?

Chalinus: [*aside*] Take him in his arms?

Olympio: [*bashfully*] Oh, OK [*Lysidamus embraces Olympio – possibly pretending that he is Casina*].

Lysidamus: When I touch you [*coming up behind Olympio and groping him*] it's like licking honey!

Olympio: Get away! Get off my back, you lovebird!

Chalinus: [*aside*] So that's it! That's why the old man made him his farm manager. Ages ago, when I'd come to escort the master home from a party, he wanted to "make me his head house slave"[36] in the same way – right in the doorway.

Olympio: How obedient I've been to you today, and how I pleased you!

Lysidamus: Yes – so I'll be wanting things to go better for you than for myself, for as long as I live!

Chalinus: [*aside*] By Hercules, they'll be playing footsies next![37] This old man really likes to chase after grown men.[38]

---

[35] It is unclear whether Lysidamus is talking to an imaginary Casina in the following lines (in which case Chalinus is misinterpreting what he hears), or to Olympio, as Chalinus believes. Both alternatives are plausible. Neither male nor female slaves would have been allowed to refuse a master's sexual advances.

[36] "Head house slave" (*atriensis*) was the urban equivalent to the farm manager (*uilicus*) – a position of authority over the other enslaved household staff. Chalinus is suggesting that he was able to fend off Lysidamus's sexual advances, since he obviously did not become the head house slave. In reality it's unlikely that a slave could have easily refused his master's sexual advances, but this is comedy.

[37] The Latin *conturbabunt pedes* apparently implies some sort of sexual activity, perhaps sexual intercourse.

[38] Literally, "to chase after bearded men" (*barbatos*). Romans considered it normal for a man to be sexually interested in beardless boys and teenagers (although citizen boys and men were supposed to be off limits), but it was considered unusual for a man to be sexually

Lysidamus: Oh, how I'll kiss Casina today – I'll do a lot of good things with her, without my wife knowing!

Chalinus: [*aside*] Oh, I get it! By Pollux, I'm on the right track now. The old man's in love with Casina! I've caught them now!

Lysidamus: By Hercules, I'm wild to get my arms around her, I'm wild to kiss her!

Olympio: Let her get married first. What's the damn hurry?

Lysidamus: I'm in love.

Olympio: I don't think your scheme can be achieved today.

Lysidamus: It can! That is, if you think your manumission can be achieved tomorrow...

Chalinus: [*aside*] I'd better really use my ears for this: I've got two wild boars nicely skewered on one spear.[39]

Lysidamus: I've got a room ready at the house of my good friend and neighbour [*gesturing to the next door house*]. I've told him all about my love affair and he said he'd give me a room to use.

Olympio: What about *his* wife? Will she be there?

Lysidamus: I've figured it out. My wife's going to invite her over for the wedding, to keep her company, and help her out. She'll sleep over too. I told her to do it, and my wife said she would. She'll sleep here, and her husband will be away from home (I'll see to that). You'll be bringing your bride to the farm – but the "farm" will be here [*gesturing to the neighbours' house*] and I'll be having my "wedding night" with Casina. And then tomorrow before dawn you'll bring her to the farm for real. Clever, aren't I?

Olympio: Crafty!

Chalinus: [*aside*] Go on, just keep plotting away towards your downfall, by Hercules, you sly ones.

Lysidamus: Do you know what to do now?

Olympio: Tell me.

---

interested in grown, bearded, men. See also note 4 on page 216 at line 963 in act V, scene iv.

[39] Literally: "I'll take two boars in one thicket" (*iam ego uno in saltu lepide apros capiam duos*) – presumably this was a proverbial saying, like "kill two birds with one stone".

Lysidamus: Take my wallet. Hurry and buy some dinner ingredients. But make sure you get some elegant little dainties, since she's such an elegant little dainty herself.

Olympio: All right, I will.

Lysidamus: Buy some little cuttlefish, and some limpets, and mini calamari, some barleyfish...

Chalinus: [*aside, in a superior tone*] You'd get wheatfish[40] if you had any taste.

Lysidamus: Some sandalfish.[41]

Chalinus: [*aside*] Why not clogfish,[42] the better to smack you in the face with, you old piece of trash?

Olympio: Do you want some chatterfish?[43]

Lysidamus: No need, with my wife at home. She's enough of a chatterfish – she never shuts up.

Olympio: When I'm at the fish-market I'll be able to choose what to buy.

Lysidamus: Good plan. Off you go then. Buy plenty of ingredients – money is no object. I need to go see my neighbour, to make sure he does what I asked.

Olympio: Shall I go now then?

Lysidamus: Yes, that's what I want! [*exeunt Olympio and Lysidamus*]

Chalinus: If I were offered three times the price of my manumission not to make major trouble for these guys today, and not to tell all this to my mistress – well, I wouldn't take it.[44] I've caught

---

[40] This joke depends on the similarity of the word *hordeia* (a kind of fish or seafood not mentioned in any extant Latin texts except this play) to the Latin word for "barley" (*hordeum*). Since wheat was considered to be more desirable than barley, Chalinus pretends to suggest that they get a non-existent "wheatfish" (*triticeia*) instead.

[41] That is, *solea*, or what we would call "sole". The Romans called this flatfish "*solea*" because they thought it looked like a sandal "*solea*".

[42] "Clogfish": *sculponeae* referred to the cheaply-made wooden shoes that enslaved people often wore; Chalinus pretends it's a type of fish to make a joke about the fact that the word for slipper (*solea*) is in fact also the name of a fish.

[43] In the Latin text, Olympio suggests "*lingulaca*", which was both a type of fish (probably a flatfish of the cynoglossidae family called "tonguefish"), and also a name for a talkative woman.

[44] We know from line 195a (act II, scene ii) that Cleustrata already knows, or at least suspects, that Lysidamus plans to have sex with Casina, but what Chalinus has now learned, and what he will now tell Cleustrata, is Lysidamus's precise plan for making it happen.

them in the act. And if my mistress just does her part, we'll win this. I'll get the better of them for sure. Luck's on our side today; we lost at first, but now we've come out on top. I'll go indoors now to add my own spices to what another cook has started,[45] so he won't get what he planned for, but he will get what he definitely hadn't planned for. [*exit Chalinus*]

---

[45] Chalinus uses the metaphor of an interfering cook ruining the carefully prepared meal of another cook to represent his own interference in Lysidamus's carefully-laid plans to get Casina for himself.

Act III

III.i Scene with Lysidamus and Alcesimus (lines 515-530)

Lysidamus: [*chatting outside his house with his neighbour*] Alcesimus, now's the time for me to find out if you're a true friend or not. Now the proof's in the pudding, now your cards are on the table![1] Don't bother asking me "why I'm infatuated" – keep your judgments to yourself. Also keep to yourself all that about "grey hairs" and "unseemly at my age" and "a married man".

Alcesimus: I've never seen anyone more infatuated than you are.

Lysidamus: Clear everyone out of your house.

Alcesimus: Actually, by Pollux, I've decided to send all the slaves over to your place.

Lysidamus: [*giddily*] Oh, how cleverly clever you are! Make sure you do what's in the blackbird's song: make sure they come "with food and everything" like they're marching to Sutrium.[2]

Alcesimus: I'll remember.

Lysidamus: There, now you're being as clever as can be. Take care of things while I'm off to the forum: I'll be back soon.

Alcesimus: Have a nice walk.

Lysidamus: Make sure your house gets all its chores done early.

Alcesimus: [*confused*] What?

Lysidamus: [*winking*] so it won't be "occupied" when I come back.[3]

Alcesimus: You really need a good thumping, you and your jokes.

Lysidamus: What's the good of me being in love if I can't make clever jokes? But don't make me have to go looking for you. [*exit Lysidamus*]

Alcesimus: I'll be here at home. [*exit Alcesimus*]

---

[1] What Lysidamus says in Latin translates more literally to: "now the evidence is seen, now the contest is decided".

[2] This is presumably a reference to a popular song about an army's march to Sutrium (a city in Etruria, north of Rome).

[3] Lysidamus's joke is nearly as bad in Latin, which translates literally to "make sure your house has a tongue... so it can invite me / be unoccupied when I come over" (involving a very contrived pun on *uocare/uacare*: "invite/be unoccupied").

III.ii Scene with Cleustrata and Alcesimus (lines 531-562)

Cleustrata: [*standing just outside her front door*] By Castor, so that's why my husband was so insistent that I hurry up and send for my neighbour Myrrhina over here – so their house would be available for him to bring Casina to it. I'm not even going to send for her at all now, so those pathetic old losers won't have the option of a free place. But look who's coming: that pillar of the senate, defender of the people, that neighbour of mine who offered his place to my husband. By Castor, he isn't worth the price of a bag of salt.

Alcesimus: I'm surprised my wife hasn't yet been invited over next door yet. She's been dressed up for a while now, waiting at home and wondering if she'll be invited over. [*seeing Cleustrata coming towards him*] Wait, though, it looks like the invitation is coming. Good day, Cleustrata.

Cleustrata: Good day to you too, Alcesimus. Where is your wife?

Alcesimus: She's waiting for you indoors in case you're going to ask her over. Your husband asked me to send her over to you to help out. Do you want me to call her?

Cleustrata: Don't bother her, I don't need her if she's busy.

Alcesimus: She's not busy.

Cleustrata: I don't mind, I don't want to bother her: I'll see her later.

Alcesimus: Aren't you preparing for a wedding at your house?

Cleustrata: Preparing and planning, yes.

Alcesimus: And don't you need someone to help?

Cleustrata: I've enough helpers at home. When the wedding's over, I'll come and see her. Take care now, and say hello to your wife from me. [*Cleustrata goes out of Alcesimus's sight, but is still within earshot*]

Alcesimus: What'll I do now? I've gotten myself into the most disgraceful situation because of that toothless, shameless old goat who's caused this situation for me. I promised my wife's help just as though we were poor enough to need the work.[4] That

---

[4] Literally: "as if (I were sending her over) to lick plates". It was beneath Alcesimus's dignity to do anything suggesting that he was poor. His worry is that Cleustrata thinks he was offering his wife's help because of the opportunity it would give her to eat some scraps off the plates at Cleustrata's house.

good-for-nothing told me his wife would invite mine over; now she says "she doesn't mind"! By Pollux, I wouldn't be surprised if Cleustrata smells a rat. But on the other hand, now that I think about it, if there were anything like that, she'd be giving me the third degree. I'll go indoors so I can put my boat back on its mooring – that is, tell my wife she won't be needed.

Cleustrata: [*giggling to herself*] I've fooled him beautifully. How the two old fools are scampering! Now I'd like that worthless senile husband of mine to come, so that I can make a fool of him too, in his turn. I'd like to set those two quarrelling between themselves. Look, here he comes. Whenever you see him looking so serious, you'd think he was an honest man.

III.iii Scene with Lysidamus and Cleustrata (lines 563-590)

Lysidamus: [*returning home from the forum*] It's very foolish, I think, for any man that's in love to go to the forum, on this day of all days when the object of his love is ready for him. I was a fool to do so: I wasted the day, supporting one of my relatives through his court appearance. I'm glad he's lost the case, by Hercules, or he'd be trying (unsuccessfully!) to call me back into court for him again today. In my opinion, anyone that summons witnesses to speak for him in court should first make very sure if his witness's heart is really in it or not. If he says his heart's not in it? Well, then send the heartless guy home.

But look, there's my wife in front of the house. Ugh, I'm in trouble! If she's not deaf I'm afraid she's overheard what I said.

Cleustrata: [*aside*] By Castor, I did overhear. Too bad for you!

Lysidamus: [*aside*] I'd better go over to her. [*to Cleustrata*] How are you, my delight?

Cleustrata: I was waiting for you, by Castor.

Lysidamus: Have you got everything ready? Did you get your neighbour over to help you?

Cleustrata: I sent for her, just as you asked, but that buddy of yours, her husband – a very good man, I'm sure – blew up at his wife for some reason: he wouldn't let her come when I invited her.

Lysidamus: You must be most to blame for that – you aren't charming enough.

Cleustrata: It's not for wives to be charming to other people's husbands, dear – that's for women in a different line of work!.

You go over and invite her back: I'll go back inside, dear, since I want to supervise what's left to be done.

Lysidamus: Hurry up then.

Cleustrata: I will. [*aside*] By Pollux, I've made him sweat, all right! I'll make this lover-boy feel even worse today, too. [*exit Cleustrata*]

III.iv Scene with Alcesimus and Lysidamus (lines 591-620)

Alcesimus: [*arriving at Lysidamus's house*] I'm checking to see if my besotted neighbour has come back from the forum, the maniac[5] – making fools of me and my wife. Look, there he is. [*to Lysidamus, angrily*] By Hercules, I want a word with you right now.

Lysidamus: [*also angry*] By Hercules, I want a word with you. What have you got to say for yourself, you worthless loser? What did I ask you to do? What did I *beg* you to do?

Alecesimus: What do you mean?

Lysidamus: How generously you made your empty house available to me, what with getting your wife to leave it and come to ours! Are you satisfied now that you've ruined me and my plans?

Alcesimus: Why don't you go hang yourself? Didn't you say your wife was going to invite mine over?

Lysidamus: She says she did invite your wife, but you didn't let her go.

Alcesimus: [*exasperated*] Actually, didn't your wife tell me that she didn't need my wife's help?

Lysidamus: ACTUALLY, didn't my wife tell me just now to invite your wife over!?

Alcesimus: ACTUALLY, I SO don't care about this.

Lysidamus: ACTUALLY, you're DESTROYING me!

Alcesimus: ACTUALLY, that's fine by me. ACTUALLY, I'm going to keep on blocking things for you. ACTUALLY, I'll enjoy –

Lysidamus: [*interrupting*] ACTUALLY –

Alcesimus: – really screwing you over!

---

5   The Latin more literally implies "possessed by evil spirits".

Lysidamus: ACTUALLY I'll gladly do the same to you – and you're not getting in more "actuallys" today than me!

Alcesimus: ACTUALLY, by Hercules, may the gods smite you down once and for all!

Lysidamus: What now, though? Are you or are you not going to send your wife over to mine?

Alcesimus: You can take her, and you can go crucify yourself on a giant cross, along with my wife, and your wife, and your little girlfriend too! Get out of here, and worry about something else. I'll tell my wife to go visit your wife there by way of the back garden. [*exit Alcesimus*]

Lysidamus: Now you're being a true friend to me! [*soliloquizing romantically*] Under what bad omen did I fall in love, I wonder? Or how often did I offend Venus, the goddess of love, since [*groaning*] so many obstacles like this are getting in the way of a man in love?

[*hearing an uproar*] What's that shouting in our house?

III.v Scene with Pardalisca and Lysidamus (lines 621-719)

Pardalisca: [*coming dramatically out of the house, and stumbling in pretended terror*] I'm a doomed! I'm doomed! I'm completely done for! My heart is dead with terror, and my knees are knocking! I don't know where I can find or look for help, for protection, for a safe refuge, or for assistance! Such horrifying things done in horrifying ways that I saw inside – strange, unheard-of boldness! Look out for yourself, Cleustrata, keep your distance from that girl, I beg! Don't let her do some harm to you in her mad rage. Take the sword away from that girl, she's out of her mind!

Lysidamus: What on earth has made this woman so frightened, so terrified that she's shot out of the house here? [*addressing Pardalisca*] Hey, Pardalisca!

Pardalisca: [*speaking like someone in a tragic drama*] I am lost! Whence comes this sound to my ears?

Lysidamus: Just look at me!

Pardalisca: My master!

Lysidamus: What's happened? Why are you frightened?

Pardalisca: I'll be killed!

Lysidamus: Killed how?

Pardalisca: I'll be killed, you'll be killed!

Lysidamus: [*even more anxious*] Me, killed? How?

Pardalisca: [*smiting her brow dramatically*] Alas for you!

Lysidamus: It'll be "alas" for you! [*grabbing her shoulders and shaking her*]

Pardalisca: Please, hold me in case I fall!

Lysidamus: Whatever it is, tell me quickly!

Pardalisca: Hold me up,[6] and fan me with your cloak, I beg.

Lysidamus: Whatever this is about is really worrying me! – unless she's got herself drunk somewhere on unmixed wine.

Pardalisca: [*weakly*] Please, hold my head in your hands![7]

Lysidamus: Get away from me and go get yourself crucified! May the gods curse your head and every other part of you![8] Unless I get out of you, right now, what's going on – I'll beat your brains out for you with this [*brandishing his staff*], you vicious old snake! You've been making a fool of me!

Pardalisca: My master!...

Lysidamus: [*exasperatedly*] My slave woman. What. Do. You. Want. From. Me?

Pardalisca: You're so angry.

Lysidamus: You haven't seen anything yet! But tell me what this is all about, as briefly as possible. What was that uproar indoors?

Pardalisca: I'll tell you. Listen. A terrible, awful thing, just now, here in the house, that slave girl of yours started doing – like she'd had no decent Attic[9] upbringing.

Lysidamus: What. Did. She. Do?

Pardalisca: [*gesturing dramatically*] Terror prevents my tongue from speech!

Lysidamus: Will you or will you not tell me what's happening?

Pardalisca: I'll tell you. That slave girl of yours, that you want to give as a wife to your farm manager. She – in the house...

---

[6] In Latin Pardalisca begs Lysidamus to hold her chest (*pectus*).
[7] Literally: "hold my ears".
[8] In Latin, he says "may the gods destroy you, your chest, ears, and head!"
[9] Remember that the play is supposed to be set in Athens, which is located in the region of Attica.

Lysidamus: WHAT IN THE HOUSE? WHAT IS HAPPENING?

Pardalisca: She's acting like a dangerous, wickedly brought up girl, who's threatening her bridegroom, his life –

Lysidamus: What?

Pardalisca: [*pretending to faint*] Ah!

Lysidamus: What is going on!?

Pardalisca: She's saying she wants to take his life! The sword...

Lysidamus: What?!!

Pardalisca: [*weakly*] The sword...

Lysidamus: WHAT SWORD?!!

Pardalisca: She's got one!

Lysidamus: Oh gods, I'm in trouble! Why does she have one?

Pardalisca: She's chasing everyone through the house and she won't let anyone go near her. So everyone's hiding under the cupboards, under the beds, afraid to say anything.

Lysidamus: I'm dead, I'm so dead! What can have happened to her so suddenly?

Pardalisca: She's gone mad.

Lysidamus: [*whimpering*] I think I'm the unluckiest man alive!

Pardalisca: But if you knew what she said in there...

Lysidamus: What did she say?

Pardalisca: Listen. She swore by all the gods and goddesses that she'd kill any man that shared her bed tonight.

Lysidamus: [*squeaking*] She wants to kill ME?

Pardalisca: Does it have anything to do with you?

Lysidamus: [*realizing his mistake*] Oh, uh...

Pardalisca: What?

Lysidamus: My mistake! I meant to say "does she want to kill my farm manager?"

Pardalisca: [*aside*] You're going down the narrow track instead of the main road[10]...

---

10   Taking the narrow track implies the less straightforward route (a metaphor for dishonesty vs. honesty).

Lysidamus: She isn't threatening ME at all, is she?

Pardalisca: It's you alone she's got it in for, more than anyone else.

Lysidamus: Why?!!

Pardalisca: Because you're making her marry Olympio. She says she won't let herself or you live till tomorrow, and husband neither: I've been sent out here to tell you this, to tell you to be on your guard against her.

Lysidamus: By Hercules, I'm in trouble!

Pardalisca: [*aside*] You deserve to be.

Lysidamus: There is not and has never been any love-struck old man so unlucky as me!

Pardalisca: [*aside*] I'm fooling him beautifully! Everything I said to him is a lie: the mistress and her friend next door made it all up, and sent me out here to fool the old man.

Lysidamus: Hey, Pardalisca!

Pardalisca: What do you want?

Lysidamus: Well, it's this way... [*pausing in embarrassment*]

Pardalisca: What?

Lysidamus: I want to ask you something.

Pardalisca: Well go on – you're delaying me.

Lysidamus: And you're horrifying me! [*stammering*] B-but does – does Casina still have that sword?

Pardalisca: She does – in fact, two of them!

Lysidamus: [*squeaking with fear*] Two?!!

Pardalisca: She says today she'll kill you with one, and the farm manager with the other.

Lysidamus: [*whimpering*] I'm the killedest[11] man alive! I'd better put on my breastplate. What about my wife? Didn't she approach Casina and take the swords away from her?

Pardalisca: No one dares go anywhere near her.

Lysidamus: She should beg with her!

---

[11] In his panic, Lysidamus invents a superlative for the verb "kill".

Pardalisca: She is begging her: but Casina says the only way she'll put the swords down is if she knows she won't be married off to the farm manager.

Lysidamus: Well she's certainly getting married today whether she likes it or not – in fact, BECAUSE she doesn't like it. Why wouldn't I carry out what I've started, and make her marry me? Oops, I mean, make her marry my farm manager?

Pardalisca: [*aside*] You're messing up over and over again...

Lysidamus: [*imitating Pardalisca's earlier dramatic utterance of line 653*] Terror – uh – prevents my speech! But please, tell my wife that I'm begging her to persuade that girl to put down the sword and let me go inside.

Pardalisca: I'll tell her.

Lysidamus: Beg her!

Pardalisca: OK, I'll beg her.

Lysidamus: Beg her persuasively, the way you often do. Do you hear? If you succeed I'll give you a pair of sandals, and a gold ring for your finger and more good things too.[12]

Pardalisca: I'll give it my best efforts.

Lysidamus: Make sure you succeed.

Pardalisca: I'm going already, unless you keep delaying me.

Lysidamus: Go on, and be careful. Oh look! Finally here's my assistant back from the marketing, bringing the hired help.

III.vi Scene with Olympio, Chytrio (the hired cook), and Lysidamus (lines 720-758)

Olympio: [*addressing Chytrio*] Hey, thief, see that you keep those thorns [*referring to the subordinate workers whom Chytrio is supposed to manage*] in order.

Chytrio: Why do you call them thorns?

Olympio: Because whatever they touch they grab onto, if you try to take it back, they slice you up: wherever they go, wherever they are, they make the masters pay twice the costs.

Chytrio: [*sceptical of Olympio's joke*] Ha!

---

[12] Enslaved people normally wore shoes with wooden soles, perhaps like clogs (see line 495), and were unlikely to wear rings. Lysidamus's promise might, therefore, imply that he would grant her her freedom.

Olympio: Oh! [*catching sight of Lysidamus*] Time to fling my cloak magnificently around myself and go to meet my master like I'm the boss.[13]

Lysidamus: Greetings, my good man.

Olympio: [*smugly accepting the compliment*] I am indeed.

Lysidamus: What's happening?

Olympio: You're in love, while I'm hungry and thirsty.

Lysidamus: [*admiringly reaching to stroke Olympio's cloak*] You've come swanning out very elegantly attired.

Olympio: [*avoiding Lysidamus*] Nuh-uh! Today... **** [14]

Lysidamus: No, wait – even if you are feeling high and mighty.

Olympio: [*holding his nose*] Ew! Your breath stinks.

Lysidamus: What's the matter?

Olympio: I'll tell you what's the matter. Won't you just stop? Ged adda mah face![15]

Lysidamus: I'll get majorly in yah face[16] I guess, unless you stop moving away.

Olympio: [*holding his nose again*] Zee-yewss![17] Can't you keep your distance? Unless you want me to puke today?

Lysidamus: Stay where you are.

Olympio: What is it? [*looking around at the other slaves*] Who is this man?

Lysidamus: [*getting annoyed*] I'm your master!

Olympio: Who's master?

Lysidamus: The one whose slave you are!

Olympio: [*in an offended tone*] I, a slave?

---

[13] "Like I'm the boss" translates the Latin adverb *patrice*: "aristocratically". Olympio's anticipated manumission is going to his head.

[14] The asterisks (****) indicate where there is a gap in Latin text.

[15] "Ged adda mah face" is an attempt to translate the Greek πράγματά μοι παρέχεις (*pragmata moi parecheis*), literally meaning "you're annoying me". Greek speech in Plautus is usually used by slaves or lower class characters (MacCary and Willcock 1976: 180: citing Shipp 1953: 105-12).

[16] "In yah face" translates *dabo tibi* / μέγα κακόν (*mega kakon*): "I'll give you big trouble", with Lysidamus imitating Olympio's use of Greek.

[17] "Zee-yewss" translates ὦ Ζεῦ, literally "O Zeus!", but perhaps with an implied reference to the stench of Lysidamus's breath.

Lysidamus: Yes, MY slave!

Olympio: But aren't I a free man? [*prancing around*] Remember? Remember?

Lysidamus: Stop that, and stand still!

Olympio: Let go of me.

Lysidamus: [*realizing he needs Olympio's cooperation*] OK, I'm YOUR slave then.

Olympio: That's better.

Lysidamus: Please, my darling Olympio, my father,[18] my protector.

Olympio: There, now you're certainly showing your good sense.

Lysidamus: I'm truly your slave.

Olympio: What's the use of such a worthless slave?

Lysidamus: Anyway, now what? How soon are you going to give me new life again?

Olympio: I'll only do it if I get a cooked meal.

Lysidamus: So let these guys [*gesturing to the catering staff*] get going.

Olympio: Hurry up, quickly go inside and immediately get that meal cooked. I'll hang around inside now. Make me that meal, and make sure there's plenty of wine! I want it made nicely – I want it made magnificently, I have no use for bland spinachy barbarian mush.[19] [*to Lysidamus*] Are you still standing around here? Get out of here. I'm staying here. There's no reason for you to wait, is there?

Lysidamus: [*nervously gesturing towards the door*] She says Casina's in there with a sword, planning on killing you and me both.

Olympio: [*looking unconcerned*] Yeah, yeah whatever. Let her keep it. They're fooling you: I'm on to those scheming crones. But [*now nervous as well*] just go on into the house with me.

---

[18] Romans sometimes used the word "father" (*pater* in Latin) to refer to someone whom one respected like a father.

[19] "Barbarian" generally means "Roman" in Plautus, because the plays are supposed to be set in the Greek world, and the characters are supposed to be Greek. Greeks called everyone who didn't speak Greek οἱ βάρβαροι (*hoi barbaroi*), or "those whose speech sounds like 'bar-bar-bar'". It must have been endlessly funny to the Roman audiences to hear themselves and their culture called "barbarian" by the Latin-speaking Plautine characters.

Lysidamus: By Pollux, though – I'm scared to! You go in, and check out what's going on first.

Olympio: My own life is as precious to me as yours is to you. Just go in.

Lysidamus: Look, if you insist, I'll go in with you. [*Lysidamus and Olympio leave the stage by going into the house*]

Act IV

IV.i Scene with Pardalisca (lines 759-779)

Pardalisca: [*having come out of the house on her own*] By Pollux, I don't believe even at Nemea, not even at the Olympics,[1] has there ever been such fun games as we're putting on in here – how hilariously we're making fun of our old master,[2] and Olympio our farm manager. Everyone is rushing around all through the house, while the old man[3] is bellowing around the kitchen and trying to hurry up the cooks: "Why aren't you getting a move on today?" he says, "Why don't you dole out the food already, if you're going to!" "Hurry up, the dinner ought to be cooked by now!"

Meanwhile the farm manager is strolling about all decked up in a bridal wreath, freshly bathed and dressed in white. And those two women meanwhile are dressing up Chalinus the armour-bearer so they can give him as the bride to the farm manager. And they're pretending so brilliantly, just as though they didn't know anything about what's about to happen; the cooks are so brilliantly helping too, making sure the old man doesn't get any dinner.[4] They're dropping the pots and spilling water onto the fire, as the women told them to do. Those women want to drive the old man out of the house unfed so they can fill up their own bellies. I know how those two can eat! They could gobble up a whole boatload of food.

Oops – there's the door opening.

IV.ii Scene with Lysidamus and Pardalisca (lines 780-797)

Lysidamus: [*coming out of the house, but talking to his wife who is indoors*] Anyway, if you're smart, wife, you two'll both eat when the dinner's cooked. I'm going to eat at the farm. I want to accompany the new bride and bridegroom to the farm. I know what men are like, and I don't want anyone carrying her off. Have a good time! But hurry up and send them off as soon as possible, so we can still get there in daylight; I'll be back tomorrow. I'll eat my share of the feast tomorrow, wife.

---

[1] The ancient Olympic games were one of four highly prestigious games held in ancient Greece, the games at Nemea being one of the other three.
[2] "Our old master" is a translation of the Latin *senex*, literally meaning "old man", and refers to Lysidamus.
[3] "Old man" (*senex*) refers again to Lysidamus.
[4] Lysidamus and Olympio are to be frustrated in their hopes of getting dinner, just like they'll soon be frustrated in their hopes of having sex with Casina.

Pardalisca: [*giggling quietly to herself*] It's turning out as I said it would: the women have sent the old man off without his dinner.

Lysidamus: [*to Pardalisca*] What are you doing here?

Pardalisca: [*glibly*] I'm going where my mistress sent me.

Lysidamus: [*suspiciously*] Really?

Pardalisca: Definitely.

Lysidamus: Why are you spying here?

Pardalisca: I'm not spying.

Lysidamus: Get out of here: you're lolling about here while the others are hurrying things along inside.

Pardalisca: All right, I'm going. [*exit Pardalisca*]

Lysidamus: Yeah, get out of here please, you no-good waste of space. [*looking around*] Has she gone now? [*moving to the side of the stage, in the opposite direction from Pardalisca's exit*] Here you can say what you want. By Hercules, when you're in love, even if you're hungry, you're not hungry for anything. But look, here's my farm manager – my accomplice and partner, my fellow bridegroom – coming along with his wreath on, and carrying a torch.

IV.iii Scene with Olympio and Lysidamus (lines 798-814)

Olympio: [*to an accompanying male slave playing a tibia*[5]] Come on, musician, while they're bringing the new bride out of the house, liven up this whole street with pretty music – with my wedding song!

Lysidamus and Olympio:[*singing the traditional marriage song*] Hymen, it's the Hymen song I sing, O Hymen![6]

Lysidamus: My hero! What's the situation?

Olympio: I'm more hungry, by Hercules, than heroic![7]

Lysidamus: [*with romantic fervour*] But I'm in LOVE.

---

[5] A *tibia* was a double reed instrument, perhaps like an oboe.
[6] At Greek weddings (it was not part of the Roman wedding ritual) the ritual cry of "*hymen, hymenaee*" was sung during the bridal procession. Whether or not the words originally had any specific meaning, at some point the word *Hymen* came to be considered the name of the god of weddings, and the ritual cry was interpreted as a call to the god to make the marriage a success (MacCary and Willcock 1976: 185, citing Maas 1907: 590-596).
[7] "My hero" and "heroic" are translations of *salus* ("saviour") and *salubriter* ("healthy"). In order to keep the pun I had to change the meaning.

Olympio: But I don't CARE, by Hercules; love may be better than food in your case, but my stomach's been rumbling from hunger for ages.

Lysidamus: Why on earth are those dawdlers in there taking so long? It's like they're doing it on purpose: the more in a hurry I am, the less anything gets done.

Olympio: What if I belt out the song to Hymen again – d'you think that'll make them come out quicker?

Lysidamus: Good idea. And I'll help you out, since it's both of us that's having the wedding.

Lysidamus and **Olympio:** [*at the tops of their lungs*] HYMEN, IT'S THE HYMEN SONG I SING, O HYMEN!

Lysidamus: [*coughing hoarsely*] By Hercules, I could strain my insides from singing the Hymen song like that – and that's not how I want to be straining my insides today! [*making a sexual gesture and laughing crudely*]

Olympio: By Pollux, if you were a stallion you'd be out of control.

Lysidamus: How so?

Olympio: You're too single-minded.

Lysidamus: [*making another sexual gesture towards Olympio*] You haven't tried me out yourself, somewhere, now have you?

Olympio: Ugh – gods forbid! [*hearing a noise*] That's the door – someone's coming out.

Lysidamus: By Hercules, saved, thank the gods! [*Pardalisca leads out Chalinus, heavily veiled and dressed in a bride's dress*].

IV.iv Scene with Pardlisca, Olympio, Lysidamus, and Cleustrata (lines 815-854)

Chalinus: [*sniggering, and talking quietly so only Pardalisca can hear*] He's caught the scent of CasinUS![8]

Pardalisca: [*reciting mock-ritual words to the "bride"*] Carefully lift your feet over the threshold,[9] my dear bride. Begin this journey

---

[8] "The scent of CasinUS": Casina sounds like it means "cinnamon" (Latin *casia*), hence the reference to its scent. "Casinus" is the masculine form of the name.

[9] In Roman tradition it would have been bad luck for the bride to trip over, or to step on, the threshold.

propitiously, so that you may achieve glorious widowhood,[10] so you'll have more power and conquer your husband and be the winner, and so your word and authority will be superior: may your husband buy you clothes while you divest him of everything he has. May you cheat your husband by night and by day. Remember all this, I beg.

Olympio: [*threateningly*] By Hercules, she'll get the worst of it as soon as she steps even a tiny bit out of line.

Lysidamus: Shush!

Olympio: [*loudly*] I won't "shush".

Lysidamus: [*hissing*] What's the matter?

Olympio: That bitch is giving the other bitch bad advice!

Lysidamus: [*in a hoarse whisper*] You'll ruin everything I've been planning! That's what THEY'd like – to undo all my schemes!

Pardalisca: [*using the ritual wedding formula*] Olympio, since you consent, take this bride from us.

Olympio: [*impatiently*] Hand her over then, if you're ever going to today.

Lysidamus: [*to Pardalisca and Cleustrata*] You go back inside now.

Pardalisca: Please, be gentle to this inexperienced and virgin girl.

Lysidamus: Yeah yeah, don't worry about it. Whatever.

Pardalisca: [*tearfully to the fake Casina*] Farewell.

Olympio: [*to Pardalisca and Cleustrata*] Go on in now.

Lysidamus: [*chiming in*] Go on.

Cleustrata: Farewell! [*exeunt Cleustrata and Pardalisca*]

Lysidamus: Is my wife finally out of the way?

Olympio: She's in the house, don't worry.

Lysidamus: Hurray! Now, by Pollux, I'm free at last! [*to the fake Casina*] My little sweetheart, my little honey, my fresh young thing!

Olympio: Whoa there, just watch it, smarty pants: she's mine.

---

[10] Pardalisca uses the Latin adjective *superstes*, which would normally be used of a victor in a military encounter who is "standing over" the body of his defeated enemy, and I have interpreted it here as referring to a desirable early widowhood, though it is also possible that it is meant here to refer only to the bride's victory over her defeated husband.

Lysidamus: I know, but I get the first go.

Olympio: Hold this torch.

Lysidamus: Can't – I'm holding THIS [*squeezing the fake Casina*] Oh all-powerful Venus, you've made good things happen for me, since you've granted me this opportunity! [*squeezing the fake Casina again*]

Olympio: [*fondling the fake Casina from the other side*] Oh what a sexy set of curves, my own little woman! Ow! What the hell?!

Lysidamus: What's wrong?

Olympio: She stomped on my foot like an elephant!

Lysidamus: Stop your noise, a cloud isn't as soft as her breast!

Olympio: By Pollux, that is a gorgeous tit... [*fondling the fake Casina*] OW!

Lysidamus: What's wrong?

Olympio: She punched me in the chest with her elbow – or should I say with a battering ram!

Lysidamus: Why are you pawing her so roughly then? She's not attacking me since I'm handling her gently. OW!

Olympio: What is it?

Lysidamus: Woah, what a feisty little thing she is! She nearly laid me out with her elbow.

Olympio: She's just eager to get laid[11] herself.

Lysidamus: So, are we gonna get going or what?

Olympio: On we go, my gorgeously gorgeous little thing! [*exeunt Olympio, Lysidamus, and Chalinus*]

---

[11] A pun on *cubitum* ("elbow") and the supine of *cubo* ("go to bed").

Act V

V.i Scene with Pardalisca, Myrrhina, and Cleustrata (lines 855-874)

Some time later, after the women have enjoyed themselves at the wedding feast without the men.

> **Myrrhina:** Now that we've been entertained so well inside, we're going out into the street here to watch the wedding games. By Castor, never in all my born days have I ever laughed so much – and I think I'll be laughing even more at what's still to come!
>
> **Pardalisca:** I'd love to know what Chalinus is doing now – the blushing bride and HIS new husband.
>
> **Myrrhina:** [*whooping with laughter*] There's no playwright that's ever devised a cleverer trick than the one we've hatched so brilliantly!
>
> **Cleustrata:** I really want my old man to come out with his face punched! There never was a more despicable old man than him. Unless you think the one providing the bedroom for him is worse [*gesturing angrily towards Myrrhina's and Alcesimus's house next door*]. ** [*some text is missing*] ** Now I want you to take charge here, Pardalisca, and keep an eye out for whichever of them comes out, so you can make fun of him.
>
> **Pardalisca:** I'm ready and willing to do that, ** [*some text is missing*] ** like always!
>
> **Cleustrata:** [*pushing Pardalisca forward so she can peak out from behind one of the out buildings*] ** [*some text is missing*] ** Watch it all from here. Tell us what they're doing indoors.
>
> **Myrrhina:** Let me see, please! [*pushing herself ahead of Pardalisca*].
>
> **Cleustrata:** [*pulling Myrrhina back*] You can say what you want more freely here.
>
> **Myrrhina:** Shush – there goes our front door!

V.ii Scene with Olympio, Myrrhina, Cleustrata, and Pardalisca (lines 875-936)

> **Olympio:** [*coming stumbling out from Alcesimus's house, holding his head*] I don't know where to run, where to hide, how to keep my disgrace a secret. We've done a GREAT job, my master and me, at being totally humiliated on our wedding night! Oh the

shame! I'm shaking all over! We've both been made into laughing stocks. Stupid me for acting out of character – I've never been disgraced before like this.

Listen, [*addressing the audience*] while I tell the whole story. It'll be worth your while to listen. The mayhem I stirred up indoors is as laughable [*grimacing*] to tell as it is to hear it. When I led this new bride of mine inside, I brought her straight into the one bedroom where the door will lock. It was as dark as a well in there. Seeing as the old master's not here yet I tell her "lie down". I place her just right, propped up, and I start softening her up and saying pretty things to her, so that I can have my wedding night before the old man gets to have his turn. I started off slow, there and then, since * * [*some text is missing*] * * and I'm constantly looking around in case the old man * * [*some text is missing*] * *. To start with, I ask her for a kiss as a lead-up to something naughtier: but she pushed my hand away and didn't let me give her that kiss! So I hurry up a bit more now – I decide to really throw myself on Casina. I want to steal a march on the old man, so I bar the door so he can't catch me at it.

Cleustrata: [*in a whisper to Pardalisca*] Come on, go on up to him.

Pardalisca: [*to Olympio*] Excuse me, where is your new bride?

Olympio: [*startled*] By Hercules, I'm ruined! All is known!

Pardalisca: Come on, be fair, tell me the whole story from the beginning. What's happening inside? How is Casina doing? [*trying not to laugh*] Is she docile enough?

Olympio: [*whimpering*] I'm too ashamed to say.

Pardalisca: [*eagerly*] Keep talking like you were, and tell me about it.

Olympio: By Hercules, I'm ashamed.

Pardalisca: Come on, be brave. I want the next bit, after you lay down. Tell me what happened!

Olympio: It's too shameful.

Pardalisca: [*brightly*] Well then, those who get to hear about it [*gesturing to the audience*] will take care not to do what you did!

Olympio: * * [*some text is missing*] * * it's huge [*sob*]. **Pardalisca:** [*snapping her fingers in front of Olympio's dazed face*] Stay focused, and keep talking!

Olympio: When * * [*some text is missing*] * * underneath – besides!

Pardalisca: What?

Olympio: Oh my gods!

Pardalisca: What?!

Olympio: OH MY GODS!

Pardalisca: Is it...?

Olympio: Oh, it was HUGE. I was afraid she had that sword, so I started to feel around for it. While I'm checking if she has the sword, I grab hold of the hilt. But now I think about it, she didn't have a sword 'cuz [*shuddering*] a sword would've been cold.

Pardalisca: Tell all!

Olympio: But I'm ashamed to.

Pardalisca: It wasn't a radish, was it?

Olympio: It was not.

Pardalisca: A cucumber then?

Olympio: Truly, by Hercules, it wasn't any kind of vegetable, unless whatever it was, no crop blight had ever touched it, 'cuz whatever it was, it was a full-grown specimen.

Pardalisca: So what ended up happening? Tell me everything!

Olympio: So then I resort to begging. "Casina", I say, "please, my little bride, why are you rejecting your own husband like this? By Hercules, you're pushing me away unfairly, just because I'm trying to get you for myself." She doesn't say a word, and just pulls her dress over her – that is – over her womanly parts. When I see she's covered up her – her nicely pruned forested ravine[1] – I ask her if she'll let me try the other route. So [I tell her to lean] on her elbows, so I can turn her around * * [*some text is missing*] * * She still doesn't say anything * * [*some text is missing*] * * I stand up so I can * * [*some text is missing*] * * into her * * [*some text is missing*] * * and her * * [*some text is missing*] * *

Myrrhina: [*to Cleustrata, with whom she's standing just out of Olympio's sight*] What a gripping narrative! * * [*some text is missing*] * *

Olympio: [I give her] a kiss * * [*some text is missing*] * * my lips get pricked with a bristly beard! * * [*some text is missing*] * * Then right away, while I'm on my knees next to her, she kicks me in the

---

[1] "Her nicely trimmed forested ravine" is a translation of the Latin *saltus* ("woodland pasture; ravine"), which was a common Latin euphemism for a woman's genitals.

chest; I fall headlong off the bed and she leaps up and punches me in the face! I sneak out of there, dressed only in what you see me in now, so the old man can get a taste of what I got.

Pardalisca: How thrilling! But where's your cloak?

Olympio: I left it in there.

Pardalisca: [*cackling*] We've played such an excellent trick on you both – have you had enough of it yet?

Olympio: I guess we deserved it. [*hearing a creak and jumping in fear*] But there goes the door! She's not coming after me, is she?

V.iii Scene with Lysidamus and Chalinus (lines 937-962)

Lysidamus: [*coming stumbling out of Alcesimus's house*] I'm burning from shame at the disgrace, and I don't know what to do! How can I look my wife in the eyes when I've disgraced myself like this? All my shady dealings are out in the open and I'm completely ruined. I'm so unlucky. * * [*some text is missing*] * * grabbed me right by the throat * * [*some text is missing*] * * How am I ever going to clear myself with my wife? * * [*some text is missing*] * Poor me, without even my cloak! * * [*some text is missing*] * * secret wedding * * [*some text is missing*] * * I guess * * [*some text is missing*] * * is my best bet. I'm going indoors to my wife, and I'll just have to take the beating for what I did.[2] But maybe there's someone who'll take my punishment for me? [*looking hopefully out at the audience for a volunteer*].

[*groaning*] What'll I do now? Unless I act like a delinquent slave and run away from home.[3] There's no saving my back from a beating if I do go home. What? [*addressing the audience*] Can you really say that's not likely? By Hercules, I really don't want a beating, even if I've deserved one. I'll take myself off and run right away.

---

[2] While no doubt there were Roman wives who physically abused their husbands, the notion that Cleustrata would beat Lysidamus is played for laughs here. In a society like republican Rome, where men had the right to beat their wives, a wife beating her husband made the husband look weak and unworthy of respect. See also line 967, where the enslaved Chalinus chases after his master to beat him: this would have been hilarious to the Roman audience because it was so highly unlikely in reality, where the right to violence was all on the slave holder's side.

[3] In a slave-holding society like Rome, running away was considered to be a moral wrong by an enslaved person, rather than a heroic break for freedom as we might view it now (as explained in note 30 on page 187). What must have made this line so funny to the Roman audience is that Lysidamus is the *pater familias* who ought not to be cringing in fear of punishment like an enslaved person.

Chalinus: [*calling from inside Alcesimus's house*] Hey! Stop right there, you womanizer.

Lysidamus: I'm screwed – she's calling me back! I'll keep going as if I can't hear her.

V.iv Scene with Chalinus, Lysidamus, Cleustrata, Myrrhina, and Olympio (lines 963-1018)

Chalinus: [*running outside, dressed in his bride's dress*] Yoo-hoo! where are you? Yes you, the one who wants to act like one of those Massilian perverts![4] If you want to get me really roused up, now's your chance! You can come back to the bedroom if you want (by Hercules,[5] you're so screwed!). Awww... just come on back here! Now I'll try to get hold of a fair judge – like this [*gesturing with Lysidamus's own staff*] – to serve in an extrajudicial capacity [*using one hand to smack the staff into his other palm*].

Lysidamus: I'm doomed! This guy's going to bust my balls with that stick there. I'll get a ball-busting back there [*gesturing back towards Chalinus*], so I'd better go this way [*dodging out of Chalinus's reach, but then realizing he is now running towards Cleustrata*].

Cleustrata: Good day to you, you womanizer.

Lysidamus: Eek, it's my wife! Now I'm between a rock and a hard place,[6] and don't know where to run to! Wolves on one side, hunting dogs on the other![7] But the wolf part of the omen is wielding a stick! I think, by Hercules, I'll switch up the old saying and go this way [*towards the women*]. I hope the dog part of the omen will be the better option.

Myrrhina: What are you up to, you bigamist?

Cleustrata: OK, husband, where're you coming from, dressed like this? What have you done with your staff, and the cloak you had on?

Myrrhina: Adultery – that's how I think he lost them. While he was cheating on you with Casina.

---

[4] According to Athenaeus (*The Learned Banqueters* 12.523c) the men of Massilia (modern Marseilles) had a reputation for enjoying being sexually penetrated. Romans did not consider sex between men to be wrong, but the one who penetrated the other had to be freeborn while the one being penetrated must be an enslaved person, or someone with no self-respect (for the ambiguous sexual status of freedmen see Williams 2010: 107).

[5] Remember that only men swore by Hercules (see note 124 on page 41), so Chalinus is letting his feminine role slip here.

[6] Literally: "I'm between the sacrificial victim and the stone knife" (*ego inter sacrum saxumque sum*) – a Roman proverb.

[7] "Wolves on one side, hunting dogs on the other" – another Roman proverb.

Lysidamus: [*whimpering*] I'm so doomed.

Chalinus: [*prancing up in his bridal outfit but no longer pretending that he's not a man*] Are we gonna get into bed now? I'm Casina!

Lysidamus: Go get yourself crucified!

Chalinus: Don't you love me?

Cleustrata: [*with false sweetness*] Why won't you tell me what happened to your cloak?

Lysidamus: [*desperately trying to think of a good excuse for having lost his cloak*] It – it was those crazy women of the Bacchus cult,[8] by Hercules!

Cleustrata: The Bacchus cult, eh?

Lysidamus: [*trying to sound firm*] Yes, by Hercules! The Bacchus cult.

Myrrhina: He's lying – there's no Bacchic women romping about any more, by Castor.

Lysidamus: Um, uh, silly me, I forgot, but anyway, those Bacchic –

Cleustrata: [*interrupting*] What, the Bacchic women again?

Lysidamus: [*stammering*] I mean, if it wasn't them...

Cleustrata: By Castor, look at you cowering there.

Lysidamus: [*trying to sound outraged*] Me? You lie, by Hercules!

Cleustrata: You're awfully pale.

* * * * * * * * * *

[*lines 983-990 are too fragmentary to decipher, but clearly Olympio arrives on the scene and confesses the whole plot, letting Lysidamus take all the blame*]

* * * * * * * * * *

Olympio: ... he even caught me up in his wicked plots, bringing down my good name!

Lysidamus: [*in a hoarse whisper to Olympio*] Won't you shut UP?

---

[8] In 186 BCE the Roman senate put a violent end to an increasingly popular and secret cult of Bacchus. These lines suggest that the play must have been written after 186. Plautus is supposed to have died in 184, which would make this one of his last plays.

Olympio: I certainly won't, by Hercules! You absolutely begged me to ask for Casina as my wife, just so you could get access to her.[9]

Lysidamus: [*trying to sound shocked*] I? I did that?

Olympio: [*sarcastically*] No, it was Hector of Troy did it.

Lysidamus: HE'd have shown you who was boss, at least! So I did all of what you just said, did I?

Cleustrata: [*threateningly*] You're still asking that, are you?

Lysidamus: [*looking crushed*] If I did do it, by Hercules, I did it badly.[10]

Cleustrata: Just come indoors. I'll jog your memory [*with a threatening gesture*] if you have any more trouble remembering.

Lysidamus: [*anxiously*] That's all right, by Hercules! I'd rather just take your word for it! But please forgive your husband my dear. Myrrhina, use your influence on Cleustrata! If I ever again put the moves on Casina, or even think about it, let alone get into bed with her – if I'm ever guilty of doing such a thing again, you'll have every reason to hang me up and beat me with sticks.

Myrrhina: By Castor, I think you should forgive him.

Cleustrata: Oh, all right. I'll forgive you, and not all that grudgingly, if only for the sake of not making this already-long play even longer.

Lysidamus: You're not angry?

Cleustrata: No, I'm not.

Lysidamus: I've got your word on this?

Cleustrata: Yes, you have my word.

Lysidamus: [*kissing her hand repeatedly*] No one ever had a nicer wife than I have!

Cleustrata: [*to Chalinus*] OK, you can give him back his staff and cloak now.

Chalinus: If you want me to! Here [*tossing the staff and cloak to Lysidamus*]. But, by Pollux, I've been greatly wronged: I've been married to two men, and neither of them has done his conjugal duty to his new bride.

---

[9] What Olympio says in Latin translates more literally to: "for the sake of your love affair".
[10] There's a double meaning here: Lysidamus admits he acted badly, but also that his plans have been unsuccessful.

Audience members, I'll tell you what's going to happen after this. It'll be discovered that this Casina here is actually the daughter of the next-door neighbours,[11] and she'll marry the master's son Euthynicus.

And now it's only fair that you give well deserved applause to our deserving actors. The one who claps the loudest will get to spend time with the girl of his choice – without his wife finding out! And the one who doesn't clap as loud as he can will get to sleep with an old billy-goat drenched in tannery water instead.[12]

THE END

---

[11] These neighbours are presumably Alcesimus and Myrrhina, and the discovery would have been made when the slave (referred to in the prologue – see page 169) who has been sick in bed throughout the play's action, confesses that it was Myrrhina who abandoned the baby Casina.

[12] The contrasting "rewards" for the married men in the audience are, for those who applaud loudly, sex with a *scortum* (sex worker), and for those who don't applaud enough, sex with a male goat reeking of the liquids used in the process of tanning hides. There is probably a pun that makes the image work better in Latin: *scortum* could mean both "sex worker" and "skin" or "hide", so the goat drenched in the notoriously stinky tanning liquid is also a literal *scortum* (Gitner 2016: 123).

ARGVMENTVM (Plot Summary)

This acrostic plot summary (in Latin called the *argumentum*) was added later, probably in the second century CE.

Conservam[13] uxorem[14] duo conservi[15] expetunt.[16]

Alium senex[17] allegat,[18] alium filius.

Senem adiuvat[19] sors,[20] verum[21] decipitur[22] dolis.[23]

Ita[24] ei[25] subicitur[26] pro[27] puella servolus[28]

Nequam,[29] qui dominum mulcat[30] atque vilicum.[31]   5

Adulescens[32] ducit civem[33] Casinam cognitam.[34]

---

[13] *conserua, -ae* (f.): "fellow (female) slave", "(female) slave of the same household".
[14] *uxor, -orem* (f.): "wife".
[15] *conseruus, -i* (m.): "fellow (male) slave", "(male) slave of the same household".
[16] *expeto, -ere, -iui, -itus*: "want", "desire".
[17] *senex, senis* (m.): "old man", "master (*pater familias*) of the household".
[18] *allego, -are, -aui, -atum*: "employ (someone) as an agent", "use (someone) as a proxy".
[19] *adiuo, -are, -aui, -atum*: "help", "favour".
[20] *sors, sortis* (f.): "lot", "lottery".
[21] *uerum* (conjunction): "but", "but in fact".
[22] *decipio, -ere, -cepi, -ceptum*: "cheat", "mislead", "frustrate".
[23] *dolus, -i* (m.): "trickery", "cunning", "deceit".
[24] *ita* (adverb): "thus", "in the following way".
[25] *ei* (refers to *senex*).
[26] *subicio, -ere, -ieci, -iectum*: "substitute".
[27] *pro*: "in place of" (+ ablative).
[28] *seruolus, -i* (m.): "a slave boy", "a young (male) slave" (usually implying contempt).
[29] *nequam* (indeclinable adjective, here modifying *seruolus*): "worthless", "shameless".
[30] *mulco, -are, -aui, -atum*: "beat up".
[31] *uilicus, -i* (m.): "(enslaved) farm manager", "slave-overseer".
[32] *adulescens, -entis* (m.): "young man".
[33] *ciuis, ciuis* (m./f.): "citizen".
[34] *cognosco, -ere, cognoui, cognitum*: "recognize", "find to be".

Acrostic Translation of the *Argumentum*

Cast out as a baby, charming Casina was raised as a slave,
And now she's pursued by old Olympio, their master's loyal
Slave. The master plans to cheat on his wife with her
If he can get her married to Olympio. But the master's wife,
Noticing it all, dresses up the male slave Chalinus as the bride   5
And both lechers get a shock. Casina, proven free, marries the son.

(Mostly) Literal Translation of the *Argumentum*

Two enslaved men want an enslaved girl from their household as a wife. The old master is using one of the enslaved men (his farm manager) as his proxy, and his son (the young master) is using the other. The lottery works in the old master's favour, but he is cheated and tricked, as follows: the shameless slave boy is substituted for the girl – and the slave boy then beats up his master and the farm manager. The young master marries Casina, who is found to be a citizen.

Works Cited

Allen, Joseph Henry, and J. B. Greenough. 1903. *Allen and Greenough's New Latin Grammar for Schools and Colleges*. Boston: Ginn & Company. https://dcc.dickinson.edu/grammar/latin/credits-and-reuse

Anderson, William S. 1996. *Barbarian Play: Plautus' Roman Comedy*. Toronto: University of Toronto Press.
http://www.degruyter.com/doi/book/10.3138/9781442671171

Aubert, Jean-Jacques. 1994. *Business Managers in Ancient Rome: A Social and Economic Study of Institores, 200 B.C. – A.D. 250*. Leiden: E. J. Brill.

Bennett, Charles E. 1918. *New Latin grammar*.
http://www.thelatinlibrary.com/bennett.html

Bhargava, Rashi, and Richa Chilana [eds.]. 2023. *Punching up in Stand-up Comedy: Speaking Truth to Power*. Abingdon, Oxon: Routledge, Taylor & Francis Group.
https://doi.org/10.4324/9781003352808

Brown, P. 2019. "Were There Slaves in the Audience of Plautus' Comedies?". *The Classical Quarterly* 69.2, 654-671.
https://doi.org/10.1017/s0009838820000099

Caldwell, Lauren. 2015. *Roman Girlhood and the Fashioning of Femininity*. Cambridge: Cambridge University Press.
https://doi.org/10.1017/cbo9781139644440

Carlsen, Jesper. 1995. *Vilici and Roman Estate Managers Until AD 284*. Rome: L'Erma di Bretschneider.

Christenson, David, and Plautus. 2000. *Amphitruo*. Cambridge: Cambridge University Press.
https://doi.org/10.1017/cbo9781139166652

Christenson, David. 2013. *Plautus: Four Plays: Casina, Amphitryon, Captivi, Pseudolus*. Newburyport: Focus Publishing.

Christenson, David, and Plautus. 2020. *Pseudolus*. Cambridge: Cambridge University Press.
https://doi.org/10.1017/9781139028363

Cody, Jane M. 1976. "The *Senex Amator* in Plautus' *Casina*". *Hermes* 104.4, 453-476.

Cook, John Granger. 2008. "Envisioning Crucifixion: Light from Several Inscriptions and the Palatine Graffito". *Novum Testamentum* 50.3, 262-285.
https://doi.org/10.1163/156853608x262918

de Melo, Wolfgang. 2007. *The Early Latin Verb System: Archaic Forms in Plautus, Terence, and Beyond*. Oxford: Oxford University Press. https://doi.org/10.1093/acprof:oso/9780199209026.001.0001

de Melo, Wolfgang. 2023. "Morphology and Syntax". In J. N. Adams, Anna Chahoud, and Giuseppe Pezzini [eds.], *Early Latin: Constructs, Diversity, Reception*. Cambridge: Cambridge University Press, 100-117. https://doi.org/10.1017/9781108671132.008

Dowling, Melissa Barden. 2006. *Clemency & Cruelty in the Roman World*. Ann Arbor: University of Michigan Press. https://doi.org/10.3998/mpub.145291

Duckworth, George E. 1952. *The Nature of Roman Comedy: A Study in Popular Entertainment*. Princeton: Princeton University Press.

Edmondson, Jonathan. 2011. "Slavery and the Roman family." In Keith Bradley and Paul Cartledge [eds.], *Cambridge World History of Slavery. Volume I: The Ancient Mediterranean World*. Cambridge: Cambridge University Press, 337-61.

Farthing, Matthew. 2020. "An Un-Humourous Treatise on Punching Up Vs. Punching Down", https://matthewfarthing.medium.com/an-un-humourous-treatise-on-punching-up-vs-punching-down-d76fa60ba0b1

Feltovitch, Anne. 2015. "In Defense of Myrrhina: Friendship between Women in Plautus's *Casina*". *Helios* 42.1, 245-266. https://doi.org/10.1353/hel.2015.0010

Fitzhugh, George. 1857. *Cannibals All! Or, Slaves Without Masters*. Richmond: Morris Publisher, https://www.gutenberg.org/ebooks/35481

Franko, George Fredric. 1999. "Imagery and Names in Plautus' *Casina*". *The Classical Journal* 95.1, 1-17.

Franko, George Fredric. 2001. "Plautus and Roman New Comedy". In Shawn O'Bryhim [ed.], *Greek and Roman Comedy: Translations and Interpretations of Four Representative Plays*. Austin: University of Texas Press, 147-188.

Gaughan, Judy E. 2010. *Murder Was Not a Crime: Homicide and Power in the Roman Republic*. 1st ed. Austin: University of Texas Press. https://doi.org/10.7560/721111

Gellar-Goad, T. H. M. 2020. "Music and Meter in Plautus". In George Fredric Franko and Dorota Dutsch [eds.], *A Companion to Plautus*. Hoboken: John Wiley & Sons, 251-67. https://doi.org/10.1002/9781118958018.ch17

Gitner, Adam. 2016. "*Nautea, notia*: A Nauseating Root in Plautus". *Glotta*

92, 110-130.
https://doi.org/10.13109/glot.2016.92.1.110

Gold, Barbara. 2003. "Vested Interests" in Plautus' *Casina*: Cross-Dressing in Roman Comedy". In Mark Golden and Peter Toohey [eds.], *Sex and Difference in Ancient Greece and Rome*. Edinburgh: Edinburgh University Press, 334-350.
https://doi.org/10.3366/edinburgh/9780748613199.003.0019

Goldberg, Sander M. 1998. "Plautus on the Palatine". *The Journal of Roman Studies* 88, 1-20.

Gowers, Emily. 2004. "The Plot Thickens: Hidden Outlets in Terence's Prologues". *Ramus* 33.1-2, 150-66.
https://doi.org/10.1017/S0048671X0000117X

Gratwick, A. S. 1973. "Titvs Maccivs Plavtvs". *Classical Quarterly* 23.1, 78-84.

Griffiths, A. 1995. "The Chiton under the Pallium: Two Greek Jokes in Roman Comedies". In A. Griffiths [ed.], *Stage Directions: Essays in Ancient Drama in Honour of E.W. Handley*. London: Institute of Classical Studies, 133-134.

Heil, A. 2012. "*Hector Ilius*. Ein obszönes Wortspiel in Plautus, *Casina* 994-5". *Mnemosyne* 65, 480-487.
https://doi.org/10.1163/156852512x585232

Hunt, Peter. 2018. *Ancient Greek and Roman Slavery*. Hoboken: Wiley-Blackwell.

James, Sharon L. 2012. "Case Study IV: Domestic Female Slaves in Roman Comedy". In Sharon L. James and Sheila Dillon [eds.], *A Companion to Women in the Ancient World*. Malden: Wiley-Blackwell, 235-237.
https://doi.org/10.1002/9781444355024.part3b

James, Sharon. L. 2015. "*Mater, Oratio, Filia* Listening to Mothers in Roman Comedy". In David Konstan, Sharon L. James, and Dorota M. Dutsch [eds.], *Women in Roman Republican Drama*. Madison: The University of Wisconsin Press, 108-127.

James, Sharon L. 2020. "Plautus and the Marriage Plot". in George Fredric Franko and Dorota Dutsch [eds.], *A Companion to Plautus*. Hoboken: Wiley, 109-121.
https://doi.org/10.1002/9781118958018.ch7

Jeppesen-Wigelsworth, Alison. 2023. "Roman Marital Ideals and Aurelia Philematium: *Casta, Pudens* ... Married at Seven?" *Phoenix* 77.1-2, 104-130.
https://doi.org/10.1353/phx.2023.a926366

Laberius, D. 2012. *Decimus Laberius: The Fragments*. Edited by Costas Panayotakis. Cambridge Classical Texts and Commentaries, 46. Cambridge:

Cambridge University Press.

Leigh, Matthew. 2000. "Primitivism and Power: The Beginnings of Latin Literature". In Oliver Taplin [ed.]. *Literature in the Greek and Roman Worlds: A New Perspective*. Oxford: Oxford University Press, 288-310.
https://doi.org/10.1093/oso/9780192893017.003.0001

Leigh, Matthew. 2004. *Comedy and the Rise of Rome*. Oxford: Oxford University Press.

Leo, Fredericus, and Titus Maccius Plautus. 1958. *Comoediae, Volumus Prius*. Berolini: Weidmann.

Lindsay, W. M. 1892. "Plautus *Cas*. 523-4". *The Classical Review* 6.3, 124.
http://www.jstor.org/stable/693190

Lindsay, W. M. 1903. *T. Macci Plauti: Comoediae*. Oxford: Clarendon Press.

Maas, Paul. 1907. "ὑμην ὑμήν". *Philologus* 66.1-4, 590-596.
https://doi.org/10.1524/phil.1907.66.14.590

MacCary, Malcolm M. Willcock, and Titus Maccius Plautus. 1976. *Casina*. Cambridge: Cambridge University Press.

Marshall, C. W. 2006. *The Stagecraft and Performance of Roman Comedy*. Cambridge: Cambridge University Press.
https://doi.org/10.1017/CBO9780511486203

Moore, Timothy. 1998. *The Theater of Plautus: Playing to the Audience*. Austin: University of Texas Press.
https://doi.org/10.7560/752085

Moore, Timothy. 2012. *The Music of Roman Comedy*. Cambridge: Cambridge University Press.

Moore, Timothy. 2020. "The State of Roman Theater c. 200 BCE". In Dorota Dutsch and George Fredric Franko [eds.], *A Companion to Plautus*. Hoboken: Wiley, 17-29.
https://doi.org/10.1002/9781118958018.ch1

Mouritsen, Henrik. 2011. *The Freedman in the Roman World*. Cambridge: Cambridge University Press.
https://doi.org/10.1017/cbo9780511975639

Nelson, T. G. A. 1990. *Comedy: An Introduction to Comedy in Literature, Drama, and Cinema*. Oxford: Oxford University Press.

Parkin, Tim G. 2003. *Old Age in the Roman World: A Cultural and Social History*. Baltimore and London: Johns Hopkins University Press.
https://doi.org/10.56021/9780801871283

Questa, Caesar. 1967. *Introduzione alla metrica di Plauto*. Bologna: Casa Editrice Prof. Riccardo Pàtron.

Questa, Caesar. 1995. *Titi Macci Plauti: Cantica*. Urbino: Quattro venti.

Questa, Caesar. 2001. *Casina*. Urbino: Quattro venti.

Quirk, Sophie. 2018. *The Politics of British Stand-up Comedy: The New Alternative*. Cham: Palgrave Macmillan. https://doi.org/10.1007/978-3-030-01105-5

Raven, D. S. 1965. *Latin Metre: An Introduction*. London: Faber and Faber.

Richlin, Amy, and Plautus. 2005. *Rome and the Mysterious Orient: Three Plays by Plautus*. Berkeley: University of California Press. https://doi.org/10.1525/9780520938229

Richlin, Amy. 2015. "Slave-Woman Drag." In Dorota Dutsch, Sharon L. James, David Konstan [eds.], *Women in Roman Republican Drama*. Madison: The University of Wisconsin Press, 37-67.

Richlin, Amy. 2017. *Slave Theater in the Roman Republic: Plautus and Popular Comedy*. Cambridge: Cambridge University Press. https://doi.org/10.1017/9781316585467

Roth, Ulrike. 2010. *By the Sweat of Your Brow: Roman Slavery in its Socio-Economic Setting*. London: University of London Institute of Classical Studies.

Shipp, G. P. 1953. "Greek in Plautus". *Wiener Studien* 66, 105-12.

Slater, Niall W. 1987. *Plautus in Performance: The Theatre of the Mind*. Princeton: Princeton University Press.

Treggiari, Susan. 1991. *Roman Marriage: Iusti Coniuges from the Time of Cicero to the Time of Ulpian*. Oxford: Clarendon.

Ussing, Johan Louis, and Titus Maccius Plautus. 1887. *Comoediae. Recensuit et enarravit Ionnes Ludovicus Ussing*. Havniae: Librariae Gyldendalianae.

Watson, Alan. 1967. *The Law of Persons in the Later Roman Republic*. Oxford: Clarendon Press.

Weiss, Michael. 2009. *Outline of the Historical and Comparative Grammar of Latin*. Beech Stave Ann Arbor: Press.

Wiedemann, Thomas. 1994. *Greek and Roman Slavery*. London and New York: Routledge. https://doi.org/10.4324/9780203358993

Williams, Craig A. 2010. *Roman Homosexuality*. Oxford: Oxford University Press.

Williams, Gordon. 1958. "Some Aspects of Roman Marriage Ceremonies and Ideals". *Journal of Roman Studies* 48.1/2, 16-29. https://doi.org/10.2307/298208

Index

A
Accent marks (*apices*), 32
Atellan farce, 3
Audiences (Roman), 1, 4–7
    Enslaved persons in the audience, 5

B
Bacchantes (worshippers of the cult of Bacchus/Liber), 5, 217
Barbarians in Plautus, 205

C
Charged humour, 2
Cleustrata, 8
    An unusually sympathetic stock *matrona*, 16, 17
    Spelling of her name, 2

D
Domestic violence, 215

E
Early Latin, 23–27

F
Fabula palliata,
    Graeco-Roman culture, 3, 4
    Greek setting, 2

G
Greek language, 208

I
Infanticide, 169, 219

L
Lysidamus (name), 8

M
Marriage (Roman), 15, 16, 209
    Adultery, 20
    Divorce, 15, 16
    Marriage *cum manu*, 15, 16
    Marriage *sine manu*, 15
Masks, 3
Mime, 3
Music and metre, 5, 28–33, 208
    Cantica, 28
    Deverbia (diverbia), 28
    Iambic senarius, 29, 31, 32
    Trochaic septenarius, 29–31

N
New Comedy (Greek), 2–4
    Plots, 7
    Source for the plot of *Casina*, 6

P
Pater familias, 6, 8–11
    Power over daughters, 15
    Power over enslaved persons in his household,
    Power over sons, 8–10
    Power over wife, 15
Peculium, 9, 11, 180
Plot of *Casina*, 1, 6
Production and performance, 7
    Casina, 2, 4, 5
Punching up, 1

S
Sexuality (Roman attitudes), 18–20
    Penetration and status, 19, 20
    Sex between men, 19, 20, 185, 191, 216
    Sexual assault, 19, 185, 191
    Stuprum, 170
Slaves and slavery, 5, 10–12
    Ancestors of enslaved persons, 189
    Manumission, 10, 11, 181, 183, 203
    Marriage of enslaved persons, 6, 13, 170
    Morality of running away, 187, 215

Seruos callidus, 4
Treatment of enslaved persons, 10, 11, 172, 183, 187, 190, 191
Vilicus (enslaved farm manager), 6, 12, 20
Power over enslaved workers under his authority, 12
Society (Roman), 1, 7, 21
Comic reversal of power, 1, 2, 4, 7, 21
Household hierarchy, 7, 8
Stock characters, 3, 4, 7, 8, 11, 12

T
Theatres, 5

W
Women
Women's power, 2, 7, 8, 15
Matrona's control of food, 175
Women's powerlessness, 6, 8
Contubernalis mulier, 13
First-time bride's lack of choice, 13–15
Unwilling brides, 14, 15
Virginity of citizen bride, 13–15

About the Team

Alessandra Tosi was the managing editor for this book.

Adèle Kreager proof-read this manuscript.

Jeevanjot Kaur Nagpal designed the cover. The cover was produced in InDesign using the Fontin font.

The author typeset the book in LaTeX and compiled the index.

Jeremy Bowman produced the PDF, paperback and hardback editions

Hannah Shakespeare was in charge of marketing.

This book was peer-reviewed by two anonymous referees. Experts in their field, these readers give their time freely to help ensure the academic rigour of our books. We are grateful for their generous and invaluable contributions.

www.ingramcontent.com/pod-product-compliance
Lightning Source LLC
Chambersburg PA
CBHW050523170426
43201CB00013B/2065